*At the
Leading
Edge*

AT THE LEADING EDGE

New Visions of Science, Spirituality, and Society

Fourteen interviews from the acclaimed
New Dimensions national interview series
hosted by

MICHAEL TOMS

With a Foreword by
BERNIE S. SIEGEL, M.D.

PUBLISHED FOR THE PAUL BRUNTON PHILOSOPHIC FOUNDATION BY
LARSON PUBLICATIONS

International Standard Book Number: 0-943914-51-5
Library of Congress Catalog Card Number: 90-63380

Manufactured in the United States of America

Published for the
Paul Brunton Philosophic Foundation
by
Larson Publications
4936 Route 414
Burdett, New York 14818

95 94 93 92 91

10 9 8 7 6 5 4 3 2 1

Photos reprinted courtesy of New Dimensions Foundation.

Dedication

To honor the legacy of R. Buckminster Fuller,
friend, mentor, and a true comprehensivist.

Contents

Foreword

I WAS HONORED when Michael Toms asked me to write a foreword to *At the Leading Edge,* a special collection of "New Dimensions" dialogues. Both Michael and "New Dimensions" dialogues were a part of my life for years before we had our first personal meeting and interview.

As I tried to find my path in life, "New Dimensions" served as a beacon to light the way. My interests and questions were responded to by the creative and exciting thinkers I heard in conversation both on the radio and on tape.

In this collection of dialogues, the foremost thinkers in the fields of science, spirituality, creativity, ecology, individuality, cosmology, consciousness, and evolution appear. All are made interesting and intelligible through Michael's inspired interaction with his unique guests.

As Joseph Campbell said, "New Dimensions" generates an atmosphere of ease and honesty which brings out from deep inside all the best that one has . . . Because of the warm, authentic environment created for a living conversation, one has the feeling that the unseen participants are also at ease and are an integral part of the play."

On a personal level, I have found "New Dimensions" dialogues to be continuously stimulating. As I reread the dialogues or listen to the tapes I find new insights and answers. They respond to the changes in me, so I hear or see what didn't seem to be there on previous occasions.

Michael Toms' conversations with Joseph

Campbell, Patricia Sun, Rupert Sheldrake, David Bohm and many others have helped me to follow my bliss and illuminate my personal path. As I continue to struggle on, "New Dimensions" dialogues remain a constant support and gentle guide that somehow make the struggle less difficult.

As an interviewer, Michael has a keen ability to probe the depths of knowledge and the psyche of each guest, with the result that you feel you are sitting with friends and sharing a wonderful experience. You will never find anyone more interesting to dialogue with. So sit down, join the dialogue and open your life to wonder, joy and awe.

BERNIE S. SIEGEL, M.D.

Preface

      THOMAS JEFFERSON was a childhood hero
for me. He was someone whose wisdom spanned many
horizons, a comprehensivist and a revolutionary thinker,
open to new ideas, yet retaining a healthy respect for the
older ones worth keeping. Jefferson inspired me with his
spirit of reaching for a wider landscape of knowledge and
ideas. Later, I was fortunate enough to spend time with the
late Buckminster Fuller, who often spoke of the value of
being a comprehensivist. Indeed, he attributed many of the
world's problems to overspecialization and the lack of an
overview.

      This book provides a larger view through ex-
ploring the edge with some of those individuals who are
breaking new ground: from Goddess spirituality to quantum physics; from morphic resonance to the warrior's way;
from conflict resolution to intuitive knowing; from global
mind change to Eco-philosophy, and so much more. As
physicist David Bohm has suggested, the process of open
dialogue is the source of creativity. True creative thinking
can emerge from the mutual exchange. You, the reader, are
part of this exchange. This is what New Dimensions Radio
is about, and the interviews included within these pages
are intended to strike the deeper chords of the creative
source within each of us. We are the solution.

MICHAEL TOMS
Mendocino County, California

Acknowledgments

GRATEFUL acknowledgment is given to those individuals within these pages who shared their wisdom so openly in dialogue on the "New Dimensions" public radio series as well as to all those persons who are not here but have made themselves available for the "New Dimensions" dialogue process. The spirit of their vision is present here.

Special thanks are due to my friend and co-worker, Tom Greenaway, whose dream inspired this volume; David Hulse-Stephens, who coordinated the project; Mary Buckley for editing and transcribing; Char Jacobs for transcribing; co-workers Robert Young, Pam Moon, Jeff Wessman, Lou Judson, and Jane Heaven for constant support; my co-publisher and friend, Paul Cash, whose inspired editing, creative suggestions, and overall support should serve as a model for all publishers; and Justine Toms, my partner, wife, and closest friend, whose generous spirit, open heart, and ready wit are always a source of inspiration.

Willis Harman

A New World View

OUR WORLD VIEW is changing. For four centuries the Cartesian-Newtonian vision of a mechanistic and material reality has dominated the scientific world-view, which in turn has permeated all aspects of Western culture. Now a shift is occurring, perhaps one of the most fundamental and dramatic transitions in history. It is nothing less than a dramatic change in the cultural belief-structure of Western industrial society.

The rediscovery of consciousness opens extraordinary possibilities and new potentials for our lives. This transformation is altering the way we interpret science and how we deliver health care, expanding our appreciation for the human intuition and creativity, revolutionizing education, and producing significant change in business and economics. Most importantly, it is bringing us to a realization that war is unthinkable, as we review our policies of national and global security. A global community is forming as we experience the shift and our minds literally change. Global mind change is upon us.

Willis Harman is the president of the Institute of Noetic Sciences in Sausalito, California. For sixteen years prior to assuming that post, he was senior social scientist at SRI International in Menlo Park, California. There he initiated a program on futures research, exploring the national and global future. In this capacity, he worked on long-term strategic planning and policy analysis for an assortment of corporations, government agencies, and international organizations. He is a member of the Board of Regents of the University of California, the author of two books, *Global Mind Change* and *An Incomplete Guide to the Future*, and co-author of *Higher Creativity* and *Paths to Peace*.

MT: *Willis, why don't we begin with science? What's changing, and what's happening in science as you see it?*

WH: What's changing I wouldn't have believed ten years ago. In the last decade there are three developments that stand out in my mind that have happened. Each one of them would be revolutionary by itself, and if you put all three together it's a total shift. I'm not really thinking of quantum physics at this point, although that tends to be what the weekend seminar circuit dwells on.

One of these developments was the recognition, just about ten years ago, in a book by Karl Popper, that science is not one thing; science is a hierarchy of things. The kind of science that works well for molecules and electrons doesn't necessarily work very well for human beings, and the kind of science that works for human beings may look a little strange when you look at it from the physicist's standpoint. The basic idea is that at the level of the physical sciences you have one kind of science which is deterministic and reductionistic. This is the science we were taught in school, and it works very well for the inanimate world. But by the time you get to the level of the biological sciences, then different, more holistic, kinds of concepts come in.

I like to think of this as a kind of bookcase where you have a shelf at the bottom that's labeled "Physical Sciences." Above that is a shelf labeled "Biological Sciences," and there you have to have some very holistic concepts, like the concept of an organism. A living organism is a much more holistic thing than what you deal with in some of the other sciences. You can't break it into bits and still have an organism. You have to deal with concepts like the function of an organ in that organism, so there's a certain kind of purposefulness, teleology, that comes in, that has no place in the physical sciences.

Then, at the level of the "Human Sciences," you have new concepts like conscious choice, intention, paying attention, and so on. And then I think we're going to have to have a level above that which we might call the "Spiritual Sciences." And there has been something known about this for thousands of years. And all of these levels fit together and make a whole body of knowledge.

So that was one new concept. It's something you can talk about rather freely now, and ten or fifteen years ago you didn't talk about it.

The second concept is what neuroscientist Roger Sperry, who has talked about it as much as anybody, calls "the consciousness revolution in science." It's essentially the idea that there are really two kinds of causation in everyday experience. One of them is what he calls "upward causation" and that is: the molecules move around, the particles move around in the fields, and that all adds up to something happening. It's the kind of causation you see when the gas molecules move in the cylinder of the car, and then the piston moves, and that causes the car to go down the freeway. So you talk about scientific causality in that sense. But, as Sperry points out, there's also "downward causation." That is, there's also the fact that I decide to go out for a Sunday drive, and *that* causes the car to move down the freeway.

Science has always dealt with the first of these kinds of causation and not the other; in fact, science has defined the second one out of existence. And so Sperry's 1987 paper "The Structure and Significance of the Consciousness Revolution in Science" was a groundbreaking paper. Not everybody's on board by any means, only a minority of scientists. But what's being opened up is that the most basic assumptions about reality that we've accepted almost without question for several centuries are now being called into question—by the public and by the scientists themselves.

The third development is one that came from the public, really; I think it probably started in the 1960s. It's essentially raising the question: Do we really need to keep on with this battle about science having defined a certain kind of territory, which excludes all sorts of phenomena in life that don't fit in, so that we are urged to believe they don't happen because they're not scientific or you can't examine them scientifically? The new suggestion is simply that we start from the other end. If certain kinds of phenomena and certain kinds of human experience have been reported down through the ages—across cultures, all around the globe—then they have a certain validity of their own, so let's start from there. What we need is a science that will accommodate what is—that will accommodate all those phenomena and experiences.

Listening to you describe that breakdown, I thought of how science has viewed the brain as a storage unit, a component to store up knowledge, and has been cutting apart the brain to try to find out which parts of it deal with certain types of knowledge. There has been an assumption that if you can't see or touch something, then it doesn't exist. But now we're seeing different scientific theories emerge. I think of Sheldrake's morphic resonance, where there may be intelligence way beyond the brain that permeates our bodies and our consciousness, that can't be seen or touched.

In a way, it's all up for grabs. That is, people like Sheldrake are talking about memory storage being not in the brain and not even in the physical body. People like Candace Pert are talking about the body's immune system being much more democratic than we used to think the body was: it's not that the brain sits on top and sends out orders to everything, but the cells and parts of the immune system are communicating between themselves, through the neuropeptide messengers and in other ways. And so in a certain sense it looks as though thinking goes on all throughout the body. Things that we've assumed, sometimes implicitly, sometimes explicitly, for centuries, to be true—everything's up for questioning now.

Matthew Fox speaks of a kind of tacit agreement between religion and science, where each has been saying to the other for centuries, "We won't touch your territory, you don't touch ours." Religion has given the material world to science, and science gave the soul and the spiritual world to religion. What's happening with religion as this incredible change starts to happen in science?

You know, there really was such an agreement, as it were. It served rather well, I think, in the beginning. It certainly protected the infant sciences from the much stronger Church.

That division of territory is tending to disappear, and that is due as much to changes in the religions as to changes in science. The changes in religion have come more quietly and more slowly, but if you stop to think about it, they haven't been so slow either. Half a century ago there were very few people claiming that there's some universal human experience which someday we will have a way of talking about that will not place one religion versus another, but will consider different religious outlooks to represent different aspects of some very fundamental human experience.

In recent years there has been more and more tolerance for that idea of a central core, of an esoteric perennial wisdom. That has made religion much more open to a reconciliation with science. In the area of religion we've had research laboratories for a long, long time; they were called monasteries and other names. And the searchers in them were just as open-minded, in many cases, as the searchers of science;

it just happened that they were exploring the realm of inner experience and had to have different kinds of rules and different methodologies, so to speak.

That change took place in the religions over the last half century. At the same time, we have seen science softening up to where the realms of experience that have been dealt with by religion are now open to sympathetic exploration from science—not a kind of exploration that will reduce them to something else, something quantifiable, but a more open exploration. I think there will always be differences in emphasis, because religion and science have somewhat different functions in our society. But the conflict between religion and science, I think, to most sophisticated minds, has just about disappeared.

In your book, Global Mind Change, *you spoke of three levels: M1, M2, and M3. Perhaps you can elucidate them.*

Well, if you're really up to that! [laughter] It's an approach to understanding the fundamental puzzle of "What's fundamentally real in the world, in the universe?" There clearly are different views on this. Science has largely been based on some metaphysical assumptions: There is the reductionistic idea, for example, that the explanation of a phenomenon is necessarily in terms of reducing complex phenomena to simpler ones. They also use the objectivist idea that there really is an objective world out there that we can be separate from and explore in a scientific way. And, of course, there's the positivistic idea that what's real is what's physically measurable. Those assumptions more or less have defined what is usually called science. That was essentially equivalent to saying that what's fundamentally real, the most basic stuff of reality, is the physical reality. In other words, what physicists study is what's real. I just called that M1—M for metaphysic—because I wanted to have some sort of a neutral designation for it.

Now clearly there are some competing ideas. A Nobel laureate in England named Sir John Eccles, as well as others, has been urging us to reconsider dualism. Dualism here means that there is matter/energy stuff, all right, and that is fundamentally real; but besides that there's something that you might call mind/spirit stuff, and that's also real, and you have to deal with it in a different way. In the minds of some scientists, that's the way it's going to come out. Science will adopt a dualistic view, which I call M2.

But then neuroscientist Roger Sperry rejects dualism and insists that we have somehow to take into account the fact that consciousness causes things to happen. Consciousness, he says, is a "causal reality" in the universe. Now, how are you going to deal with that? Well, in the esoteric core of the spiritual traditions, they've dealt with it in another way. They've said that consciousness, mind, the mind/spirit stuff, the universal mind—that's what's real. And everything else is created out of that. So I just call that M3.

There is a contest going on among those three, and even variations of them. There are several variations of M1, the materialistic paradigm, in science right now. Whether we know it or not, each one of us is in that dialogue, in that debate. We're making up our own minds: which way are we going to bet our lives on as to what's most real, and by which way are we going to have our social institutions guided?

The realm of psychic phenomena and paranormal activity, what's known as parapsychology today, has previously been excluded from science. The idea that consciousness produces matter and everything else has served as the base of a lot of the esoteric traditions. As you describe M3, I think of the manifestation of objects in certain psychic situations and that sort of thing. How do you view what's going to happen in the area of parapsychology?

The psychic phenomena which are so much anomalous in the M1 world seem much more natural to the M2 dualistic idea that there is matter/energy stuff and also mind/spirit stuff. They are even more natural to the M3 idea that consciousness is what's ultimately real, and since out of that is created everything, it's not so surprising when there's an intrusion of consciousness to produce some psychokinetic effect, for an example.

Now you ask, what's going to happen in the area of parapsychology? I'll make a guess. But first I have to guess what's going to happen to science in general. It seems to me that where we are is that there's a widening group of people in this society who are really betting their lives on a very different proposition than what they were taught in science class. They're betting that mind/consciousness does bring about effects in ways that are not explainable by the old M1 science. And that's not just true of the United States—it's happening through much of the industrialized society.

This is having some effect on the scientific community as well. After all, there's no fundamental difference between being a graduate student in science and being a person! And a lot of this, of course, did start in the 1960s. So you're finding that there's a shift taking place. The question about causality and science is being raised in ways that even a couple of years ago it really wasn't. It's an open question so far as to how this is going to come out.

I'm going to make a guess that Roger Sperry's position will probably gain in favor, and let me just be a little more explicit about what
that is. In his 1987 paper describing his position, causality does involve consciousness, and consciousness is qualitatively different—
mind is qualitatively different—from matter. But mind is something
that occurred in the universe in the course of a long evolution, starting with the Big Bang and going on for thirteen or fifteen billion
years. Eventually you get the human brain with complex networks of
neuronal cells, and then the creation of consciousness. From then on,
it's qualitatively different. That particular outlook he calls "mentalism," and he's urging that on science now.

My guess is that scientists, by and large, will go either with Roger
Sperry and his mentalism, or with another Nobel laureate, Sir John
Eccles, and his dualism. In other words, consciousness will be admitted, as it really is in some sense already, to the cognitive sciences. But
there will be as little perturbation of the original basic assumptions as
possible.

Meanwhile, there's a rather complete ignoring by scientists of the
esoteric perennial wisdom, even though that's a little bit arrogant of
them. After all, that wisdom has been around for a long time and it
has been supported by the experience of many people. So the M3
proposition—that behind everything is universal mind and that we
all potentially can tap into the universal mind with our conscious
awareness—that proposition is not taken very seriously in the scientific community yet. I'm guessing that there will be a two-stage process: that science will go to some variant of materialism or maybe
dualism, and then later on—and by later on I don't think I mean more
than a generation—it will shift over to this M3 assumption.

Now if that's the course of things, we're going to become much
more comfortable with the psychic phenomena. We already have, in
the last quarter-century. We'll recognize, for example, in the case of
channeling, that something is going on there that's pretty mysterious.
Sometimes it comes through with pretty flaky stuff that doesn't seem
to have much value, but sometimes it comes through with material
that has astounding depth to it, and it's in some sense testable. So this
is an example of something you just can't ignore. It fits into one set of
assumptions reasonably well—the perennial-wisdom, M3 kind of
assumptions. It doesn't fit very well at all into the materialist assumption.

We will come to view such things with less discomfort. We will learn more about them, but not through the external experiments of parapsychology so much as through more and more people realizing that we have another tool to work with—namely, the deep intuition. We'll begin to accept that more as something that can lead potentially to knowledge which is not improperly called scientific knowledge.

You're someone who travels in business circles from time to time, doing seminars for corporations, and so forth. How is business being impacted by these changes you've been talking about? There has been an emergence among business people of a deep interest in the area of intuition, hasn't there?

Oh, it's a very hot area right now. First of all, intuition is a word you can now talk about in business circles, which was not true much more than a decade ago. You never used to find the word "intuition" in any of the business journals—*Harvard Business Review*, *Fortune*, or anything like that.

It was all management by objectives.

That sort of thing. But now intuition is there for sure. It's a new codeword in business. Now the question is, "Is this another passing fad or is this something that's here to stay?" There are a lot of indications that could lead you to either conclusion right at the moment. First of all, the most exciting thing, I think, is in the executive development, management training courses. The principles being taught there are being used because they're practical, because they work, and yet they're principles that just don't fit in our contemporary scientific picture. They really don't.

Now, of course, there's always a reaction to something like this. After all, this is a new heresy. We're not talking about something trivial here. It gets right to the heart of some of the assumptions that our whole society's built on.

Might even burn witches, if you set yourself . . .

[laughter] We don't do that now, we just write reports! Recently the National Research Council came out with a report entitled "Enhancing Human Performance," commissioned by the federal government. The purpose of the report was to look at all of these various new kinds of trainings that are available and ask the question, "Is there any scientific demonstration that they accomplish anything?" And essentially the report says, "No, there's not much."

So there's where we are. If you ask the people who went through the courses, they'll tell you how their lives were changed. They'll tell you what the tools are and how they use them. And it's an exciting story. But if you go to scientific evidence, there's not much.

That reminds me again of how if you look at something in one box, it looks differently than if you put it in another box. It may be that the very rules that govern how you look at something affect how you perceive it.

I think that's one of the questions being raised.

It's certainly true that paranormal phenomena frequently don't stand up under "scientific" investigation. But they aren't necessarily invalidated just because they don't fit that box.

You said that.

I said that, yes. [laughter] That's my view, my bias, as it may be.

We've touched on intuition and business, and I would like to look into the whole area of creativity. You wrote a book with Howard Rheingold on higher creativity. How do you see what's happening in this new world-view as it affects human creativity?

Well, we've had human creativity in every society whether or not there were any beliefs about it, so it's not terribly clear what's going to happen if we change our beliefs about creativity. I think, in a way, that creativity and intuition are sort of code-words that we're using for something that lies beyond. We're reclaiming a part of ourselves, in a way, that we tended to lose.

Think about the shift, from the Middle Ages to modern times. It stretches over a fair period of time, but the seventeenth century was more or less the critical time. There was not only a scientific revolution but also an economic revolution, and the very early democratic political revolutions were starting. It was a time in which the basic assumptions underlying Western European and North American society—and later on it spread around the globe—really shifted in a very fundamental way. We began to have our social decisions guided by economic rationality and scientific and technical rationality; creativity became downplayed somewhat, even in the arts. Other things were so exciting—technological revolutions, the onrush of science and so on.

So it's kind of a rediscovery that creativity isn't just putting things together to give some sort of novel product or some sort of innovative process. "Creativity" or "intuition" is used to describe the process by which we tap into our deeper selves and discover a wisdom and an inspiration and a spirituality and an aesthetic sense that can be trusted. And all of that, we're not taught a whole lot about in school. There's not a very rational approach to go with it, but it's there. It's being rediscovered, and as it's rediscovered we use these words to communicate with one another about it. It's less taboo than it was a couple of decades ago, but we still need the code-words.

So I think we are paying more attention to creativity. Certainly in business we are. Certainly it's being honored. In the managerial revolution that's taking place, the new management is not using the resources of the corporation to achieve some goals that have been decided by the board; instead, management is really bringing out the creativity in others. This is happening because the competitive corporation in the future is going to be the one that can attract and hold the very best people, the most creative people. The management practices and the structure of the corporation have to be redesigned to accommodate that.

So we're going to hear a lot more about creativity. It's a word with much more positive connotations that it used to have. But it's also a word whose definition is expanding as we go along.

Creativity used to be kind of put off in a box; it didn't permeate all of the professions like it does in music and the arts. There were certain areas where creativity was OK to use, but when you moved into other, say, "hard-core" or more "real" or practical concerns, creativity kind of went by the boards. What I hear you saying is that that's no longer true, that creativity is entering these very pragmatic and practical arenas.

I certainly think you're right. Creativity is becoming a way of life, and it is more important than a lot of other dimensions now—status and economic dimensions, for example. And that's true for a widening group of people.

Perhaps the most important effect of all of this change is that we are starting to review how we conceptualize security, both national and global. Having the challenge of nuclear weapons upon us may be part of the reason that we're doing this. But also it seems directly related to the shift that you're talking about in the level of our world view. Would you speak to that?

I think that's true. You know, there's always a question of what causes what, and in history that's probably a question you shouldn't be asking because it's probably not answerable. But we're going through a dramatic, a very fundamental change. Partly, I think, this is pushed by problems such as the danger of a nuclear holocaust and all the environmental problems and other global problems. We have to change our way of thinking, because it's just an untenable situation that we're headed for if we don't.

On the other hand, we've got this other kind of shift taking place, where people are awakening and realizing that they've only been using a part of their potentialities, and that the heavens are wide open for learning more and using more. I think that both of those forces are operating in any aspect of what's going on in the world today, and national security is certainly one issue that's affected.

The word *peace* is another code-word, of course. It connotes more than just laying down your weapons and then shaking hands. And again what it does connote varies a great deal. But it's an awkward word right at the moment, because you never know what somebody means when they use it.

Some of the more sophisticated talking these days is in terms of alternative ways of getting national security. We pay our taxes, we have a big government operation that's labeled "National Security," and what has it given us? Total insecurity. That paradox attracts people's attention. We have to do something about that.

So there's a good deal of thinking about how we could possibly satisfy the need of people for security, but still not try to do it with nuclear deterrence, because that won't work; with or without "Star Wars," it won't work. As you probe this issue more deeply, you find that there's no way in the world that we can have national security unless everybody else in the world has national security as well, because we're not going to forget how to make nuclear weapons even if we do decide to dismantle the ones we have.

Then you have to think about national and global security, and you realize that nobody feels secure when they don't know where their meals are coming from tomorrow. So you can't separate security from the problems of poverty and hunger. And you certainly can't separate security from the problem of environmental deterioration and impacting the life-support systems of the planet; dealing with that problem necessitates a total change in attitude with regard to our relationship to the planet. So all of these things are interconnected in such a way that there's no solution to one problem—national security or any other—without a solution to them all together. At first glance, that might seem to make the problems much harder and the situation much more complex. To the contrary, it really doesn't, because what it says is, "What we need is one fundamental global mind change, and all of the problems will become much more solvable than they were before."

And I think that's what we are somehow intuitively being led to.

What evidence do you have, personally, of this kind of thing, this kind of perception changing in parts of the world other than the United States?

Oh, a tremendous amount, so we can only hit a highlight or two. Certainly one of the most impressive and inspiring things to me that I've been involved with recently is the citizen summit, the Soviet-American citizen summit that you and I both attended in early February, 1988. This brought a hundred citizens of the Soviet Union and roughly four hundred citizens of the United States together to create joint projects, to *do* things together. It doesn't matter what we do. What's important is that we just do *something* together to build trust between the two peoples. As the trust level gets high enough, our governments will find that they just have to lay down the weapons, because that's really what the people want.

There's a very, very basic cultural change taking place in the Soviet Union which we don't notice very much because it's not reported in our media. But it's as dramatic a change as has taken place over here. And it's in the direction of a widening group of people awakening to the idea that they can take a hand in their own destiny. And of course under Mr. Gorbachev's leadership there's a lot more permission from the government. These things are not independent; each one feeds the other.

So there's a mind change taking place in the Soviet Union, and it has all the same dimensions as the mind change over here. It has some different characteristics because that's a different kind of society.

Another impressive thing is that wherever you go in business these days, you find an interest in the new concepts of management and of management training. Everybody's talking about them, though they're not all talking in the same ways. The code-word "intuition" is widely talked about; but it's understood with different levels of depth in different circles, as you might imagine.

It's like wearing different glasses as you move around in different arenas.

Willis, I was thinking about the paradoxes in the shift. It occurred to me that as we review what national and global security really mean, then we can come back much more to the personal. For example, here in the United States we see that as we create more and more weapons, we have more and more homeless; we have more and more people who don't have enough food to eat. And it's also true in the Soviet Union, I think. There seems to be a direct relationship. So it's almost as if such paradoxes are creating this shift, and I suspect that the global concern is going to create a re-emphasis on the personal in some ways.

I think that's right, Michael.

Willis, I think it would be useful to go into some of the details about the kinds of training and seminars that are now occurring in the business community. Can you do that?

It's really fascinating to see what's going on these days. The other day, for example, I was sitting with a group of business executives. One of them had come late to a meeting, and he was explaining that he was a little surprised to even be there because there was a whole series of coincidences that had resulted in his arriving. Then somebody at the table said, "But there are no coincidences." And every head around that table nodded. Now, that could not have happened a decade earlier. What it means is that people are sensing that there's another kind of causality around them, beyond the ones that we ordinarily take into account.

In one of these executive development seminars, the instructor starts out by writing on the blackboard: "Imagination creates reality." Now that just doesn't fit with our scientific picture of what creates what. Then the rest of the seminar was an elaboration of that idea.

For at least twenty years now there have been seminars on the power of the vision, the power of the inner image, the power of the affirmation. This is a very profound principle, that we see the world in a certain way. We perceive in a way that's shaped by certain kinds of unconscious assumptions, unconscious beliefs that we have. We call some of them expectations, but some of our expectations are quite unconscious. We have certain assumptions about the nature of reality that shape what we see.

It's well known that if you change your unconscious expectations by hypnotic suggestion, then you'll see something different. You'll experience a different world because the hypnotist told you to see it a different way. Well, hypnotism doesn't last terribly long. But we carry around these other kinds of cultural hypnosis that have been years in the building, and they are lasting.

Sometimes these include some beliefs that get in our way, such as the belief that "I am inadequate, I am fundamentally unworthy, I am inferior." And if you carry around a bunch of baggage like that, then of course you are inferior and you are inadequate. So discovering the power of changing all of that, the power of changing it by a kind of self-hypnosis—by affirming yourself otherwise, by affirming, for example, that "I am totally adequate; everything I need will be present" and so on—that has been a part of these executive training courses for quite a while. Although it came in slowly and quietly, and without a lot of talk, the basic idea is that you can deal with the unconscious, you can reprogram the unconscious mind to your own advantage.

It's only a slight extension beyond that to believe that if you vividly hold the image of the goal to be achieved, then that goal will tend to come into being in some ways that are really quite startling. It's somewhat like the person in athletic training who vividly imagines going over the bar time after time, higher than he ever jumped in his life.

So you hear stories of how executives put this idea to use. For example, it might be that in order for a particular goal to be achieved, a certain kind of information was needed; but the person doesn't know where to go for this information, and then a book just falls off the shelf and opens up to a page that has the information in it. That sort of minor miracle seems to happen with people who have taken some of these courses. So those are examples of what I meant by saying that the principles that are being taught don't fit the old pictures.

I'd like to tell you about one of these courses, where the learnings are rather explicit. I used this example for the concluding section in *Global Mind Change* because I thought it was so useful as well as indicative of what's happening.

At the Pecos River Training Center, four learnings are being taught. The first learning is that I don't have to have fear; fear is an unconscious choice. I don't have to perceive that which is fearful, and if I change my perceptions so that nothing is fearful, then I don't feel fear. To put it another way, I can learn to trust the universe. I can learn to trust my total environment, and I do that by just programming the unconscious in ways that are perfectly safe and take a little time. It's just a matter of self-suggestion.

The second learning is the power of the affirmation, the power of the inner image, the power of vision, and the power that a vision has. If a group of people in a corporation, in an organization, hold the same vision, and then just go about their activities, but holding that vision, it does remarkable things.

The third learning is that every one of us, whether we're consciously aware of it our not, feels some deep sense of purpose in our life. And it's a very, very strong urge to make sense out of our lives, to find out what that sense of purpose is, what that purpose is in doing. If you manage an organization in such a way that you honor that sense of purpose in the people in that organization, and you let it be known that the organization's activities are going to be such as to give that purpose a chance to actualize, then you'll have an organization that will really flourish in a sense that is different from any of the old management styles.

The fourth principle is sort of like the non-attachment in Buddhism, but it's in a much more attractive package for the modern business mind. That principle is that all experience is feedback. Whatever happens—failure, your plans didn't work out, unexpected opposition, whatever it is—it's OK. It's alright if things go well, and it's alright if they don't, because then you learn something. So all experience is feedback. It's a very profound kind of message.

Now, if you infer the kind of picture of the universe, the kind of picture of reality that lies behind those four learnings, you realize that it's essentially what we were earlier talking about as the M3 kind of picture.

Very metaphysical.

Yes, that's the old word for it—metaphysical. The fundamental stuff in reality is mind and universal mind, and you live differently once you're sure of that.

All four of those learnings seem to have behind them consciousness, which wasn't present in the old model.

That's right. Call it mind, or call it consciousness, that's essentially the implicit message. And it implies a discovery that everyone has to make for themselves, because there's no external demonstration. The discovery is that there's no limit to mind other than what we believe in, only the limits that our own beliefs set. You know, that doesn't fit with the old picture, but it's very comfortable with the new one.

That reminds me of the truth of the old saying, "Be careful what you wish for because you're going to get it."

Absolutely.

Well, it's really quite exciting as I listen to you talk about your view of what's happening. When some of us look at existing institutions that are permeated with the old view of the world, it's sometimes difficult to see that there really is a new view emerging. But I think it's important to point out that sometimes you don't see this new view present in the existing order. You have to look beneath the existing order, and see that it's happening in other areas. Isn't that true?

I think that's right. If I go to any organization—say, a modern corporation—I can find it there, but I'll find it in individuals, in small groups. It may be a small group that went off to some executive training program, or it may have come about in some other way. Some of these people are still feeling a little lonely because they realize that most of the organization isn't on board yet with that picture. But it has been growing. I've been tracking it professionally for twenty years. It has been gaining in strength, and the group of people involved has been expanding. Now that doesn't necessarily mean it's going to continue to grow, but all the indications so far are that it will. It's much, much stronger now than I would have ever guessed, ten years ago, it would be by this time.

We've touched on the citizen summit and our experience of that as a unique and transformative event. What about the area of politics? How do you see the global mind change affecting politics?

Slowly. Slowly. [laughter] There are some institutions that are more leading-edge institutions, for a variety of reasons. And corporations are very, very flexible; when they sense something new is coming, they respond to it quite quickly. This is especially true of small corporations and small entrepreneurial organizations, particularly small entrepreneurial organizations that were started by women, because women are starting corporations for quite different reasons than men used to start them.

In the area of politics, you find a lot of awareness of this in the Congress, in the House of Representatives, because those people are very much in tune with their constituents. As the constituents change, sometimes they lead a little, sometimes not. But they're in tune. There's less of this awareness in some other parts of the government, though, and less in some of the bureaucracies. And if you don't mind, I'd just as soon stay out of conversation about the Administration, which is strangely unaware of a lot of this, it seems to me. I don't know exactly why.

What about the multinational or global corporation? How do you see it being affected?

I think the multinational corporations, first of all, realize that they do have to take responsibility for the whole planet; there's no way of avoiding that. What they're doing about this varies tremendously from one case to another, but there is a change of mind taking place in them, of necessity. And there are some corporations where I've talked with the leadership and they really are sensing very, very fundamental change involving responsibility for the planet. You can talk with others and find that they're mainly trying to get along.

I think of some of the exploitation that has taken place with multinationals, and particularly in developing countries. Do you see that changing?

Oh, it has to change, obviously. But it has to change not because the corporations have been led by bad guys, but because there has been a tremendous economic pressure not to do things that another part o1 your being would tell you were sensible things to do. I find that a lot of business leaders these days are relieved that the economic logic that led them to exploit the planet is really weakening enough, and other kinds of values are becoming stronger, that they can do more things that they're going to feel good about when they go home at night.

Matthew Fox

Creative Christianity & Ecumenical Visions

FOR TWENTY-SEVEN years, Thomas Merton lived the life of a Trappist monk. Trappists take a vow of silence and live simply, growing their own food and spending much time in silent prayer. Merton was an unusual Trappist, since he wrote more than sixty books, many still in print, and wrote many journals and letters, most of which remains to be published. During the early 1960s Merton ran afoul of religious superiors and Church authorities, who tried to silence him because of his writings against nuclear war. A quarter century later, and twenty years since his untimely death in 1968, Merton is respected and read by more people than ever before, including his writings against nuclear war.

I refer to Thomas Merton because Dominican priest Matthew Fox, like Merton and many others before him, has faced censure and censorship by Roman Catholic Church authorities. He was sentenced to a year of public silence because of his views on Creation Spirituality. Matthew Fox is founder of the Institute in Culture and Creation Spirituality at Holy Names College in Oakland, California. He is the author of numerous books, including *Original Blessing* and *The Coming of the Cosmic Christ*. His work reflects the early stirring of Christianity, the Gnostic tradition, ecumenicism and the mystical streaming of Catholicism, more than it does current interpretation of Church dogma—and therein lies the rub.

MT: *Matthew, we're going to be talking about some of the contents of your books, but I'd like to begin with a fundamental question. When did the view that you have, which is very different than one normally associates with the traditional Church, first become fully alive for you? There had to be a turning point, a transition point. Where did it happen for you?*

MF: Well, Michael, I think I got a basically sane, holistic, creation-centered approach to spirituality from my family—especially from my mother, probably—but this was kind of beaten underground as I went deeper into American education. For example, I used to write poetry as a child. But as soon as I hit college, I just went underground for years. And it was when I went to study in Paris, at the advice of Thomas Merton, that it all came washing back.

     It was there that I met Father Chenu, who is now an eighty-six-year-old radical French Dominican, who named the Creation tradition for me. It made so much sense! It named the burden of dualism, the fear of the body, the put-down of artists, the put-down of women, and so on, that had characterized so much of my formal training in the seminary but did not correspond to my deepest spiritual needs. My own spiritual awakening as an adolescent had come through reading Tolstoy or Shakespeare or hearing Beethoven and all those things that represent a much larger cosmic view of reality. But somehow a combination of academia and formal seminary training had reduced all this to almost a trivial-sized soul.

     And then I met Chenu, who is one of the founders of the Liberation Theology movement. He had been silenced by Pius XII for twelve years, forbidden to write in the 1950s, and was later vindicated by the Second Vatican Council. He was the one who named the two traditions for me: the dualistic tradition in the West, that has certainly dominated, and the holistic tradition that we need to know an awful lot more about. It was like a coming-home for me, and I threw myself into the holistic tradition. That's what I've been doing since. And every place I go, people respond with similar enthusiasm. It's a coming-home for many people.

     How did Thomas Merton enter into the picture? You say he advised you to go to Paris.

Well, I had a lot of respect for him, from his writings and his journey, and I was struggling with where to go to get a doctorate in spirituality in the late 1960s. The advice I had been given so far was not appealing to me: "Go to Rome," "Go to Spain," and so forth. So I wrote him and he said, "Go to Paris." I'll always be grateful to him for that advice, because that's where I met Chenu and the naming of this tradition.

The tradition that we're talking about here, the tradition of Original Blessing instead of Original Sin, is far older. It's the oldest tradition in the Bible. It goes back to the ninth century B.C. The first author, the Yahwist, J, source in the Hebrew Bible, is of this tradition, as was Jesus. And the idea of Original Sin came in only in the fourth century A.D. with Saint Augustine—very late! Jesus never heard of Original Sin. And no Jew has.

Elie Wiesel, for example, says that "the idea of Original Sin is alien to Jewish thinking." A very strong statement. Original Sin introduces a suspicion of our right to be here in the universe, and of the beauty that we bring to the universe. We're talking about our origins, and the way people feel about their origins is very significant. It's a question of how we feel about ourselves, about the twenty-billion-year history that has brought us to this point of existence.

Meister Eckhart, who represents so beautifully the creation tradition, says: "When I flowed out of the Creator," meaning when he was born, "all creatures stood up and shouted, and said, 'Behold, here is God!' and they were correct." Now *that's* Creation theology, which says that we're not only *not* worms—and guilty worms!—but that we are divine. We bring an image of divinity into the universe that is unique and surprising, and that's why the whole universe celebrates our existence. When parents start teaching children this, and our institutions—educational, religious, governmental, political, psychological—have this supposition in dealing with people, we will have a totally different society.

I think you're right. [laughter] Are there other examples, like yourself, of individuals who are functioning this way within the institutional structure? I mean, you're still a part of the structure—albeit, perhaps, on the fringe, or on the edge. But is this something that's happening in the Church?

It's definitely happening in the Church. We're here to be catalysts, to see it happen. I think that the Church, like any other institution, runs onto bad times from time to time. I think that the despair of our times is urging a lot of people to take another look at what their religious roots are—why they say what they believe, or believe what they say. And I think that the harder look you take at the Christian roots, the more you have to go back to the Jewish roots, and the harder you look there, the further back you go, the more you realize you are talking about a Creation theology, a holistic theology. And this is happening. The feminist movement, the awakening, the fact that now more than fifty percent of seminarians in Protestant seminaries are women—all this is putting a whole new light on questions asked in seminaries.

Many of the invitations that I accept now are from Protestant seminaries, because there's this demand. The young people, the seminarians, are for spirituality; but most of the left-brain-trained theologians not only don't *know* the mystics, they're afraid of them! So you have to call in an outsider to put this fire out, so to speak. But it doesn't go out, because the fact is that as Protestants discover that they, too, are capable of mysticism, and as Catholics begin to realize their holistic instead of their dualistic mystical tradition, what you're really doing is generating fire. There's fire happening in the seminaries and in churches and wherever this tradition is catching on. It's by no means limited to the churches, and that's what's so exciting about it—it's so ecumenical.

This whole tradition links to the native traditions—the Native American, native European, and native African, among others. I've had African students, Latin American students, Asian students, who catch on to this immediately. Just a week ago, for example, during a program in Philadelphia, a young Filipino man came up to me and said, "I can hardly wait to go back and teach this! I'm going to have our people dancing our traditional dances, singing our traditional hymns. Now I see a link between Christianity and our native roots." I find this constantly, that native peoples everywhere have been deprived. Part of the colonialization of native peoples everywhere has involved the wiping out of the wisdom of their spiritualities. But the Creation tradition welcomes this wisdom, and it's a real bridge from Christianity, which is a latecomer, to these traditions that are tens of thousands of years old—including, of course, the deep women's experience of ancient Europe, for example.

This is like a breath of fresh air coming out of a smoke-filled room in some sense. You mentioned Original Sin. What about the concept of sin in the creation-centered tradition?

To begin with sin, to begin a theology with sin, is to leave out 19,996,000,000 years of the universe's work—and of the Creator's work—which I think is a rather substantial lacuna. What it ends up doing is trivializing sin. We don't even have the words in our vocabulary today for the real sins of our times. Our religious vocabulary doesn't have the words because it has no cosmos. It's the sins against the cosmos that we have to address, the sin of ecocide, for example— destroying the marvelous network and balance between trees, animals, fish, and two-legged ones. And there's the sin of geocide, our pouring of chemicals willy-nilly into the waters and the earth that will poison generations of all living things, including our own children, for a hundred thousand years to come.

In other words, to begin with sin is to trivialize sin. And doing so is typical of the anthropocentrism, the homocentrism of zooming-in on the two-legged ones, that has dominated Western thought not only in religion but in everything for three hundred years. So I think we should begin with the good news which science is just in the last ten years now in a position to talk about—the amazing gift that the universe is. Take the fact, for example, from what we now know about the universe, that the only water we know of in the whole universe is here, on this earth. We're talking about water, the sacred, holy gift of water, that it took the universe twenty billion years to invent and make flow on this earth. It's so sacred, it's so holy! You don't have to re-baptize the water.

We have to get back to the holiness of our existence, the fact that this earth, four billion years ago, had to maintain a temperature within a few degrees. If it had gotten a few degrees hotter, the oceans would have evaporated. If it had gotten a few degrees colder, the oceans would have frozen over. There'd be no life as we know it. During this four billion years the earth maintained a temperature overall of within a few degrees, even though the sun increased its temperature. When you learn these truths and facts about our universe, you're just in awe about the gift of our being here. You realize that there would be none of us without this gift of the Original Blessing of the universe.

So I think this is where we should begin all our theologies, with the wonder and the gratitude which is really what prayer is about— thankfulness for existence. Then you move into the responsibilities, and from there you move into areas of sin. But the fact is, everyone is talking about sin. Practically every headline of every newspaper is about sin. Sin is seldom news, and is not good news. If Christians claim to have some good news, they should begin with Original Blessing. Then, by developing the wondrous powers of the human race—especially for imagination and creativity, which is our divine power—we can work ways out of sin. So the Creation tradition does indeed deal with sin, but we refuse to *begin* with it.

Matthew, when we talk about spirituality, spiritual growth, personal growth, sometimes the criticism is that as one pursues that part of oneself one becomes less socially conscious, less involved with the social problems of the world. There's a kind of image or myth, as it were, of the monk on the mountain being totally not involved in what's going on in the world. In some sense, we're all conditioned by that image of leaving the world to go off and pursue one's "spirituality." But your work is very much involved in the social fabric of the society and the culture. I'd like to hear you talk about the connection between one's spiritual development and the real problems that we all have to wrestle with.

Yes, you're talking about something really important there—the dualistic split in our minds, if nowhere else, that you must go away from the world to be spiritual. That is so in the Original Sin tradition, but it's not so in the creation-centered tradition. This is a tradition of the prophets, who were very much involved in the struggle, the pain, the suffering, and the responsibility for their culture. Meister Eckhart, who was the greatest single articulator of this tradition in the West, was fully involved in the Bingen movement, which was a women's movement of his day, and in the peasant awakening of his day. And this, in fact—it's now proven—had everything to do with his condemnation. It was a political condemnation, as so many have been. Hildegard of Bingen, the great twelfth-century Benedictine nun, was painter, poet, prophet, criticizer of popes, bishops, archbishops, abbots—she was thoroughly involved in the politics of her day.

So the real tradition of Creation theology is persons involved in the social struggle of the day, because the social struggle is a struggle for visions. It's a struggle for what we believe in, what we want to enact in terms of institutions. It's about whether our institutions are worthy of us, whether they're as beautiful as we have a right to be, and as we want to pass on to our children. Father Chenu, my mentor, was silenced by Pius XII in the 1950s because he had joined the worker-priest movement in the late 1940s in France, and he was their theologian. He left academia, and the privileges of academia, to go there and help them articulate their experience, for twelve years. He paid the price of a prophet. But then, as I say, he was reinstated by the Second Vatican Council, which urged Catholics to find their spirituality in the world. This is very much a lay spirituality.

I do believe that monks have a right to be monks. But I don't believe that others of us should be closet monks. I think we have a right to spirituality in the world, a spirituality of work, for example, which is so beautifully developed by Eckhart in this whole tradition. And it has *everything* to do with art, because really our work is our self-expression, our gift back to the community for the time that we're on earth. In this tradition is the spirituality of pleasure—there's a right in our lives and a beautiful place for it. Pleasure, including sexuality and sensuality, is celebrated as holy and as a meditation experience, ecstasy, an experience of God in this tradition. So there is no dualism, no dichotomy.

When you look at the prophets, the mysticism there has an energy that allows you to enter the struggles of everyday life, earthly institutions, birthing new ones, letting the old ones go, or surviving in ones that are half good and half bad. We need energy to do that without selling our soul. We need to be *in* and not *of* these things. And that is where mysticism plays its authentic role—to bring the cosmos, to bring creativity, to bring beauty, to bring what I call erotic justice, which is personalized justice, into our institutions. To do this, you need a grounding in mysticism.

One of the real tragedies of Western culture, for the last few centuries, is that we've put mystics in a closet—which means we've put ourselves in a closet, because every human being is a mystic, at least potentially. But academia has cut the mystic off from knowledge; as a result, we don't have *wisdom* in our universities anymore, we have only knowledge and information. And churches have cut the mystic out of worship, so you have a lot of words and a lot of verbiage going on. But where's the dance? Where's the letting-go? Where's the childlikeness? Where's the spontaneity? What Eckhart calls "unselfconsciousness," developing unselfconsciousness? All of this is what the churches should be teaching people. It can be done, especially through art. That's what we're doing in our institute, recovering art as meditation—play, dance, massage, painting, music—not to produce something, not capitalist art, but to enter into it, as process. This is what heals us and brings the cosmos in, helps us to realize, and makes us young again. Jesus said the same thing, that until you adults turn and become like children, you'll not receive the Kingdom and Queendom of God. So this turning and becoming like children is what churches and synagogues should be doing—inviting people to turn, to let go of some of our adult ways and become childlike again. And it's in recovering this that we recover our wonder, our appreciation, and our responsibility to the universe. Effective justice-making results from this. The prophet is the mystic in action.

You mentioned the Second Vatican Council, and I think of Pope John XXIII and the impact that he had, not only on the Catholic Church but on the world. There was a vision that he expressed that it seemed like the world resonated to. In some sense I want to ask, "Where's John XXIII [laughter] twenty years later?"

Well, I couldn't agree more. He was *so* special. But, you know, he was also creation-centered. I met a priest in New Jersey a few years ago who told me this story. Back in the late 1950s, he was visiting Spain, and he stayed overnight in a seminary there. At one in the morning there was a knock on his door. A short, fat Cardinal woke him up at one in the morning and said, "Come with me, come with me." The priest said, "I'm sleeping." The Cardinal said, "Come with me." So they went down to the dining room and there was an entire banquet laid out. The Cardinal said, "It's the middle of the night; I couldn't sleep. I had to cook myself something. I never eat alone, so *mange, mange!*" So at one in the morning they were eating this incredible banquet. He said, "A year later the guy, Cardinal Roncalli, was elected pope." This was after the ascetic Pius XII. The priest shook his head and said, "There are going to be some changes around here!"

I remember the first picture I saw of John XXIII. He had a cigarette in one hand and a martini in the other, and he was kicking because his short, chubby feet never touched the ground. But he was always kicking, telling stories. He was an Italian peasant. He was thoroughly creation-centered, you see. This is why he could tell the stories and people could relate to them, whether Jew or Moslem or Buddhist and so forth. He had a humanity, a radical humanity about him.

Now, I think that his spirit is alive and well in many places—and it certainly is in our institute and in the work we are doing in the creation-centered spirituality. The importance of humor in the man's life, the art of storytelling, and of course the humanism that what people have in common is so much greater than these minor things that we make separate us—these were the keys. So there's no question that there was a very special spirit, an avatar who went our way in the person of John XXIII. I think that he allowed things to happen. I certainly am indebted to him. I'm a child of his generation. That is to say, I grew up, theologically, under the Vatican Council. And the spirits that he brought back into the core of Catholicism, including Chenu and Teilhard de Chardin and these other theologians who had been on the fringes! John allowed these people right back in the core of things.

How has de Chardin influenced your work?

Well, de Chardin is, of course, part of this Creation tradition too. Here's a man who was scientist and poet and priest. He had a vision of what could happen when Western civilization would bring science and theology together again. And from that point of view, you see, we're carrying on his work. We have a full-time physicist in our program. It's so important, because you can't create a cosmology, which is the vision that moves people, without both your scientific myths and your religious myths.

You know, the Western culture, in the last three centuries, is the only tribe of human beings that we know of that imagined it could get along with religion taking the soul and science taking the cosmos. And what has happened? Well, today we're seven minutes away from science blowing up the world because some scientists, going the way of the cosmos without conscience, discovered the ultimate power of the cosmos. And religion, as I mentioned earlier, has so trivialized the soul that it puts people to sleep, in church and out of church. Even when they talk about their favorite subject—sin—it's sleepytime.

Now we can stand on the shoulders of Teilhard, with a more mature science, on one hand, and a fuller grounding of theology on the other. He was *such* a pioneer in trying to bring together the two disparate parts—that is, parts that were disparate for the last three hundred years.

There's been a kind of unspoken agreement, or sometimes spoken agreement, between science and religion—and even between the political structure and religion. It's like all these agreements have been made between governments and the church. It's like each is saying to the other, "OK, we'll stay out of your ball park and you stay out of our ball park." You can see that happening in the Iron Curtain countries, especially, where there's a tacit agreement because there has been a realization that you're not going to wipe out the Church—it has got to be there. "We'll stay out of your ball park and you stay out of ours." What about that? I mean, you're talking about institutions and agreements that have gone on for centuries.

Well, yes, but only for three centuries. That is the point I was making: You can't create a people; you can't create a global civilization or a global spirituality without the cosmological shared vision. All people celebrate how their scientific and religious myths came together. This is what creates a vision for the people and gives them excitement and energy to move on.

Now, what's so wonderful about the times in which we live is that scientists are writing the best works on mysticism being written in our time! That is of no small consequence. It's a real awakening.

Can you give us some examples?

Well, sure. There's the work of Fritjof Capra, and *The Dancing Wu Li Masters*, for example. The fact is, with Einstein, mystery has returned to the universe. And there are the few examples that I gave before, that we're learning about the wonder of water, the wonder of how our earth has survived these last four billion years. It's all so full of wonder. Mystery has now returned to the universe, thanks to Einstein. Newton thought that the universe was essentially inert, it was settled, it was just getting along. But now we find matter is anything but inert. It's so exciting that the physicists bubble when they talk about it. Matter is dancing. "A scenario of dance," Capra calls it at one point. That, combined with the Creation Spirituality, allows for amazing cross-fertilization, because scientists are human beings, too, and they are waking up to the issues of conscience that they've often turned off in the name of "objective science" in the last few centuries. But now, again, Einstein has shown that no science is objective; it's all relative to the viewer, the observer. And the facts we're learning about what human arrogance is doing to our planet, much of it in the name of technology and science—these are waking up a lot of scientists.

You see, the year 1600 broke in with the burning of Giordano Bruno at the stake by the Church. Giordano Bruno was, actually, a Dominican like myself (ex-Dominican), but a theologian and scientist who wanted to bring the two together. Now, scientists weren't dumb. They had already witnessed 150 years of war between Protestants and Catholics. So they said, "Well, if we're going to do our work, we've got to form a truce." And essentially the truce was, "Well, you religious people, you take the soul, and we'll take the cosmos." And, as I say, the result of this truce has been the pathology of the times in which we live, in which religion has been trivialized, on one hand, and science has lost its conscience, on the other. So I think more and more people are waking up to this need for a cosmology, a spiritual cosmology that brings together the best energies of both sources.

One of the ironic and perverse spectator sports of our time is to observe the fundamentalist religious people on one hand and the fundamentalist scientists on the other, fighting each other head on in their ego-clashes. It's really a pity. I think that we can let go of fundamentalist science, which is science which does not take into account mysticism and mystery, and we can let go of fundamentalist religion, which is still arguing about whether the world was created six thousand years ago or twenty billion years ago, whereas in fact the Bible teaches that creation is going on all the time. Every time a flower blooms or a child is born or a friendship is struck up or a song is composed or a movement is organized, there is God creating, co-creating with us and with the rest of creation. So I think we should let go now of those fundamentalist, dualistic, either-or approaches to science or to religion, and begin to move with the cosmology that's emerging out of the new creation story from science, which is a global story. It has so many implications for a global spirituality, a global celebration.

Here's an example. Rusty Schweikart is an astronaut who came to our program last year. He was a macho, jet-fighter pilot for the American Air Force. He told how he was up in space in the late 1960s. Usually NASA keeps you very busy; they're not into making mystics, but as he left the Apollo capsule, something went wrong inside the capsule that had to be repaired. For forty-five minutes, he was left alone floating around the whole earth. And his first awakening was that he had been lied to—that, in fact, the world is not marked "Socialist," "Capitalist," "Communist." That the boundaries of Russia and Europe are not clearly marked. The rivers serve capitalist, socialist, and communist countries together.

Now there's once again a view of the earth which is how the earth is, which is its whole entirety. The ideologies of nation-states—the politics and the education and the religions that are built on nation-states—completely wither, melt away. And Teilhard predicted this twenty-five years ago. He said, "To really recover the sense of earth would mean letting go of our sense of nations and nationality." It would mean relating to something, I think, more global but also more rooted. We can also learn to love the earth in our local places of living and gardening and celebrating and dying and burying with more sacredness, at the same time that we relate to the bigger picture. They go together. It's a " both-and," not an "either-or."

I'm interested in something that you were talking about, and have been talking about throughout your conversation: the connection of the creation-

centered tradition and Native American peoples, the Indians. Could you talk
more about that, and what it is?

For the last couple of summers, I've gone to the Tekakwitha Conference—attended by about 1500 Native American peoples—that lasts
about a week or so. One summer I led a workshop on creation-centered ways and Native American ways with a Native American
priest. When we ended, a large Navajo woman turned to her parish
priest, who was sitting next to her and who was very small and puny.
She started beating up on him and said, "Why did I have to come all
the way to Montana to hear about this?" She said, "All of my life has
been a split down my middle, between my native ways and my
Christianity, and now I realize the split has been between my native
ways and Saint Augustine"—who is the namer of the Original Sin,
dualistic tradition in the West, the very patriarchal tradition that has
dominated. She said, "I feel healed." And ten other Indians stood up
and said the same thing. They said, "We've never heard a Christian
preacher talk about creation. All we hear about is sin and redemption,
sin and redemption. And creation is in fact the basis of our spirituality."

I am convinced, Michael, that the wisdom of the native peoples—
not just Native American, but also native European (the wicca tradition), native African, native Asian—this is one of the great gifts of our
time. I'm convinced that our efforts at genocide have not been successful precisely because one of the ways the earth has of saving itself from human chauvinism and arrogance is to bring back the wisdom of the native peoples. And I'm not talking about romanticism.
I'm talking about the fact that they have developed over the centuries
ways of teaching people to befriend the earth, to befriend darkness,
to deal with pain—in ways that are gentle and celebrative and truly
form community.

I've had African, Asian, and Native American peoples in classes,
and every place I go they recognize us immediately. I met twelve Es-
kimos at one of these conventions. We were eating dinner together,
me at a table with twelve Inuit people, and I happened to ask the
woman sitting across from me, "Did you make that dress?"

"Oh, of course," she said. And they told me, "She makes parkas
too."

And then I asked the man next to me, "Did you make your brace-
lets?"

"Oh, yes, from the tusks of walruses." We went around the table that way and learned that twelve out of twelve were artists. It's taken for granted in native traditions, everywhere, that everyone is an artist! Well, that's what the Bible teaches, too, that we're all images of God. But industrial society and a dualistic theology have made us think that only geniuses are artists, only professionals are artists, et cetera. The fact is, as Eckhart teaches, the only work that is human and satisfying is art—that is, what we give birth to that goes from inside out.

And this is why the recovery of art as meditation is so essential, not only for putting everybody to work—which is one of the key issues of our time, for everybody to work—but to *good* work, where the returns are good for the community, for celebration, for love of life, for exercising imagination so we can begin to imagine different economic, political, educational relationships and ways of worship that will do us justice instead of bringing more pain. So I am continually affirmed in seeing the wisdom of native peoples and how the tradition of Creation Spirituality that I speak of is their tradition—and they recognize it immediately.

Frederick Turner wrote a book called *Beyond Geography*, which is a history of America from the moment Columbus landed, from the point of view of the Native American—a little different reading. Turner calls it, in his introduction, "an essay in the history of spirituality," which amazes me. His thesis—he subtitles it "Western Spirit Against the Wilderness"—is that white, European Christianity repressed the wilderness, that is, the sensual, the mystery, and the sexual, and then came over here and projected this repression on to the native peoples, calling them "savages" who needed "redemption." And in that process genocide was legitimized.

It's a very sobering thesis, and there's a lot of truth to it. What we're doing, in recovering Creation Theology, is getting at the wilderness tradition, if you will, which includes the women's experience—the women mystics like Hildegard, Julian, Mechtild, and feminists like Eckhart—that has been forgotten in the Western churches.

Would you say more about Hildegard?

Hildegard was a twelfth-century Benedictine nun, poet, preacher, painter, scientist, and doctor also. She wrote books on stones, trees, animals, the cosmos, the stars—an amazing Renaissance woman. She has been called the greatest intellectual in the West, but her works had never been in English until we came out with one of her works this year. And we'll be doing more next year. It's typical of a patriarchal culture that we have even many Benedictine nuns who have not heard of Hildegard, one of their own. You know, we've been so one-sided—especially since the seventeenth century, with the Enlightenment, with science, with the left-brain or with patriarchy taking over—we have missed the wisdom of women through the centuries. The Creation tradition is full of these wonderful women.

I met a woman who came up to me this past year after a lecture. "You know," she said, "I don't believe there's ever been a mother who believed in Original Sin."

I said, "Now that fathers are present for the mystery and the mysticism of birth, there'll be fewer and fewer fathers who believe in that too." As a starting point for religion, it makes a big difference whether you begin your view of the world in terms of blessing or in terms of sin.

Matthew, you've talked about patriarchy, including the patriarchal aspect of the Church, as suppressing women and the role, particularly, of women mystics. It brings to my mind the subject of the Virgin Birth, which does exist still within the Church. Is that some kind of leftover that got left in when Augustine came along and started the whole patriarchal tradition?

Well, there's no question that there was a reward put on virginity around the fourth century that is totally un-Jewish. And it really upped the stakes in this whole story of the Virgin Birth. Part of the story of the Virgin Birth is, of course, a celebration of the unique individual. The idea of the Virgin Birth is not unique to Christianity—the idea that an avatar comes into the world in a special way. But I read something about a year ago that I found one of the more interesting comments on Virgin Birth, and it came from Otto Rank, who is, in my opinion, the most prophetic psychologist in the twentieth century. He remained a Jew all his life, but he talks about Christ and the Virgin Birth. He emphasizes that Christianity had to talk about it because the Middle Eastern religions celebrated the Mother Goddess and so forth, but she always has a sexual relationship with her son. And this, he says, is the real reason for Virgin Birth. It was to put distance between Jesus and Mary, so that there was not a sexual relationship between the two. And according to Rank this puts more emphasis on how Jesus brought about the awakening of the Goddess mentality—the women's religion, really, of the Middle East—without inheriting some of the more peculiar sexual aspects of that tradition. Jesus is freed to be a *prophet*—to leave the mother, to disturb the peace through bigger acts of compassion.

I found that analysis to be *astounding*, because it names a political-social reason why the Virgin Birth has hung around with such intensity. I found it a very interesting analysis of why it was necessary. Because, up to that time, in the Middle East, you couldn't have the man really awakening civilization to the gifts of the Mother without a sexual relationship. So, I just threw that in because I had never read that anyplace else, and I think it's a very interesting thesis. Otto Rank is no lightweight when it comes to looking at the history of human cultures, human religions.

What about a Mother Teresa, and her work with poor people in India, and particularly the relevance of her work to social ills? She was acknowledged with a Nobel prize. Would she be an example of creation-centered spirituality?

Not really. I would celebrate Dorothy Day before I would celebrate Mother Teresa, especially for the North American scene. I would not venture to judge what's possible in India, and I'm sure that Mother Teresa is doing superb and generous work in India with the destitute. A lot of people have worked with her there, and I admire her and respect her for that. But I do think there's a lack of social consciousness that is typical of the old dualistic spirituality. It's Band-Aids. I mean, it's one thing to give a person a fish; it's another to teach them to fish, and I'm interested in a more justice-oriented and social and intellectual approach—a creative approach—to the overall malaise of the human race. There are reasons why there are so many destitute on the streets of India, and Mother Teresa cannot address herself to that because she's dealing with the front lines.

I respect her for that, of course, but I don't see that kind of charity, really, as the ultimate solution. I think that that kind of giving, a charity, is of course a part of the gifts of the human race. But we need something much more than that. We need creative awakenings as to why it is that we have such gulfs between haves and have-nots, and what we can do about it. The fact is that the human race has enough imagination to do whatever it wants. Buckminster Fuller said in 1977 that we could close down every university, every library, every computer in the world, and with the knowledge we then had we could, within two and a half years of work, clothe, house, provide basic education, health care, food, and work for everyone in the world.

Now that's the kind of approach I'm interested in. We've had the poor for centuries and centuries, and now we have more poor because we have more people. There's really no reason for it except, as

Buckminster Fuller said, "We have the knowledge; we don't have the will." We don't have the willingness to let go, to change our patterns of living and our frozenness in the institutions, in the closed structures we now have, to get on with the task of celebrating one another. So I really see Mother Teresa, as much as I respect her on an individual basis, as representing basically a familiar—and really a too-familiar—spirituality.

Pretty challenging philosophy that you present. I'm wondering what kind of responses you get from people as you do seminars and workshops in different parts of the country—particularly for people of the Judeo-Christian tradition. What has been the response?

It comes close to ecstatic, really. We just finished a summer program for 270 people in Philadelphia, and I was getting some letters back today. All kinds of people—there are artists, there are people who have been living in ghettos with the poorest of the poor for years, there are social workers, there are teachers, musicians, young people and old people, people in their twenties and people in their seventies, people out of Protestant traditions, Catholic, Jewish, people who left formal religion years ago—experience this as a coming-home, as an affirmation of their struggle. And one thing they love is that they realize they're not isolated.

I consider that my main task—to articulate the fact that this is a tradition, and that we're not isolated. Once you begin to get over that feeling of isolation as a mystic or as a prophet, or as both, then energy returns. And it's amazing. Our program requires artists of all kinds—masseurs, painters, dancers—working with feminists, working with theologians and physicists. And the teachers all say that this is a coming-home. Just a week ago, the dance teacher in Philadelphia said, "I've taught dance for years in the university, but this is the first time I can really be myself."

I asked, "Why?"

"Because spirituality is involved," she said. "This is why I'm in dance in the first place, and I always have to leave that level out when I teach dance at the university. This is without doubt the happiest teaching of my life." So it's a coming-home for people, and that bodes well for the future, because that means there's energy being created here. And I see it happening all the time.

[Between the preceding interview, *Creative Christianity*, and the following interview, *Ecumenical Visions*, Matthew Fox encountered censure and censorship from Roman Catholic authorities. He was sentenced to a year of public silence, which began shortly after this next interview.—Ed.]

When you wrote Original Blessing *and some of your other books, did you have any idea that your writings would cause such an uproar in the Church?*

No. I thought I was doing my job, recovering the spiritual tradition of the Church. But as Jung points out, the mystics bring what is creative to religion itself, and the mystics—how does he put it?—are always a cross to the Church. When you look at Church history, of course, it is that way. Eckhart was condemned, and he was our greatest mystic. Thomas Aquinas was condemned three times. John of the Cross had to run from the Inquisition his whole life, as did Teresa of Avila, who got her autobiography condemned—it wasn't allowed to be published in her day. So there is a certain tradition in our Church of not dealing real happily with the mystics.

The problem today, though, is that we cannot afford the luxury of being patient and obedient in this regard, because the issue today isn't how am I getting on with Rome, it's how is the planet getting on with our species. And I think that way of putting the question takes us far beyond the sensationalism of a North American priest's being honored in the fashion of these others of the past.

It seems almost like doing this creates the very thing that Rome would prefer not to happen. I mean, it brings great attention to this issue—perhaps to people that wouldn't have otherwise noticed. Why do you think something like this would be done?

First of all, you're absolutely right about that. Leonardo Boff, a liberation theologian from Brazil whom they silenced two years ago, pointed out long afterwards that it was a monument of evangelization: millions of people heard about Liberation Theology who would not have heard about it otherwise. I've often felt that if it came to this it would be a providential way of getting the seed spread.

Why do they do this? Why do they pour gasoline on a fire? Well, I analyze it in my open public letter to Cardinal Ratzinger as the machinations of a dysfunctional family. If you live in an isolated situation, which is how dysfunctional families survive, you don't think about the consequences. You're so busy dealing with your own struggle, your own neurosis, that you don't see the world around you as it is. So, I think that in the long run what they're doing is foolhardy. If they want Creation Spirituality to go away, they should be as quiet as they can. But it's not going to go away because, in my opinion, this is the best of our tradition.

In the opening part of The Coming of the Cosmic Christ *which was re-*

*leased in the fall of 1988, you deal with the number of deaths that are occur-
ring on a planetary scale, and one of the deaths you refer to is the dying
Church. What do you mean by the dying Church?*

Well, I think that the Church in its present form, in its institutional
form and its patriarchal expression, is clearly dying. In fact, it's on a
kind of a suicide binge. I have an image of this great patriarchal dino-
saur that is dying and its tail is flashing around and kind of bringing
others down with it in its suicide wishes—and the real problem is
that it's dying on top of its own treasure. Our job is, one, to stay away
from that tail, and two, to try to get it to roll over enough so that we
can retrieve the treasure. Because I think that there are treasures there,
especially around the mystical tradition and around the prophets and
the gospels and so forth.

It's dying, just like other patriarchal institutions are dying, because
the paradigm—the way of seeing the world—that the institutional
Church has run on for centuries is no longer adequate. The irony is
that deep within the bosom of this same tradition there are useful
paradigms. For instance, just this morning in class I was lecturing on
the Goddess tradition of the twelfth Century that gave us Chartres
Cathedral and 580 other churches the size of Chartres in France, all
built in a hundred-year period in the twelfth century and all dedicated to the Mother Goddess—that is, Mary. This was an amazing
period, a period of renaissance and cosmology—which is what we
need today. Patriarchy doesn't have a cosmology. It reduces everything to mechanism and control. What we need is this influx of the
Goddess tradition which I have found is the Cosmic Christ tradition:
It's the cosmological tradition of the West.

How would you view Mary in the context of Catholicism?

Well, Henry Adams makes the point that Protestantism rejected Mary
altogether, and Catholicism has trivialized Mary. To the extent that
we've emphasized Mary as Virgin and Mother in a totally human-
centered context, we've missed the point. Mary is a cosmic center,
she's like the Mother Goddess of Africa, Isis. The Black Madonna that
you see in the twelfth century religious art—you see it at Chartres
and many other places—the Black Madonna stands for the throne.
Isis is always sitting on a throne, the throne of what? It's the throne of
heaven, of the cosmos. So Mary is an archetype of Sophia, of the
wisdom that lies at the heart of the universe—and that is available in
the heart of every human being. And, of course, that's the essence of

mysticism—which is heart knowledge.

The great line from Rilke, "the work of our eyes is done, now go and do heart work" really moves me. That is the essence of the paradigm shift: we have to move more into mysticism and incorporate that into the accomplishments that our left brain has gifted us with. And, of course, this is happening in science today. Beginning with Einstein, scientists are talking explicitly about mysticism and how we can't get along without it. In a recent study, for example, Stanford scientist Paul Ehrlich talks about the greenhouse effect and all the issues of survival for Mother Earth today. He says, "Curiously, science itself points to the need for a quasi-religious transformation of society." And that, of course, is what I'm talking about. There has to be a spiritual awakening—I call it a global renaissance. And it has to be grassroots. The great church historian Pere Chenu says that the only renaissance that was effective in the West was the twelfth-century renaissance. Not the sixteenth, which is what we think of when we hear the term Renaissance, but the twelfth—because it was grassroots. It was women, it was peasants, it was the young, and that's what's needed today. It could happen if all the world religions would let go of their excessive institutionalization and get more deeply into their mystical traditions. That's why the archetype of the Cosmic Christ is so meaningful—because this tradition is in all the world religions. It's called the "Buddha nature" that's in all of us, if you're a Buddhist. It's the divine light that's in all of us.

Religions of the world have never related at this level of mysticism because, when Western European Christianity encountered the wisdom of Native American, African, and Asian cultures for the first time in the sixteenth and seventeenth centuries, we had already deposed the Cosmic Christ. We had lost our own mystical tradition. We didn't know the wisdom we had encountered. So we were busy slaying the other religions. Today's a different day, and I think mysticism could lead the way to a really authentic renaissance.

You mention the twelfth century. Wasn't it the Church that put down that renaissance through the Albigensian Crusade? And other peasant, basic grassroots movements that were in some ways opposed to the Church of the time eventually got wiped out.

That's true, but it took a while. And in between you had the movement like Francis and Dominic's. You had some powerful new movements, including, of course, the University movement. And you had a few popes like Innocent III and Honorius III who in effect supported these things. But then you could get into questions such as: Did the Franciscans in fact co-opt the commune movements of the twelfth century and Did the Dominicans—who, of course, got before long into the Inquisition, along with the Albigenses as you say—also do this. So, this door that opened, you might say, this window that opened, didn't last more than 150 years. But during that time, something did happen. It began in the psyche. I think that's why Henry Adams is such an interesting figure: Being Protestant, being an American intellectual, nevertheless he was so awakened by Chartres Cathedral. That whole period was a breakthrough in Western consciousness. Yet, you're right—it only lasted 150 years. I tend to put the closing date as 1276 or so, when they condemned Aquinas for the first time. Aquinas represented the culmination of so much earlier effort—much of which, of course, came from the great intellectual input from the science of Islam. And it was so *ecumenical.* We use that word in the twentieth century and it usually means Catholics and Protestants being nice to each other. But there you had, for example, Ramond Lull, who set up centers all over Spain to teach Christians the Islamic tradition and the Arabic language. Lull was a layman, who had studied with Meister Eckhart in Paris. We don't have anything like that today. We don't have Christians studying Islam, but we should—especially with the rise of Islam. We have nothing comparable. We don't have Christians studying Taoism, you know, or . . .

We have Christians and Jews and Moslems fighting one another in the Middle East, that's what we have.

That's our accomplishment. So I'm hoping that this archetype of the Cosmic Christ that I'm trying to rename could elicit deep ecumenicism, because I think many people yearn for this. Many Christians, as you know, have left the Church to go East to find Taoism, Buddhism—to find mysticism someplace! But it's exciting when you can find it at home and then relate, and see, we haven't tried this.

So Matthew, what do you think will become of the Church? We speak of the paradigm shift and a new consciousness emerging.

Well, I think that the Church is going to have to strip down its institutional structure considerably and become more and more the work of the people. And I'm not even content with defining it as People of God, which the Second Vatican Council did—though they presently seem to want to take that back. It really should have something to do with the Cosmos. People of God is still really anthropocentric, and that's the basic disease in Western Civilization—anthropocentrism.

But within our own tradition we do have the idea of the mystical body of Christ, or the cosmic body, and I think this is where we have to move with understanding of "Church." It has to do with awe and wonder, as well as with justice and the struggle for justice. And this means justice toward all creatures, not just the two-legged ones. I think that's implied in this Cosmic Christ tradition and in the Goddess tradition. You know, the Goddess—the idea that the Goddess is divinity intrinsic to all things—that is exactly what the Cosmic Christ means. It means that every creature, as Hildegard said, is a glittering, glistening mirror of God—the image of God, you see. That's a *wonderful* image. It applies to every galaxy and every atom and every whale and every leaf and every horse and every human. We have to get back to that sense of raw reverence. And by *reverence* I don't mean this bourgeois thing of nodding your head and being pious. Reverence comes from the word to revere, which means to stand in awe at. In fact, we've had this idea mistranslated in the Bible; where we read that wisdom begins with *fear* of the Lord, that really means with *awe*. Awe is the beginning of wisdom. Awe does have something to do with fear—not with fear of the Lord as a person, but awakening to the awesome story that *we're here*. It's amazing! This awakening, I think, has to become the beginning of all authentic spirituality, and it's happening.

I think of the basis for awaiting the return of Christ, the mythological tale of Christ coming back. The title of your book, The Coming of the Cosmic Christ, *suggests that in some sense the Cosmic Christ is already here—it's our coming to that understanding.*

Exactly. The "coming" would be our awakening to it. Yes, definitely. It's really a matter of consciousness, isn't it?

Why do you think there is this difference, this constant dichotomy and dualism, between the literal and the metaphorical, the linear and the intuitive? Why do we—particularly institutions like the Church—want to interpret the literature, the liturgy, the scriptures in a literal sense?

Well, it's control, isn't it? And it's also distrust, which is interesting. I point out in *Original Blessing* that the basic meaning of faith in the New Testament is *trust. Pistuein* means to have trust, not to have an intellectual concept or a dogmatic position. So really we're talking about a lack of faith among churchmen, who don't trust the process of the Spirit to make order out of chaos. But every artist knows—and there's an artist in each one of us—that part of the artistic process is undergoing the *via negativa*, the chaos that precedes creativity, and that you have to trust the process.

One thing I found in doing this book that really amazed me was that in the first century—when the gospels and the epistles were written and Jesus and Paul lived—the number one scientific question of the day was about angels: "Are the angels our friends or our foe?" Angels represented the cosmology. It was believed that four elements—earth, air, fire, water—were pushed around by angels. So this was a cosmic question: "How much anxiety should we be living with here in this universe?" Well, Einstein was asked in the twentieth century, "What's the most important question you can ask in life?" And his answer was, "Is the universe a friendly place, or not?" It's the same question! So there is something in our tradition that speaks to the cosmology of the twentieth century. If you go back to the Cosmic Christ hymns, they all talk about how Christ has power over the angels, the dominations, the thrones, the principalities—meaning that whatever angels are busy doing you can relax about, because the universe is essentially a friendly place. So, as I point out to people who want to read the Bible, every time you see the word "angel," you should think Albert Einstein—that's what's going on there, a whole cosmological world-view. We haven't had cosmology for three hundred years in the West, so we have been misreading all our traditions. We've been anthropocentrizing them and worried about whether we're saved or not, but the issue is much bigger than that. The issue is how glorious is the universe, how much are we empowered by it—and let's get on with healing.

What would the Church find wrong with what you just said?

You mean the hierarchy in the Vatican. Let's not give them the credit to be called the Church. The folks who understand this in the heart are Church. And I think other creatures are Church—my dog is my spiritual director. I'm notorious for saying that creatures have a lot to tell us about the wisdom of the Cosmic Christ.

But what would the Vatican have trouble with? I don't know. They complained that I called God "Mother" in *Original Blessing*, and I proved that all the mystics of the Middle Ages did that. All the creation mystics and even Pope John Paul I called God "Mother." And the scriptures call God "Mother." So, I'm not here to defend the Vatican— I don't know what their problems are. Essentially, of course, they're stuck in patriarchy and probably a lot of it is unconscious. It is so irrational that they would object to calling God "Mother." I think that they're stuck in a totally male world-view and want to keep their images of God totally male. Keep it clean. And needless to say, the implication is that if you open up our images of God to gender justice, then you might be opening everything else up—including the Vatican Library.

In The Coming of the Cosmic Christ, *you refer to the work of Thomas Kuhn and the idea of paradigm shifts. You say Kuhn mentioned that with every paradigm shift comes resistance. It's one of the principles that occurs when we're in the midst of such a transition.*

If the resistance weren't there, then you probably wouldn't be really naming something at its core—where it matters. So, sure, resistance is the sign of doing something right. Jesus certainly met a lot of resistance, and Gandhi met it, and Sojourner Truth met it. We're all going to be meeting it these days as, you see, a paradigm shift is something we're all involved in. The more we commit ourselves to it, the resistance will be there.

You're dealing with the shadow side of a society, of people, of individuals. And where there are shadows that are unnamed and uncared for, you are also dealing with the wounded child. A lot of people who have found a safe haven in religion—as comfort or as safety or security or literal doctrine—a lot of these people have a deeply wounded child inside. And that child has to be cared for or it's going to emerge as a killer adult. There is a certain amount of that going on, as there always has been in organized religions.

Today the fundamentalist movement is alive and well not just in Christianity but also in Islam and in Judaism. That is very frightening. There's no violence like that of a religious fanatic. When you think that you're doing it all for God, or you're on God's side, or God's on your side—that kind of ups the ante of assault.

You refer to some other "dyings" in the opening of the book—the dying of the planet, for example. What about that?

Well, it's real, of course, and every day there's more evidence in the papers. There are more scientific congresses meeting around the world now, finally, making it clear. The rain forests *are* disappearing. I was in Australia this summer and saw the encroachment of the desert there. Now, we're destroying in our country six billion tons of topsoil a year, but in Australia it's more visible because their topsoil is not as deep as ours is. The desert is moving faster. And of course, there's the hole in the ozone layer over Antarctica, the waters that are being so polluted, and the disappearance of species. Ordinarily a species disappears one every two thousand years in the course of evolution. Currently we have a species disappearing one every twenty-five minutes—and a species is a once-in-a-universe event.

All this has to do with the Cosmic Christ. The reason we allow our soil to be raped by multinational agribusiness interests is that we don't believe the soil is divine, we don't have reverence for it. If we had reverence for it, we would realize that small farming is essential for preserving the divinity of the soil—the sacredness, the holiness of the soil. And this applies to all the species, to the forests, to the water and the air and so forth. So again, our problem is lack of reverence. We have no reverence because we don't live in a cosmology. We think food comes from supermarkets, and water comes from spigots, and all of it is wrapped in plastic! The paradigm shift requires that we go from anthropocentrism to cosmology, and with that shift will come a new sense of awe at our being here—seeing the gift that water is, appreciating all the other creatures that have served us so generously on this planet, and realizing that we could change our ways.

It has to happen in our generation or it will be too late. Time is not on our side. But that makes our times very exciting times, indeed, to live in. And it's like water boiling—you know, it doesn't look like a lot's happening until it moves just a degree or two. I think that underneath there's a lot of water boiling in the human psyche today, including the fear of the fundamentalist movements. That alone is a sign that something deep wants to change, and that's why fundamentalists—whether it's in the Vatican or in the Bible Belt of this country or in Islam or in Judaism—want to put tighter and tighter clamps on things. Their psyches are getting the same message that my psyche is getting—that there's an earthquake we're involved in here, a psyche quake or, as you said, a second coming of Christ. If you're a fearful person—perhaps you've had a very wounded background—your first response is *control*. But that really won't do. None of us got here by control. We got here because our parents loved each other enough to lose control and I think that sense is part of all the universe's ecstasy and going with the flow.

Matthew, when you were doing your research for The Coming of the Cosmic Christ, *you found that there were other traditions that had similar leanings. Perhaps you could take about that.*

Yes. Again, that's what I call "deep ecumanism." It is the coming-together of all the world religions to unleash their traditions of Cosmic Christ or cosmic wisdom. I alluded to the Goddess tradition—there's a real bridge here between the Goddess tradition and the Christian tradition. The Buddha nature—and also the Mother of all Buddhas—is part of the cosmic wisdom tradition of Buddhism. The Cosmic Christ is not Christian, you see, in any exclusive sense. In Israel there's a Cosmic Christ in the pre-existent wisdom tradition and also in the prophets and in the apocalyptic literature—which, by the way, is why your liberal theologians have turned the Book of Revelations over to the fundamentalists. They can't deal with cosmology. Jarislav Pelican, a professor at Yale, pointed out recently that "the Enlightenment deposed the Cosmic Christ and made the quest for the historical Jesus necessary." In that period, we just put the tradition of the Cosmic Christ on the shelf and went after an anthropocentric quest for the historical Jesus. That's why liberal religion today is boring and the churches are emptier and emptier—because the gospels aren't about pursuing the historical Jesus, they're about the Cosmic Christ, and people want some mysticism in their lives. They want some experience of their own, they don't just want to know about Jesus' experience.

The Native American tradition, for example, is rich in this tradition of the Cosmic Christ. I wrote about the pipe, their sacred pipe, as an experience of the Christ. You put the tobacco in the pipe and bless all four directions, and the tobacco represents all the elements and all the creatures of the universe. All of them are sacred, and they come together in fire—the fire of the pipe. Well, that image is like Eckhart talking about the soul as *ancilla animae*, the "spark of the soul." So what's at stake here is what Eckhart calls "one underground river" which is Divinity, with many wells that plug into it—Buddhism, Taoism, Judaism, Sufism, certainly Native Peoples and Christianity. We all have different mystical wells, but they empty into one underground river. And the amazing thing is that the same archetypes keep coming up from our same naming of the experience, for the same river. A person who has plunged his or her well understands the other mystical traditions out of that experience—I'm convinced of that.

What about artists and creators, people in the creative arts, and their relationship to the coming of the Cosmic Christ?

In the West, especially during this era of Newtonianism and mechanism and religious anthropocentrism, it's the artists who have kept alive the tradition of the Cosmic Christ. I call on poet after poet to name that for us. Whitman has some great lines about "Divine am I inside and out" . . . "I see God every day in the faces of men and of women and in my own face when I look in the glass" and "I find letters on the street dropped by God, every one signed by God." That's Cosmic Christ theology. You have it in Hopkins talking about us all as "immortal diamonds." You have it in Adrian Rich's work: She has a marvelous line where she says, "I would have loved to have lived in a world of women and men gaily" and then she goes on to describe green stalks and building mineral cities, and she builds and builds, and then she ends "being in union with the Crab nebula, the exploding universe, the mind." It's all one sense, it's just a delicious sense. But it's all about cosmology. She says she would have loved to have lived in a Cosmos, but no one invited her to. And the key word in that whole phrase is "gaily," women and men *gaily*. When you live in a cosmology, there's delight, there's joy. That's what Proverb 8 talks about, you know—the joy that is present with wisdom before the creation of the world.

Our civilization has not done a good job with the energy called delight and joy. We have people getting their ecstasies from a wheel of fortune and waiting for the next lottery ticket. There's a real repression of everybody's capacity for cosmic joy in our civilization, and that's a tragedy. Out of this repression comes a lot of our shadow side, our violence. We're cosmically lonely, so we're cosmically violent— they go together. Again, the Cosmic Christ is such a rich archetype to lead us—with the help of today's science, which is so mystical in it's rediscovery of the mysticism of the cosmos—to lead us out of this painful existence. The addictions, for example, that so-called First World people are caught in—whether it's drugs or alcohol or entertainment or television or shopping—where do these addictions come from? I define alcoholism as liquid cosmology. I think a civilization that can't offer up a cosmology is in trouble. People have to get cosmology someplace. In a civilization that doesn't offer one, they're going to get it from drugs or alcohol or racism or fascism or nationalism. These are pseudo-mysticisms.

In saying what I'm saying, of course, I'm deeply criticizing the churches and the synagogues in the West. They've failed in this primary task of eliciting from all of us the mystic inside and teaching us ways to honor and nurture that mystic. Your Native Peoples, in contrast, have wonderful ways to do that. The sweat lodge, the drumming—those are experiences of cosmic prayer. What does a drum do?

It brings back your nine months in the womb, when you were next to your mother's heart. Drumming was very important when we began our journey in the universe. I can't imagine any religious services worthy of the name that don't bring us back by way of drumming. It stands for the heartbeat of Mother Earth as well, and the heartbeat of cosmic wisdom. So, when religion gets true to itself, there are ways to elicit this experience for us ordinary folks on a regular basis. We have to give that more attention.

I've come very reluctantly to the conclusion that worship is more important for changing Western civilization than the media is. If we could redeem worship, if worship could become an instrument in bringing about the paradigm shift through the love of the earth and the experience of the Cosmic Christ and so forth, our renaissance would really take off. Our civilization, which needs to be a global civilization, would truly be healthy again.

How would you see that happening? How would you see a renaissance in worship?

Well, we have to get rid of pews and all the benches we sit our tired bodies on and we have to start using our bodies to symbolize the curvature of the universe. As Otto Rank points out, all authentic ritual is a microcosm/macrocosm experience. We have to start playing again. The whole issue of the repression of the child and the oppression of the youth in our world today is paramount, and I'm convinced the key to a solution is mysticism. I think this is so because the mystic inside is the child inside—the divine child wanting to play gaily in the universe. If we adults have repressed the child inside, as our religions encourage us to and everything else in our culture does, then we resent the youth when we see it. That resentment comes up as oppression and projection onto the young, and that is why the young are in such despair around the world today.

Consider that in ten years fifty percent of the human race will be under sixteen years of age. We need some radical changes in adults so that we can connect again. We need to pool our senex power, the healthy older person, with a healthy child inside of us. Then we can appreciate the young. So, part of worship must be to allow the old to play again and this means circle dances and spiral dances—playing in the universe. No books!

We've got to get rid of the books. Prayer is not about being read at or reading from—that's reading class. Prayer is about *heart*, opening the heart up. If we can't pray out of our hearts, then we're doomed.

So I go through about six stages of redeeming worship and, really, they're quite practical. We've tried them.

One I call cosmic Masses. We put on cosmic Masses in gymnasiums, because you can't pray in churches that have benches that prevent your body from moving. I remember, after the third cosmic Mass we sponsored, a woman came up—she was about fifty—and she said, "I just want to thank you for leading us in ways of worship in which we'll all be praying forty years from now." I thought that was pretty nice intuition on her part. But there are so many ways that humans can pray and reinvent processes today that take us into the darkness.

Here's another example, Lamentations. Jews and Christians have a Book of Lamentations in our Bible, but it's a book—it's on a page. No one of our dominant culture knows how to lament or wail any more. We have to get that ability from the natives. We have to start lamentating and wailing for our youth, for Mother Earth, for the wounded child in us, for all these deep, deep griefs that we have to go through if we are going to be empowered, first of all, to name the suffering of our time, and secondly to do something creative about it. Authentic religion has always led people in ways of lamentation, but you can't find white folks today in any church or synagogue who are at home with lamenting and wailing.

I think of gospel singing.

You bet. The black people still have it, and the native peoples still have it—absolutely. That's why there is so much to be learned from these native traditions. I was in New Zealand recently, for example. When we landed, we were taken to a Maori school—Maoris are the native people in New Zealand. Sixth-grade boys and girls, about sixty of them, put on a welcoming ceremony for us that lasted about forty minutes. It was so powerful and so beautiful! It ended with the boys doing a canoe chant that was very powerful, very masculine, and I realized that the sixth grade marks exactly the age that children on a Native American reservation usually go into drugs and alcohol and depression. These Maori youngsters were just getting into their power, because they were getting into their spiritual tradition.

There is a wonderful awakening happening with Native Americans in their own traditions today. But they have to be truly allowed to explore their own tradition, which is where they are going to recover their power. Could you imagine moving from a tradition as rich as these native people had regarding cosmology into our world offering McDonald's hamburgers and what not? There's such a culture shock! It's no wonder that those people are especially struck with the disease of alcoholism. Depression replaces energy.

Also, sixth grade is where boys discover girls and vice versa.

Absolutely. That's puberty. There's not going to be a renaissance without an unleashing of erotic energy. There's no creativity without eros, as Jung says. I call for churches to cease being houses of sublimation, and to be instead oases of recovering sexuality, mysticism, and cosmology. The Song of Songs is a wonderful example of this. It is a cosmological poem about the Cosmic Christ, about meeting the Cosmic Christ in human love, *in* the universe. It ends with the woman saying to her lover, "Come play on the mountains of myrrh." In Hebrew, the word for mountain also means breast—breast of Mother Earth. So this woman sees herself as Earth, Mother Earth. All that dimension of play and cosmology has to return to our understanding of sexuality. We have to take eros back from the pornographers. It belongs in religion. Healthy religion deals healthily with sexual energy and mysticism, but this can only come about within a cosmological context.

At the end of The Coming of the Cosmic Christ, *you have a piece about Vatican III. It's kind of a vision. Would you talk about that?*

Yes. I had a dream, actually, when I thought I'd finished the book. I dreamed that there was a new pope, John XXIV, who was a black man from Africa. I thought that that was interesting—the whole Mother Africa returning, getting more to center stage in terms of Church history. This fellow first put out an apology to all the native peoples of the world—also to women, homosexuals, artists, scientists, and some of the others who have been victims of the Christian church over the centuries—asking forgiveness. Each of these groups went into its prayer houses and consciences, thought about it for a while, and then accepted the apology. The result was that there was a tremendous unleashing of energy—a creative energy—in the world, and this pope called the council Vatican III to define the tradition of the Cosmic Christ as an essential way our species can look at itself in the universe. There was an authentic ecumenical council with representatives from all world religions, from all different kinds of backgrounds.

One of the results was that a Jubilee Year was declared for the year 2000, when all debts would be erased between First and Third World countries. It also would mean a restructuring of our economic systems that would be more global, more appropriate, and more interdependent for the species. We'd realize that the basis of wealth is not money, gold, securities, stock, but it's the health of our earth—the health of the air and the waters, and the animals, and our own bodies. As a countdown for the year 2000, every nation agreed to cut back ten percent each year on its military budget. Imagine what Americans would do—what would we all do? You know, we're now spending 1.8 million dollars a minute on weapons. What if we had that money back again? How could we put it into something more interesting, from education to extended families to art and creativity? That's how we're going to put the 700 million unemployed adults to work—through creativity. Again, this is part of the Goddess tradition, that we honor creativity. I talk about a new devotion to creativity, taking a vow to creativity. The only hope Mother Earth has for survival is our recovering creativity, which is of course our divine power. Creativity is so satisfying, so important, not because it produces something but because the *process* is cosmological. It's spiritual, it's centering. There's joy and delight in giving birth.

So my dream was something along those lines. And I might add that all the *opus dei* bishops were put on an island for renewal for two or three years. They had a special retreat, and the native people taught them art as meditation, and their vacated dioceses were taken over by women bishops. It was an interesting dream. I don't think even the Vatican can condemn me for publishing a dream.

Did this include the Congregation for the Doctrine of the Faith?

Well, that was part of it. The Congregation for the Doctrine of the Faith was dismantled and in its place was a council of grandmothers who would decide on doctrines of the Church and, above all, the orthopraxis, the practice of the Church—whether it was healthy for the people, for the young, especially for the children who are born seven generations from today.

And another part of it was that you saw the armies of the world actually becoming defenders of the environment.

Yes. Wouldn't it be wonderful if national defense really meant defense? It's time to defend the environment, to defend the DNA, this precious, precious blessing. You know, all the DNA in the entire human race that's ever lived can fit into one tear drop. This is where we should be putting our defense department—into defending that tear, that eye drop of precious DNA. And it should be defending the soil and the waters, which is the same as the defending of our children. This is what a defense department should be about. These are the issues. Anthropocentric patriarchal ideologies between socialism and capitalism, these are tired issues that are melting in our midst. The issue today is creation, it's earth. Chernobyl is a perfect example of that and so too now is the greenhouse effect. All this is raising our consciousness, and we have to pay attention. As all the mystics say, pay attention! If we don't pay attention, we're doomed.

You've said that you're going to abide by the decision that's been put upon you by the Congregation for the Doctrine of the Faith, that you're going to go into public silence. What do you see yourself doing now in the future?

Well, I don't know how long I'll be in that silence. In other words, I have to wrestle with my conscience every day. I think the issues which Creation Spirituality is speaking about, as I said earlier, cannot afford the luxury of unending patience. So I'm willing to do this for a few months to express my continued goodwill and to give the Vatican an honorable way out. But I can't be silent for too long.

During the period that I am silent, I want to go to Latin America. I want to visit with Father Boff and other liberation theologians. I thought he and I could have a party where no one talks. And I want to go to Africa. I met a fellow this summer who has been twenty-three years in Zimbabwe. He said that the most exciting thing happening in the African church is Creation Spirituality. They're watching our video tapes, reading *Original Blessing*, and they recognize instanteously that this is the heart of their own African traditions. He said that the last Mass he was at in Africa, before he came to America, went on for two and a half hours and an hour and a half of it was dancing— everybody dancing. So I want to experience that. And I'm sure I'll be doing some writing and reflecting and relaxing.

We have maybe a minute left. What would you like to leave our listeners with? Is there anything you'd like to say before you go into silence, at least on these microphones?

Well, here's one thing no one has ever said before that I discovered in my Cosmic Christ research. Each of the four gospels begins with a hymn to the Cosmic Christ. Obviously, John I does. But I'm saying that the synoptic gospels also are set in a cosmological context. Every event in Jesus' life is set in a cosmological context, and we've missed that because we've been reading the scriptures through our anthro-pocentric glasses. So the paradigm shift we're talking about is to move from the quest for the historical Jesus in religion to the quest for the Cosmic Christ. That could unleash a lot of energy in the churches and seminaries and theology schools. I envision renting ten thousand moving vans, parking one at every seminary and theology school, and loading in all the apparatus that for three hundred years we've used to go after the historical Jesus. This would help make it possible now to go after the Cosmic Christ, which would be an authentic pursuit of love of the earth, of love of wisdom in all world religions, of creativity and art at the personal level, of sexual mysticism, all this, and of the relationship to the child in us. All this has to be explored, deliberately and with vigor, in our lifetimes.

Marsha Sinetar

Daily Life as Spiritual Exercise

IN OUR SANER moments, most of us probably regard ourselves as average, ordinary persons, living our lives as best we can, although we may sometimes secretly wonder why we're not rich, famous, and very attractive like those who are. Perhaps by being ordinary, in the true sense of simplifying our life, pursuing our own sense of values, and meeting the demands of everyday life in a new and more integrated way, we can truly become more healthy in body, mind and spirit.

Marsha Sinetar has discovered that ordinary people may indeed live extraordinary lives, and that the realm of the mystic and the ultimate goal of the vision quest may be much closer than we imagine. Marsha Sinetar heads Sinetar & Associates, a human resource development firm based in Santa Rosa, California, and she works with major corporations throughout America. Her research has focused on the characteristics, workstyles, and thinking of gifted leaders, creative entrepreneurs, and self-actualized persons. She holds a degree in psychology and is the author of three books, *Ordinary People as Monks and Mystics, Do What You Love: The Money Will Follow*, and *Elegant Choices, Healing Choices*.

MT: *Marsha, what got you interested in studying ordinary people, or even think-ing about ordinary people?*

MS: I guess people themselves. I have always been interested in talking to people, learning from people. All through my school years, I wanted to get to know everybody around me. I was one of those kids in school who made friends both with the hoodlums and with the honor students. I never wanted to have to choose which group to belong to. Fortunately, nobody ever made me choose, and I became sort of a liaison person between groups.

When I grew up, I found myself in that same role—the role of help-ing different kinds of people understand one another. People who have been influenced too much by the media, who have too little experience of their own, can learn a lot from ordinary people. Each person has everything within them. We can learn from one another, and doing this makes us one another's best friends, one another's best teachers.

You chose a rather unique way to find the people that you studied. Please tell us how you did that.

I asked myself, "What would I respond to if someone wanted to talk to me?" Then, because advertising has always been interesting to me, I took out an ad in some journals. One was a national journal, and the others were local to California. I was looking for certain characteris-tics: a sense of ethics, a sense of the universal order of things, and so on. I listed, in the ad, the traits that I thought would be characteristics of people that I'd want to talk to. And I said, "If you know someone who has these characteristics, please contact me." It was not a gim-mick. I simply wanted to find certain kinds of persons.

And people did respond to the ads—not in droves by any means, but I got mail. In one case, a man's wife told him to respond to the ad. In another case, a mother said to her daughter, "Gee, this kinda sounds like you! Why don't you see what it's about?" People were very trusting from the very beginning.

So these people filled out questionnaires? How did you connect with them?

The initial connection was their letter to me. That was the only screening device I used. In my ordinary work, I'm working with people all the time, in corporate environments. I regularly have to make immediate assessments with very little to go on. So if the letter to me sounded coherent, if it was legible, and if the person seemed sincere, then I simply believed that the individual had something to offer.

Then I sent them, at their request, a lengthy survey. It was about six pages long. Some of it was check-the-box or fill-in-the-blanks and part of it was in essay form. The essay was long. Some people weren't willing to fill this out, but others loved it. In fact, some people wrote me that the survey itself set them to thinking about things in such a way as to make a change in their life.

The questions I asked were very broad-gauged. They asked the kind of thing that would make you reflect on where you've been, what has been important to you, how you solve your problems, and the kinds of people that you tend to be drawn toward. I was really looking to relate to the whole person.

And then you interviewed some of them personally?

Yes, I interviewed about half of the nearly fifty people in the study. Their ages ranged from twenty-seven—that was the youngest— through about seventy-eight.

Didn't the ad say you had to be over thirty-five?

Yes, it did. The one person that I took who was under the age of thirty-five came at the suggestion of a friend of mine who had met this individual and told me, "This person has the maturity of an adult. She has her own business, she's raising her own child, you'll be missing something if you don't interview her, and she wants to be in the study." Well, that's all I needed to hear!

You're not going to turn that down. So who was the oldest?

The oldest was a gentleman from southern California who sailed a boat into nuclear-ridden waters in order to protest some testing devices there. He's seventy-nine, or seventy-eight, and a peace activist.

I had all kinds of people. There were men and women, people who were retired, people who were working, entrepreneurs, people who lived in the South, people who lived in urban areas in the East, people from along the California coast—I mean, just about every possibility.

Was each one uniquely moving along his or her own path, or were there common characteristics?

A little of both. Each one was unique. And there were common characteristics.

What were some of the common characteristics you found?

The single strongest link was a sense of self-definition, a sense of "I AM this kind of person." I would say that this is also the most important characteristic, because it really is what self-actualization is about.

What do you mean by "self-actualization"?

I mean wholeness, authenticity of being. I don't mean, as so many people in the human potential movement and in media have defined it, "doing everything well." For example, someone might say, "I jog, and then I play tennis, and then I ballet, and then I also crochet."

Like the trend to excellence or peak performance, that kind of thing.

Right. I don't necessarily mean that. I mean being the best that one naturally is. For instance, one might feel, "I am the kind of person who is quiet, and so I'm the best quiet person that I know."

So it's something that comes more from internal values, or internal looking, as opposed to external.

Exactly.

The pursuit of excellence, albeit a fine one, or the pursuit of peak performance, albeit fine also, may involve some more external than internal looking.

It may. And that's a very important point. Everything we do is driven by motives. We need to ask ourselves: Where is the motivating urge coming from when we want to be excellent or to be a peak performer? If the motivation is coming from within ourselves, we can be sure that it's natural to us and right for us. If it's coming from "Oh, I want my boss to pat me on the head; he's the father I never had, and so I want his strokes," or "My mother is finally going to approve of me if I am the president," or whatever, then we're being externally driven.

All the people I interviewed had a strong sense of who they were, a sense that came from within themselves. In varying degrees, each was also successful at living that out. The ability to live out their sense of self is another characteristic they shared.

It's a twofold situation here. One issue is that I have to know what I am. The other issue is, Can I live this out? Can I live my knowledge out in my actions? The people that I interviewed were, to one degree or another, successful in both. And that's what I mean by being the best self that one is naturally. We all have a best self, and we all have the potential to live out that self. In fact, that's our birthright, and that's what we're longing for. But doing it takes tremendous courage.

So a third characteristic that the people I interviewed share is that they have a lot of courage. They're *alive*. They are able to strike out on behalf of what's important to them, even when it means saying good-bye to things that are externally programmed for them—things that are toxic, perhaps, or even pleasant to them. This may include relationships, types of work, places that they are living, lifestyles, foods, or even friends. They are able to say, "Yes, I like this," or "No, this is not comfortable," and "Yes, it's not me. I want *this*." They are willing to be what they know they are.

So a fourth characteristic that people share is that they are willing to let go. And that's a very difficult thing to do. We're all attached to people, places, relationships, work, approval of others, the comfort of being at home or belonging to a group. But these people are able to cut those cords. It's not that they actually have to move away. But they have to be willing to take a risk that when they define themselves—"I am the person who is quiet," for example, in a family of extroverts—there's a risk that their family will let them go, or that others will be so unhappy that moving away *will* be necessary. So letting go is another shared characteristic.

A fifth characteristic—I'll mention only five, although in my book I have quite a list—is that these people are very creative and resourceful. Normally these are people who embark on an uncharted path. They may begin in childhood, when they find that they have something in them that needs to be expressed. Or it may happen as they grow into maturing adults. They begin to hear from within that there is a direction they must go. And then, very often—in fact, more often than not—they don't know quite how to go there. "There" is to be somebody that they have had no experience of being. Or it's to do a work that they're not sure is actually in existence. That's why I had the thirty-five year-old age cut-off; I wanted grown-ups who knew what making a decision and a commitment is about.

One woman, for example, wanted to be an artist. No one in her family had ever been an artist. They had always been housewives, mothers, bookkeepers, and so on. So she had to embark on her own path, create her own livelihood.

So we're talking about people who are very resourceful at making ends meet. Some make a lot of ends meet; they're well-off. We shouldn't equate self-actualization, letting go, being creative, and so on with poverty. There's not necessarily a connection. If there is a connection, it's because the person has chosen a simplified lifestyle which involves minimizing his or her possessions.

But even some of the more wealthy people that you found had simplified their lives. They had extracted themselves from the hustle-bustle world and created a much simpler approach to their lives—even though they may have had a lot of money.

Yes. I would even say that that was also another shared characteristic. There were many examples of people who simply gave things away.

One man—a successful businessman—said that everything he owns fits into a chest of drawers. He doesn't wear a tie, ever, anymore. He does have a few sports jackets; but he wears them only to make other people comfortable, not for himself.

Another man, a very successful financial adviser, found that he had to separate the week into two parts in order to keep his practice. One part was for business—that was Monday and Tuesday. Then he took three days to organize his mind, his creative activities, and his investments for people. He discovered that he made much more money for people this way. But again, this took letting go.

Marsha, in your book you referred to an article from Psychology Today *magazine about super kids. The article was about some research that had been done with children. Please tell us about that, and how it relates to your work and your survey and study.*

It's a wonderful article by a woman who has since done subsequent studies of children from disadvantaged and abused home situations. She has found, as others now have who are studying along these lines, that some children whom we would expect to grow up to be totally demolished, actually grow up to be exemplary human beings—about fifteen percent of them, as a matter of fact. I particularly like what that article expresses because it brings a lot of hope to people who, despite having had very difficult early childhoods, have managed to survive and flourish.

In my own book, I describe children who make a link to a healthy adult. It may be a teacher, it may be the parent of a friend. These are children who learn early on in life that they must use their minds to solve their own problem, because their parents won't or can't solve it for them. They are children who, because of circumstances, learn that they have to rely on themselves.

As I point out when I interpret the study in my book, these kids make a bond to *themselves*. We hear so often now, in the literature about child-rearing, that children need to have a bond to the parent—especially to the mother. Yes, this is so, but sometimes that just doesn't happen.

It's heartening to know that we can do the needed repair work any time in adulthood. We mustn't believe that because Mother wasn't at home, or because Mother or Father or a sibling was abusive when we were young, that we can't function well when we're grown up. We can.

Healthy people are people who have made a bond to themselves; they have a trusted, trusting relationship with themselves. The bottom line of being self-actualized is optimal emotional health. And that's what children who overcome great difficulties have.

People who are healthy have done what I call their psychological homework. They know that if all else fails, they do have this sacred entity within themselves—what I think Saint Peter called the inner man of the heart. They are aware of the inner core of themselves that is always there, that never ages and never dies. And it's that knowledge and that sense that brings health.

Children whom we call "super kids" are ones who learn, in the midst of extremely difficult early circumstances, that they have the capacity to solve problems. They may have, for example, parents who are mentally ill or otherwise dysfunctional; there may be extreme poverty or abuse. But these children discover something in themselves that can deal with these problems. So they experience themselves as worthwhile and powerful, even while simultaneously feeling vulnerable. They see themselves in their own corner. They keep the promises that they make to themselves, and they work toward what they need.

We form our self-esteem out of the experiences of our youth. People with healthy self-ideas, such as high self-esteem, learn early that they can alter their thoughts and change their minds for the better.

I think of what Krishnamurti would say about how the brain gets patterned. The brain creates who we think we are, and we become the patterns that are in the brain.

Yes. And what I'm suggesting is that the possibility exists for us to create ourselves.

You know, we often hear today that people have to find themselves. But sometimes it's actually not so much finding ourselves as creating ourselves. It takes tremendous commitment and tenacity and ingenuity to create yourself, because you have to adopt an idea and then manifest it. But it's really not that difficult to do. Self-actualized people are those who have said to themselves, "I understand or I experience who I am to such an extent that I will act that out."

Most people seem to feel they can't do that. Somehow they feel blocked from being able to make the jump, or make the move. It may be for any of a variety of different reasons. I can easily imagine someone saying, "Oh, that's all fine and good, but I can't move to the woods," [laughter] or "I can't move to the country," or "I can't give up my job; I've got a family to support." There are all kinds of reasons that keep us in place. And some of them are very valid reasons.

Yes, they're valid.

What about that?

Well, the reason I liked writing this book was because the people I wrote about fit all of the reasons and profiles you could possibly suggest. There were housewives with children. There were men with families to support . . .

So you weren't talking to total dropouts.

No. And I wasn't talking only to hermits, although there were some hermits. But basically, as the title implies, these are ordinary people. They are people who have to earn money in order to survive. Often they had to do a job other than what they wanted to do. They are examples—not every conceivable example, of course—but some examples of how one can go about breaking away if one wants to.

What these people did is difficult, because it's scary to be that good. But when I say "that good," I don't mean just good at what one does—as in peak performance or the search for excellence. I mean "that good" as a human being. I mean "that responsible," "that authentic." It's scary to be transparent, truthful, so that what we are is known to other people. So we adopt any number of ways to hide ourselves, to appear more like everybody else.

It takes tremendous courage to be authentic, and yet it's so easy because it's simply being what we truly are. And that's the paradox: As people move in this direction of authenticity, their own goodness charms them and encourages them along the path; at the same time, their own vulnerability threatens them away. Sometimes we're stuck for years at a time. So it's important to learn not to push, not to want to go too fast.

Patience was another of the shared virtues you found, I think.

Yes. It could take ten years to change a habit or an attitude. The people in my study were willing to take the time they needed. And the more time they were willing to take, the less time they needed. Too often, people want to force themselves into changing overnight at one of those "quick-fix" seminars or weekend workshops. They're tantalized by images of glorious, stupendous success, and they give very little thought to just "ordinary" success.

At the same time that we're inundated with the weekend growth workshops where "instant enlightenment" is offered, there's also an idea that only a few people get to be saints, only a few people get to be enlightened, only a few people make it to Buddhahood. It's an interesting paradox.

It is such a paradox. And we're never warned adequately about how the workshop dynamic can breed dependency. If you take an expert as your only guide, the expert sets up the criteria of what you should try to be. The expert sets an example for you, and then our job is to become just like him or her. And only a few get to be that way! This kind of dependency takes you away from your own inner voice.

I was raised a Catholic, and I went to Catholic school. I remember what it was like to hear about the saints. They were real. They were very special people. Now maybe it has changed since I was in school, but at that time there was an idea that what the saints exemplify is achievable by only a few people; what they achieved is not available to everyone. You had to be totally good. [laughter] Totally good! And nobody can do that.

It's very unfortunate that we are taught that way. Children really do want to be saintly. If you can just touch them correctly, work with them correctly, they are saints. They can also be little demons, but they have a strong desire to be good. I saw this often when I worked as a teacher.

Yet we tell them that it's impossible for them, that only a few people can get such realization. So of course, they think, "Well, I'll be a baseball player, because *that* I see on TV!" It would be so much better if we encouraged them in their original desire to be good, if we strengthened the impulse toward goodness in one another.

My own belief is that many more saints exist than we know of. People who are just considerate of one another and sweet to one another are saintly in their acts. They might not be that way all the time, but perhaps this is the time for us to be emphasizing those traits.

The people whom I've interviewed certainly have that potential. I don't want to inflate them into something they're not—they're normal people. But normal people have the potential for goodness, if we will simply begin looking at it. Anything you put your attention on grows stronger in your life. So why not put our attention on those good qualities? If we put our attention on these virtues, especially with younger people, there's the opportunity to draw these virtues out of ourselves. We have the potential of becoming anything we want. I believe that.

Well, I think I do too. [laughter] It's really interesting, though, how the patterns of how it's supposed to be get created early on; and then we spend our adult life trying first to discover the patterns, and then to unravel them so we can get back to where we started from.

Some people are what I call "pattern-literate." They understand their own patterns, and they are also able to look around in society and read the cues there. With very little training, they seem to understand the whole picture. That's another characteristic of people who are moving towards wholeness: They begin to see in a whole fashion. They look at things globally as opposed to in a fragmented fashion.

We often fail to recognize the deeper significance of some of our common experiences. I'm thinking of an example you used of an executive you worked with in a counseling situation. You started to talk about meditation and he said, "Oh, no, I don't want to get into that; I don't do that." It turned out that he was an avid skier, and as he described his experience of skiing, it sounded like skiing was something very close to a mystical experience for him.

Yes, and I've had that experience time and again, primarily with executives who are fairly closed to these issues. Often, though, the problem is just one of language or context.

One client of mine, for example, plays tennis. He says that when he plays tennis well, he sees the ball as if in slow motion: He can see the threads on the ball. Well, that's a perfect example of the kind of experience I'm trying to discuss when I talk about meditation. Time just seems to stop. You're so totally in the moment that there is no other distraction. If I can get someone to see the connection between their own experience and the topic they were closed to, then we can move. This just amounts to speaking to people in the language that they're comfortable with.

You wrote that, for some people, simply walking through the woods could bring a sense of union, a sense of no longer being a separate self. Part of what you're talking about there is a transcending of the self. But self-transcendence involves a social transcendence as well.

Yes, it does.

It may be about that. Or it could be either-or.

I found that people had many different ways to get to that state.

One woman talked about sitting at her dining-room table. She lives on the coast, and in the afternoon she just sits and looks at the ocean. Sitting there seems to transport and heal her.

Another person—a man who recently read my book—wrote to me about listening to music in the afternoon. When he gets home from work, he puts on some of his favorite music and sits quietly by himself. After that, he is ready to give quality time to his family. But first he needs this time for himself. In his case, he likes to listen to Bach.

Since reading the book, he has invested in better-quality stereo equipment for himself. He wouldn't have done that before, because he had a tendency to think it would be selfish. But now he realizes that getting the better equipment acknowledges something important in himself. Something is not necessarily selfish if, in the long run, it feeds the greater good.

We're exploring how seemingly ordinary people can lead extraordinary lives, or how extraordinary people can live ordinary lives [laughter]. I think both ways of saying it are right, in some way. More people need to know that it's possible to achieve deeper states of being and more profound levels of consciousness without having to go to India or to a mountain for forty years. These experiences are available to us right where we live. The various levels of awareness are available to most people most of the time. But I don't think we generally believe that.

Generally, we don't. In the process of "legitimizing" ideas of enlightenment and religious achievement, we have burdened them with kinds of academics. It's as if you have to go to college now to have chance of being enlightened. First you take Enlightenment 1-A you go to 1-B, and then you go to an advanced seminar.

Or you have to study with a master.

Yes. Or, if it's approached in a traditional religious form, you may go on for years and years and years. You may be seventy-five before someone tells you that you've done it. And that's another thing—that someone tells you when you are "There."

Yes. You get the imprimatur. The seal. The initiation.

Right. The seal. But I believe in self-definition.

Which is not to deny that there's value in churches, or working with a teacher or a master. It's not to deny that there's value in discipline and in learning precepts.

Absolutely. It's an additive process. I'm not denying the value of any part of the process. I'm not saying, "Don't go to India." But I am saying that you should think about *why* you might go. Don't go because someone is telling you it's "the only way." But if you find that you're genuinely being prompted from *within* yourself, go.

No matter what you do, the very fact that you desire to be enlightened will give you the power to be enlightened. Your desire is the fuel. And you can fan the flame by paying attention to it.

Pay attention to what you resonate with. It's really important to acknowledge that you're being driven internally and not externally.

That's right.

A lot of people get involved with groups and teachings because they think they may be missing out on something that Charlie or Mary is doing. Then it's not really an inner quest. The motivation is not really coming from their own deeper being.

There's a tendency to think that what someone else is doing may get them "There," capital T, first. We can drive ourselves nutty if we let that tendency rule us.

The inner quest, pursuing the values that come from within, is frequently criticized as being self-centered and selfish. Critics say that it takes one away from the "real world," away from shared problems that have to be solved. What about that?

That's a really good point. It may look selfish on the surface. But I don't think any of us can ever judge anyone else. We have to be very,

very careful when we're about to judge another person. We don't really know whether what they're doing fits well into a bigger picture we don't have. Only each individual's inner person knows that. Even the conscious mind of the individual may not know.

The person, for example, who is selling everything in order to follow what he or she thinks is his good may be following a call of destiny. Selling the home, paying off the mortgage, getting rid of the family pet, and so on, may look like a very selfish thing to us now. But ten years down the line, it may look like the only sane thing that person could have done.

So we have to be very cautious. I don't have a general answer for this. It takes tremendous tenacity to be able to do what one needs to do in the face of criticism from people around us whose love we have worked for. And we have worked for their love! Love is seldom given unconditionally.

Speaking of love and the people around us, another characteristic that the people in your study share is that most of them have very carefully selected the friends that they involve themselves with. They either chose new friends or limited their involvement with people they already knew in a way that serves their path.

Yes. They make choices that reinforce what is good for them. If you socialize indiscriminately, you can get undermined. You can lose your one-pointedness and become indecisive. These people in my study have all said to me, in one way or another, "I can't afford to be undermined in my present journey. It has cost me a lot to come as far as I have, and it's very important that I have supportive people around me."

Saying this reminds me of another characteristic these people share. They are truly loving. They have the psychic energy to do what Erich Fromm, in his book *The Art of Loving*, calls "standing in for the other." When someone else needs something, they have the strength and the reservoir of energy to give something tangible—their energy, their resourcefulness, their real help. Many other people just don't have resources like that to share. In their work, self-actualized people show a stewardship pattern. And in their day-to-day interpersonal interactions, they stand in for the other.

Stewardship pattern—please explain that.

I simply mean a tendency towards taking care of the greater good. For some, that means looking after the land. For others, it means taking care of the family or the community. Or it may mean serving the cause of world peace. But however the person defines it, it means taking good care of other things and people, being a good manager.

So the apparent dropouts really dropped into a much larger reality.

Exactly. The dropping-out was a necessary phase. It allowed them to get the energy, understanding, wisdom, and strength to eventually drop back in at a deeper level.

Getting a better sense of the whole picture helps us to see more clearly what our own role is within that picture.

Exactly.

It also explains, in part, the energizing power that keeps individuals like this going.

It does. The energizing power is life itself expressing itself in an ever larger and more complex way.

Perhaps in an ever more simple way.

Yes, more simple also. Both complex and simple.

I'm reminded of Krishnamurti saying, "The most complex problems of the world, of which there are many, have the simplest solutions at their core."

The core of the self-actualization process is life expressing itself. As we know from looking at nature, and also from common occurrences around us, life cuts itself back only in order to grow into a larger life.

Robert Fuller

From Physics to Peace

SOME PEOPLE are content to mold a career and climb the traditional ladder. Others find neither their niche nor their passion, and meander through life like lost sheep. A few persons continue to push their edge, exploring the farther reaches of their creative potential, leaving their mark wherever they may roam.

Robert Fuller has been a physics professor, a teacher in Seattle's inner city, and a college president. Disenchanted with institutional life, he took an extended sabbatical, during which he re-educated himself. He emerged with a new and expanded global view that, in only a few years, has led him to create several projects of worldwide significance.

He has traveled the planet—working to eliminate hunger, rearrange the game of global politics, and understand the root causes of social ills, unrest, and war. A past president of Oberlin College, he holds a doctorate in physics and is particularly interested in the nature of conflict, creativity, and personal power. He is the founder of the Mo Tzu Project, through which private individuals work toward world peace and understanding by traveling and making personal contacts in areas of conflict throughout the world.

MT: *Bob, how did you make the transition from being a trained physicist to work-*
     ing for social and political change?

RF: A better question is: How did I get into physics in the first place? I've
     been probing my youth lately, in connection with my writing, and
     I've come to see that I may have been seduced into physics by the
     glamour that surrounded the field in the forties and fifties, when I
     was a student.

     When I was nine, World War II suddenly ended as a result of a
     physics discovery: the bomb. All of us were enamored with physics;
     physicists were gods. I think anyone who had any scientific ability
     wanted to be a physicist. I feel that I was drawn away from a more
     fundamental interest and that I returned to it when I left physics.

     That more fundamental interest was a fascination with my class-
     mates in grade school. I was fascinated with how they learned. I was
     puzzled that they could be so bright and lively and interesting on the
     playground, yet so dull and apparently stupid in the classroom. I
     never believed they were stupid, although, as the years passed, it
     seemed increasingly evident that most kids are. I knew from experi-
     ence that many children who are considered slow are as quick and
     insightful as anybody else. So it has been a lifelong puzzle to me that
     children get sorted into two groups—the smart and the dumb—and
     that far more find themselves in the second group.

You said you were "seduced into physics." How did that happen?

I was good at science. My father was a scientist, and I had an advantage because he worked with me. That career path was attractive
because in the sixties there were more jobs than people in that area.
Right after Sputnik, there was federal funding for science, and physics was glamorous, exciting, and intrinsically interesting. I loved the
miraculous correspondence between symbolic models and how the
world works.

It's amazing that you can make a mental representation of gravity
or electromagnetism or nuclear physics and, from those verbal or
mathematical models, predict the behavior of the world. The congru-
ence excited me. I think I cared less about how the world works than

the fact that I could build models of how it works. That drew me into physics.

Finally, however, my model-building interest gave way to my earlier interest, which concerned how my friends learned, or failed to learn. I've always had those two interests—science and education.

John Wheeler influenced you a great deal. Could you tell us about him?

John Wheeler is alive and well and doing research in physics at Princeton, where I knew him, and where he has trained so many physicists during the past forty years. His first student was Richard Feynman. I was one of his later students. There have probably been several hundred of us.

His eyes sparkled with excitement, almost with boyish glee, as he figured out how the world works. He came to prominence in the mid-thirties, when he joined Neils Bohr and predicted that one of the two kinds of uranium in the world was relatively inert, but that the other kind, uranium 235, could be the basis for a great explosion. That crucial prediction affected the outcome of World War II. Wheeler played a role in designing the bombs. He also did other kinds of fundamental physics at the same time. And then as Einstein's career drew to an end, Wheeler picked up on Einstein's great program and carried it forward more than anyone else had since Einstein.

He also had an interesting habit of being nice to everybody?

He always treated you as if it were an honor to him that you were willing to work with him—although, of course, the reality was just the opposite. For example, when he took a sabbatical from Princeton to work at Berkeley for a year, I was a student of his. I desperately needed his counsel almost daily to make any progress on my dissertation. He said, "Well, why don't you just come along to Berkeley?" He thought he could find a little money to pay me to do calculations for him.

My wife and I jumped into our Volkswagen, drove to California, and spent a year in Berkeley. I did a little calculation for him, and when it came time to publish the paper—which he had thought of, I had just assisted with it—he credited me as a co-author. He was always putting people's names on papers, even if they had contributed little to them. He was generous, but that alone wouldn't have made him a great teacher; and I do think he's one of the greatest teachers in the history of American physics.

What made him great was his infectious enthusiasm for the subject. He would leave you with a problem at eleven o'clock at night and then call you at six-thirty in the morning to ask you how it had worked out. He assumed, of course, that you'd been up all night. He would have done that himself, and he assumed everyone else would. He was fascinated with the world, and respectful of it, and he reasoned in a most unusual way.

He reasoned by analogy more than most physicists do. In other words, he didn't just explore the mathematical consequences of equations in a formal way. He would compare the nucleus of the uranium atom with a drop of water and use hydro-dynamics to figure out how a nucleus might work. He had the view that God does things as simply as possible, and that if He has something working in one realm, He's going to use the same idea in another realm to get it working. So if you penetrate one realm, you also penetrate others, where similar things probably work in the same way.

By using that kind of metaphoric reasoning, Wheeler was the first to come up with some of the most important results of the last forty years in physics. His analytical work is almost poetical, and it's complemented by his ability to do formal mathematics. Neither talent alone is that fruitful, but when someone can combine metaphorical, analogical reasoning with formal mathematical skill, that's dynamite.

You had some other mentors. I think of Peter Putnam. Will you tell us about him?

Putnam was another student of Wheeler's at the time I was there. He was ten years older than the rest of the class because he'd gone off and done other things. He was interested in understanding how the objective world of science can exist simultaneously—yet seemingly without connection—with the world of ethical or moral law. In the years since I met him, that has been my question, too.

Putnam wanted to establish the connection between the laws of science and the "shoulds" of the world—the things your mother taught you when you were five, things that seem to have an independent existence. He tried to understand how the mind works, how the brain works, psychological laws. The brain ought to be the link because, ultimately, it's probably as understandable as a computer. Although it's admittedly a great deal more complicated than a computer, the brain probably will come to be understood in the twenty-first century.

When the brain is understood—since it's the gadget, if you will, that's coming up with these moral principles—there ought to be a relationship, finally, between the laws of science, through which you understand the brain's function, and the moral principles the brain produces.

Now that's a long program of study, and it's incomplete. But it was Putnam's program. As we worked on it together, he became an important teacher for me.

Was he a good teacher in the same way that Wheeler was?

No, he was the opposite kind of teacher. He was highly eccentric and individualistic, and he developed his own language. I think he had to; the problem he tackled was so fundamental, and he was so far ahead of his time, that he had to be original to make headway. He wasn't a well-known figure. Quite a few people know of his work and continue in the same spirit. But, unlike Wheeler, he wasn't a public figure.

So when you finally decided to abandon physics, or at least to leave physics behind and move on, what happened?

I had been working with Putnam while teaching physics at Columbia, and I was increasingly drawn back to human problems. That was in the sixties, when undeniable political, human problems were drawing the attention of the whole country. I also had all my memories of my elementary and high-school classmates, who hadn't been stupid but had been destroyed by the system.

Working with Putnam, I had studied how the brain works, how the mind works, how intelligence is formed. I had a theory, derived partly from studying some of Pavlov's experiments, that with a different kind of teaching, kids who are labeled "dumb" would shine, too. I wanted to try that theory. It was pulling at me in an emotional way. I had a great passion for education and a diminishing passion for theoretical physics. Physics just didn't seem relevant to what the world needed or to what I cared about most.

That's what I meant when I said that the question isn't, "Why did I drop physics?" The question is, "How did I manage to do a fifteen-year interlude of physics?" My passion has always been to understand why some people appear stupid. Perhaps the question really is, "Why do I sometimes appear stupid to myself and other people?"

Most people, looking at my credentials, would say, "Of course he isn't stupid." But I know myself. I know that sometimes I am stupid. Sometimes I'm inarticulate. But I have an education that allows me to cover that up most of the time.

I think that's how it is with all people who are labeled bright and intelligent: They think of themselves as covering up a fundamental ignorance. And the kids who get destroyed in elementary school never learn the tricks of covering it up. They get caught out, defeated, and consigned to humdrum jobs for life. Of course, then they do stop learning. Their alleged inferior ability becomes a self-fulfilling prophecy.

Pavlov's experiments suggested that people learn in different ways?

That's right. Pavlov discovered that, with regard to learning styles, there are at least two classes of dogs. Actually, of course, many learning styles exist in any species. But he noticed that the dogs that he liked best—the rough, tough, macho dogs—were apparently dumber than the docile, introverted dogs, which, from Pavlov's point of view, were cowardly. It embarrassed him. He didn't want his favorite dogs to seem less intelligent!

He resolved to find a way to train them that would result in their doing as well as the "model student" dogs. The situation is similar to that in an elementary school classroom, where the model students sit patiently and steadfastly and the rowdy kids won't learn anything. Pavlov wanted to find a way to teach his rowdy students.

Here's how he did it: He simply never forced them to pay attention any longer than they were naturally inclined to do, which was often for only three to five seconds. He conditioned them to the metronome (or the bell or buzzer, or whatever) for just five seconds. His previous method had been to go on for minutes at a time, and he had been boring the dogs. After five seconds they hadn't paid attention anyway. So he gave in to their natural rhythm. He began to teach in synchrony with their willingness to learn. And, lo and behold, they learned incredibly well.

At first they didn't seem to learn anything. But he gave them five seconds of the buzzer on Monday, another five seconds on Tuesday—stopping when he noticed they were bored—another five seconds on Wednesday, and so on. By Friday they had had half a minute of the buzzer, and they knew the buzzer. They salivated when the buzzer went on.

The docile dogs might manage to pay attention for a whole half-minute at a time, so on Monday they might salivate to the buzzer by the end of the learning session. And by the end of the Tuesday session they might salivate to the bell.

The rowdy dogs, the extroverted dogs, wouldn't salivate to anything until Friday, when suddenly they would know five things, because they had accumulated enough learning time with each of the five stimuli on five different days.

The situation reminded me of my classmates in Chatham, New Jersey, in the forties. Half of those kids were so restive and jittery that they couldn't pay attention. But they learned wonderfully on the playing fields and outside of school, where they weren't put to sleep by the lullaby rhythm of the teacher.

I applied my new theory in Seattle's inner city. My students were certainly extroverted and rowdy. I never tried to teach them anything if I saw their eyes glaze even the slightest bit. I would force myself to stop, even if I was passionately interested in whatever I was doing. They called the shots. After a year, there was a lot of evidence that they were learning and retaining far, far better than they had been. They were learning as well as anyone else. Their retention rate, in fact, seemed close to one hundred percent. They were illiterate, and they couldn't demonstrate their achievement on written tests. But they could do so on oral tests.

I felt Pavlov's experiments did apply to human beings, and I concluded that if you look carefully at any learner and adjust your teaching style to that learner's natural cognitive style, then you get a resonance. That learner will come out just as smart as anybody else. That's my basic belief, and I think its implications for education and for the future of the human species are enormous.

Your theory challenges traditional educational methods in which a single teaching approach is used for large groups of students.

That's right. Traditionally, everyone is exposed to the same cognitive style, to the same teaching method. Teachers and administrators assume that everyone has the same natural learning style. But we don't, any more than we all like the same food.

I finally understand why I didn't get along with the Jesuits.

Right. But, you know, it doesn't follow that the Jesuits' methods wouldn't work wonderfully for someone else. That's why educational reform never seems to be the answer. We jump from one system to another, forcing all the students into either the first system or the second. Half of them may do better under the first, and half of them may do better under the second.

There's a placebo effect in any educational reform. For a while, everybody's shaken out of old patterns and has a certain amount of fresh energy. So it's probably always better to undertake a reform than not. But educational reform on the institutional level never produces Utopia. Utopia resides in subtle, secret relationships, one-on-one, between individuals. There's no "group Utopia" in education. The teachers who are geniuses sense the differences among pupils and tailor the way they communicate with each individual.

Rhythm—the factor that Pavlov explored, and that I explored in the Seattle inner city—rhythm is an important factor, but modality is equally important. Some people learn through pictures; other people learn through numbers. Some people learn best through speech and sounds; others learn best through kinesthetics, through movement and touch.

I encountered an example of that with my teenagers in Seattle. I tried to teach them fractions, and naturally I tried the same old method of drawing the segments of a pie on the blackboard. Their eyes glazed over immediately. Zero. Failure.

I had noticed, however, that the kids had a tendency to drum on their desks. So I tried teaching fractions in terms of quarter-notes, eighth-notes, and sixteenth-notes. When they drummed out the fractions—hearing them and feeling them, rather than seeing them—they learned fractions like lightning. If I had had to learn fractions through the kinesthetic modality when I was ten, I don't think I ever would have gotten the idea. I would have been a dunce.

So you can switch not just the rhythm but the modality, and lots of other variables, in reaching any individual. Intelligence is formed in relationships between two individuals. The kids who come out of the system as successes are probably the kids who were fortunate enough to have had a parent, or two, or a teacher, early on, who struck a resonance with them. Someone helped them develop that native intelligence that I believe everyone has in approximately equal measure at the outset.

Does that mean the effectiveness of education in the future will depend on our finding ways to adapt teaching methods to the needs of individual students?

Yes. It does mean that. It means that education must have a large diagnostic component. Teachers must not think in terms of mastering history and then presenting history in lectures to thirty kids at a time. What a deadly business! The goal must be to discern how a given student will learn optimally and then to coach that student in the appropriate ways. That may involve using films and computers or sending the student to someone else. And it may involve, to some extent, encouraging teachers to change their methodology from student to student. That's hard to do. Few teachers have a repertoire of rhythms and modalities and skills.

We can at least become sensitive to what makes other people come alive. We can help students get what they need—even if that takes them away from us. A good doctor doesn't try to treat everybody. He or she sends people to specialists who can treat them better.

The food analogy is wonderful. Some people don't like spinach, some don't like sweets, and some don't like meat. But we all know instinctively what we need. Students know what they need, too.

I'm reminded of Colin Wilson, who, I think, was a high-school dropout. He has written more than sixty books in widely varied fields. Clearly, he's an intelligent person, but somehow school didn't work for him. Self-education did. You provide an explanation for the success of self-education: If you can pursue your own interests, it stands to reason that you learn faster.

Yes. Yes. The great leverage comes when you're responding to your own passion rather than trying to acquire information that you can then return to someone on a test, information that someone else is interested in but that you may very well not be. If you use the leverage of a child's passion and curiosity, you can do anything.

Your students in Seattle had been expelled from school?

They had been. They were abject failures according to the school system. They had failed every class and had been expelled. To get into my class, you had to have flunked every other one. I wanted people who were so written-off by the system that, if they showed any success, people couldn't say, "Well, they were bright in the first place." Those kids had already been severely damaged. And yet they had a tremendous spark. I enjoyed working with them and teaching them, more than I had enjoyed working with graduate students in physics, the year before, at Columbia. They had more for me; the Columbia kids were almost exactly like me.

You discovered, in one sense, that the clearest way to learn something is to teach it.

Yes.

What had you discovered at Columbia?

When you get out of graduate school, there's nothing greater than to teach what you've learned, to fully own the material by virtue of teaching it to someone else. It's a great way to consolidate the material you've struggled with for so long.

But after doing that for a few years, I found that it became boring to me. The experience was like gold the first year, silver the second year, and mud the third year. I tired of teaching the same thing because I wasn't learning any more in doing so.

When I taught in Seattle, of course, most of what I was saying wasn't something I was consolidating. We talked mainly about subjects that interested the kids in the class—things like sex, drugs, justice, the absence of justice, and racial issues. But the human interaction with those kids—who were primarily of racial backgrounds other than my own—was priceless. I learned something, I acquired something, by working with them.

And then you went to Oberlin.

Yes. After Seattle, I returned to Oberlin as president. I thought the country had become ripe and ready for a real transformation of the educational system. The country was demanding that minority peoples be accorded personhood, full citizenship, and that women be granted personhood in the eyes of the rest of us. Two great revolutions were under way in the late sixties: the civil rights movement and the feminist revolution.

Moreover, we were changing the definition of adulthood—lowering the age of majority from twenty-one to eighteen. All that ferment drew me back into formal education, and I spent a number of years making basic educational reforms at Oberlin.

My earlier remark—that educational reforms don't amount to all that much—comes partly from that experience. I had high hopes at the outset, but I came to see that the main value of reform lay in shaking the place up, breaking it out of ruts. Afterwards, things went on much as they had before. The great transmissions of mind continued to occur between sensitive teachers and students who wanted to learn. The change of the outer forms, the educational reforms, didn't have much impact on those transmissions of mind, which are the real foci of educational success.

Is that because the decision-making process didn't change?

No, it's deeper than that. It's just that you learn the hardest things, the subtlest, most important things, through apprenticeship. You learn them by doing with teachers what I had the good fortune to do with John Wheeler and Peter Putnam, which is to work with them day in, day out, close enough to them to see them making their mistakes and to see how they recover from their mistakes.

The great teachers, as Wheeler always said, are great because they make more mistakes than anybody else. They just make them faster, and they have the ability to recover from them. It's not that they don't make them. By living closely with someone like that, you learn how to dig yourself out of the holes you fall into.

That's what good teachers do. They don't always appear infallible, invulnerable. They share their vulnerability and fallibility with their students and show how to recover—sometimes not the next hour, sometimes only the next day or the next week. In my work in Seattle, the students often asked questions to which I had no answer. But they would then see how I went about preparing myself to deal with their questions the next day. I'd tell them what I'd done, so that I'd be in a better position to respond. That's more valuable than just always having the right answer.

In all the educational reforms of the sixties and early seventies, I don't think the governance of our American colleges and universities and schools changed one iota. The faculties controlled education before the sixties, and they ended up controlling things after the sixties. Many changes had been forced during those years of change, but the governing bodies remained intact. Students started with no voice and ended with no voice.

I think that's wrong. I think the system would be much better if the students and administrators and staff all had proportional voices. The faculty should remain the main voice, but when you add in the other voices you get a better mix and a more responsive educational system. I believe that will be the next round of educational reform and that it will occur sometime during the next twenty years.

So you left Oberlin and went into a process of what you called re-educating yourself.

Yes. I had left science, you see, and, between Seattle and Oberlin, I had done about seven years of educational reform of one kind or another. During all that time I had pretty much stopped reading. I learned a lot experientially, but I hadn't kept up with reading and with living. So when I left Oberlin, I came to California and spent a few years reading, traveling, and attending workshops. I was young then, in my late thirties, and I wanted to prepare for a second go at the world, using what I'd learned in the fifteen years since I had completed my formal education.

And for the last ten years or so you've been traveling around the planet. That began with a train trip across the Soviet Union on the Trans-Siberian Railway.

My wife and I took our new baby across all of the Soviet Union. Our impulse was to get to know the people whose leaders, we realized, could destroy us in half an hour. It seemed a good idea to go have a talk with them about the situation that had grown up because of nuclear weapons.

That was before many people were doing that.

It was hard to get permission and support for that kind of trip. Most people thought it was a waste of time. But it was in the spirit that Eisenhower had suggested, back in the fifties, when he said that the people have to take responsibility for peace. He warned that we shouldn't count on our leaders to do it; that we should just do it ourselves. And he said that when people demand peace from their leaders, their leaders will have to give it to them.

In our small way, we wanted to go out and start talking about that with people in the society that most threatened our own in the seventies—the Soviet Union. And we did talk to hundreds, thousands, of Russians about war and peace issues. Since then we've been doing what's known as citizen diplomacy. Citizens with no formal portfolios or diplomatic powers nevertheless take responsibility for doing whatever they can about establishing conditions where war won't happen anymore.

Do you think there's really any positive value in those efforts?

There's tremendous value in them. They represent an historic step in that the public is taking responsibility for the conditions in which it lives. Five hundred years ago a warlord could make war on anybody he felt like attacking. About a hundred years ago, when that kind of thing was getting out of hand, politicians decided that war is too serious a business to be left to generals and warlords, that it should be decided by parliaments.

That was a tremendous step forward at the time, because it meant that the people's representatives, at least, were involved in those life-or-death decisions. It didn't change the frequency of war much. In fact, wars got bigger, partly because we were more technologically advanced. The twentieth century has seen the world's worst wars—wars worse than they were when the generals could fight autonomously.

Taking the decision to fight away from the generals did represent a spreading of responsibility for declaring war. I think we're in the middle of another historic extension of that responsibility, where everybody who now is vulnerable in war—given nuclear weapons—has a say in the business of war. In other words, war is now too important to be left to politicians, just as it was once too important to be left to generals. Everyone needs to address it directly. By doing so, we change the climate in which our elected representatives function.

For example, during the last ten years a lot of people have made linkages with Soviets. There have been many television exchanges, so-called "space bridges." And those have grown to the point that members of the U.S. Congress, our elected representatives, want to be part of them! We did a space bridge with members of the U.S. Congress and the Supreme Soviet. They related to each other differently because of the work of citizen diplomats, who have created a new way for Soviets and Americans to talk with each other. For the first time, the Soviet and American publics are watching their representatives relate to each other.

Citizen diplomacy doesn't replace formal diplomacy. Formal diplomacy, as the Department of State and the Foreign Service conduct it, still has a crucial role to play. But we can affect the climate within which the professionals do their jobs, and we can change our expectations. We can also create a public that is immune to, inoculated against, demagoguery and bad leadership.

The Germans never would have elected and followed Hitler had they known more about the world. Neither would the Japanese. Neither will the Americans or the Soviets be inclined to follow bad leaders once they've seen more of the world and understand the situation. The citizen diplomacy movement is an historic and necessary step toward outmoding war.

In 1988 you visited Afghanistan, just as the Soviets were planning to withdraw their troops. What was it like?

For ten years, no Westerners had been in the country legally. A few years before, I had gone to the border of Afghanistan and Pakistan and had seen all the refugees from Afghanistan living in tents. But getting into the country became possible only in April 1988, after the Geneva accords were signed. Then the Soviets arranged for a dozen Americans to go in. I think they did it because they wanted us to see that they were indeed leaving. They were trying to go out with their heads held high, but the truth of the matter is that they went out with their tails between their legs, just as we left Vietnam. They were re-signed to the fact that, without their assistance, the government they had supported for a decade was going to fall. Whether it would fall was the subject of continual discussion while we were there. But ulti-mately that's not the most important thing about Afghanistan, just as the fall of the government we supported in Vietnam isn't the real point.

The real point, I think, is the searing experience of impotency that we had in Vietnam and that the Russians had in Afghanistan: Even though you're a superpower, even though you pour in billions of dollars and the lives of countless young people, you can't defeat a resistance movement that believes it has a just cause and that the other superpower is supplying with weapons. They can't win, either, until you give up. But you can't defeat them. So they wear you down, and then they win. It's a bleeding wound, in Gorbachev's phrase. The Soviet Union learned that in Afghanistan. They've sobered up, as we have.

I couldn't resist the invitation to go to Afghanistan, despite my misgivings. I knew that, once we were there, we'd be in the hands of the regime that was in power, the puppet regime, and that they could use our presence to make themselves seem more legitimate. And they did do that. They controlled the press; they filmed us arriving and misrepresented our presence. But I went anyway, because I couldn't resist the temptation to see the end of imperialism on earth. We may have seen that in Afghanistan. I think the lesson learned is so deep and so sobering that, with a little luck, Afghanistan might mark the expeditionary force's high-water mark in the history of human af-fairs. Afghanistan might mean the end of the Age of Empire. It could become a great symbol, a turning point, in human history. I had been thinking that for several years, and what I saw there confirmed it.

Do you think it's possible to discover a better game than war?

Well, war is a hard game to top. It serves deep human purposes, re-solving conflicts that we've so far been unable to resolve in any other way. It's a game in which you can go all out, and people love games in which they can go all out. Battling, all out, is a way we seek truth.

I should say that war *has been* a game in which you can go all out. The amazing thing is, we've come up with a weapon that we dare not use. For the first time, war is not a game in which you can go all out. There were already intimations of that in the first two world wars, where we had gas that we didn't dare use. Now we have most of our money in weapons we don't dare use. Maybe that is going to put war out of business—the fact that it's no longer a game in which you can go all out.

I see the possibility of a better game than war. It lies in the realm of human learning and education. Learning, model-building, creative work—those are areas of human endeavor where people can go all out. You usually pit yourself against your own ignorance, not against another person. Sometimes, however, in a scholarly debate or an argument over which theory is correct, you can go all out to win.

War also has the beautiful feature of putting everybody in a society on the same side. We like that feeling of camaraderie. Creative work doesn't do that in the same way, although teams of investigators can all work on the same side to solve a problem.

I regard it as an open question: Is there a better game than war, and if so, what is it? Such a game would have to meet two conditions. It would have to be something you can do all out, and it would have to be something that has to do with finding new truth. In the past, war has done both. We tend to forget that wars were the ways in which we consolidated new social insights. If you look back for centuries, you'll see that many of our deepest human values were born in strife and consolidated in wars.

What can do that for us? What can put us on the same side and give us that feeling of working together for something bigger than ourselves? Through what activity can we risk our own identity, as war has made us do, and thereby discover that we're not who we thought we were, that we're not our personality, that we're something deeper? War brings those realizations to people. There must be a better way to do it, since war is no longer an activity in which we can go all out.

My goal now—my koan, my investigation—is to design a better game than war. I think such a game lies in the realm of human learning and human creativity, in working together and in working alone against one's own ignorance.

Most people think that most people are too stupid to play intellectual games, to play artistic and creative games. I think that's not the case at all, that most people are perfectly capable of playing those games, of doing intellectual and artistic and creative work. They haven't been able to, thus far in human history, because economic conditions didn't support it.

But we're creating economic conditions now where more and more people have time for creative activity. In the long run that's a necessary condition if creative, intellectual work is to replace war. It has to be the case that most people can do it. I believe that most people can, and I think the experiment in the Seattle inner city shows that.

Andrew Bard Schmookler

Beyond Power and the Thought of War

IN A DANGEROUS world, civilized people depend on the warrior's spirit for protection. Indeed, we use the metaphors of war in all areas of life. Football teams have battle plans. Civil rights activists carry on the struggle in the trenches. President Bush launches a war on drugs.

Fighting to defend our lives and liberties may be rational, but it may also be that conflicts and fears between individuals lead to conflicts and wars among nations. Because we can no longer rely on our instincts to govern our lives, we feel constant uncertainty as we face a hostile world. To compensate for our insecurities, we adopt a posture of aggression, which leads to violence.

Resolving interior conflicts that drive the cycle of war is imperative in the nuclear age. If wars arise out of weakness, humankind must travel beyond weakness to create harmony and peace.

Andrew Bard Schmookler has explored the roots of conflict and war and considered what it means to create a peaceful world. His books include *The Parable of the Tribes* and *Out of Weakness: Healing the Wounds That Drive Us to War*. His view helps us understand the nature of fear and power, the causes of war and conflict, and how power has influenced the evolution of civilization.

MT: *Andy, I'd like to go back to the time before you wrote* The Parable of the Tribes. *How did the idea of writing a book about the issues of power emerge?*

AS: A fair chunk of my life history is bound up with that quest. For the first two decades of my life, I had a clear sense of purpose, a sense of how I might make a contribution in the world. But by the time I had graduated from college, several things had happened to upset that. Some were personal, such as the death of my father, and some were more global, such as the Vietnam War and the 1968 Democratic convention in Chicago. The times seemed out of joint.

The world seemed full of destructive energies, and I decided to take some time to find my way. I wanted to understand what I could do that would make sense in such a world, and I felt the tension of that search in my body. Looking back, I see that physical tension as the preliminary work for *The Parable of the Tribes.*

In 1970 I had a couple of visionary experiences, in which I saw my true nature as a human being and understood my place as an animal on this earth. My vision of our connection with nature stood in juxtaposition to the forces of civilization that operate upon us and around us. I saw how it is that the systems we've created have an autonomous existence and a logic of their own. I saw how those systems have used our energies without being governed by our needs.

I also had a sense of being charged to develop what I had seen and communicate it to my fellow creatures as effectively and clearly as I could. And I received that charge at a level of my being that was so profound that I had no choice but to fulfill my assignment, whatever the obstacles. Now, almost two decades later, I feel the satisfaction of having completed that mission.

I understand that you wrote The Parable of the Tribes *as a dissertation for your Ph.D. degree. Is that correct?*

Although I was bold or reckless enough to take on the assignment I just described, I tried to satisfy the demands of prudence at the same time. I had committed myself to completing that task whether I earned any credentials for it or not. But I spent two years on the East Coast and then on the West Coast trying to find a way to write my book and receive a Ph.D. degree at the same time. Eventually I found an institutional niche and a committee that believed in what I was doing. By 1977 I had finished the first—and considerabiy longer—version of *The Parable of the Tribes*.

That kind of project often remains in the dusty, murky halls of academia. Yet you were able to transform a dissertation into an eminently readable book for the general public. Can you explain that next step?

I never thought of the book as just a dissertation. I felt myself in the service of something for which I had considerably more reverence than I would expect an academic institution to have. On the other hand, the original presentation wasn't as effective as I knew it could be. I wanted to make *The Parable of the Tribes* into a work of art—something that conveyed ideas and, at the same time, moved people. I always had one audience in mind: concerned, caring people in the general public who are passionately committed to making the planet a more humane place.

What is the message of The Parable of the Tribes?

To understand what we are and how we've arrived here, we need to recognize that we're not fundamentally creatures of civilization. We've been born into civilization, we see civilization all around us, and we trace our origins to classical civilizations. But we've also evolved on the planet for three and a half billion years. The three thousand years since Moses and the twenty-five hundred years since the golden age of Greece are but moments of time.

When we see ourselves as parts of the biologically evolved order—and grasp the nature of that order—we discover that the problems that torment civilized people are new in history. The problems of civilization are separate from our essential nature; we were human long before those problems arose.

What's the nature of the system out of which we emerged? The insights of ecology and evolutionary biology indicate that we're products of a natural system characterized by an intricate harmony of creatures. The nature of each of those creatures has evolved over countless eons to fit into the community of creatures. Even the relationship between predator and prey, between parasite and host, is critical to the life cycle of both species. The outputs of one species are the inputs of another and vice versa. Everything cycles. The living system as a whole protects life. Air and soil are artifacts of the living system. In the absence of civilization, the living system is a perpetual motion machine that requires only the energy of the sun as input.

After millions of years the biosphere has become adept at creating the safeguards and homeostatic conditions that maintain the well-being of the entire living system. That's not to say that deaths don't occur, or that individual creatures aren't injured. But until civilization emerged, threats to the perpetuation of the living system could come only from outside the system—for example, a comet streaking out of the cosmos could demolish the planet. The living system created only safeguards.

What happened with human beings? We became creatures with the capacity to learn, to create, to break out of the niche into which we had evolved, and ultimately to fashion our own way of life. That emergence into a world of new social possibilities *appears* to have been a breakthrough into freedom. Hunter-gatherer societies can become only so big and so complex. In their essential nature, their relationships to the surrounding world, and their interaction with each other, they remain like primate bands. But when we started to rearrange the ecosystem to serve our own purposes, all things seem to have become possible for humankind.

After five thousand years, however, what's the result of that apparent freedom? For civilized peoples, the road of civilization has led substantially downhill. War has become chronic and destructive. Tyranny has emerged. And most people live as virtual slaves. Human activity has begun to spread the rough and rocky desert. Why did civilization develop such an ugly face? That's the question *The Parable of the Tribes* answers.

The breakthrough into freedom was only apparent. The breakthrough that appeared liberating unleashed new forces—forces people didn't choose, *couldn't* choose, and that aren't part of their nature. Civilization didn't free us. It subjected us to new and harsher necessities.

So the ways of power inevitably spread throughout the entire system?

Creatures in that situation inevitably will engage in a struggle for power—not among themselves as individuals, but as social groups. The problem is like that described by Thomas Hobbes in *Leviathan*, which is about the pernicious effects of anarchy. But he misnames anarchy "the state of nature." Anarchy doesn't characterize the living systems of nature. Anarchy is a state of un-nature. It arose only when living entities—civilized societies—broke out of the regime of nature, yet were subject to no other law.

Once the struggle for power begins, there's an inevitable selection for the way of power instead of the way of peace. That's the parable of the tribes. If the interacting societies in a system choose the way of peace, then all may live in peace. But if all but one choose the way of peace, and that one is aggressive and intent upon extending its domain, then that one can impose upon all the necessity for power.

In an anarchic system, power is a contaminant. What choices are available to the societies that confront a single society in their vicinity that wishes to extend its domain? The aggressive society can attack and *annihilate* one of its neighbors, taking over its territory. That's destruction. Or the aggressive society can attack, conquer, and *absorb* a neighbor—making the conquered people part of an underclass in the imperial society, with its homelands coming under the aegis of the expanding society. That's transformation and absorption. A third possibility is that a society, seeing the threat of aggression, might leave the system and withdraw to remote jungles, islands, or arctic regions. That's withdrawal.

The fourth possibility is that societies, recognizing a threat, decide to protect themselves. Ironically, to protect themselves against power, they must be able to wield power. And if the society that threatens them has magnified its power—by technological, political, economic, or psychological innovations—the societies that resist the threat must, to be successful, become more like the society that threatens them. That's imitation.

Though different from each other in important ways, those four possible responses to aggression—destruction, transformation and absorption, withdrawal, and imitation—have one thing in common: In each case, the way of power spreads inexorably and inevitably throughout the entire system.

It's therefore an illusion that that emerging creature, with its new capacity to invent a way of life, could have developed its social evolution in whatever way it wished. Of the many cultural options that seemed available, only those that conferred sufficient power for success in the inescapable competitive struggle could survive and spread. All other possibilities—however beautiful, however fulfilling to the human spirit—would be swept aside if they entailed weakness in the arena of competition.

In *The Parable of the Tribes* I show the enormous ramifications of that simple idea. Many of the trends and problems of history can be illuminated by an understanding of the process that—through the centuries, through the millennia—has sifted among the cultural possibilities and left only those that have brought success in a destructive, unwanted, and inevitable selection for power.

We usually think of the agricultural and industrial revolutions as milestones in the progression from primitive to contemporary society. Yet in a sense those technological revolutions have created the problems we now face. Do you see such advances as progress?

The thrust of history is "progressive" in the sense that some things increase. What increases most reliably is the *power* of societies. The first horticultural societies were more powerful than the hunter-gatherer societies among which they arose. Then the agrarian societies—emergent in certain areas, like the Nile, Tigris-Euphrates, and Indus valleys and China—were more powerful than the horticultural societies around them. As societies developed new subsistence technologies, they also created political structures that provided more efficient ways to control land and wield power.

Sometimes that kind of change constitutes progress in the sense of increasing human well-being, and sometimes it doesn't. During the considerable period between the time of the hunter-gatherer societies and the full flowering of civilizations in Egypt and Babylonia, for example, the changes were detrimental for most of humanity. For you, me, and most of our readers—living in one of the most powerful nations on earth and enjoying material comfort and sufficient liberty of the spirit that we can have this conversation—civilization has been kinder. But it would be a mistake to be complacent.

Social evolution during the last four centuries may have improved the human lot in some societies. But it would be a mistake to assume that the benefits to us are the *reason* for those changes. The forces that led many free human beings in hunter-gatherer societies to become slaves in ancient civilizations may still be at work. Although the selection for power is not hostile to human needs, it does tend to be indifferent to them.

The nuclear arms race is the most florid contemporary example of how the struggle for power warps social evolution. Two ambitious and frightened powers strive against each other, taking resources away from meeting human needs to achieve what they hope will be security. At the same time, they increase the likelihood of a final destructive cataclysm. Truly we must contain that process before it undoes us.

In the midst of that gigantic race between two huge monoliths, what can we, as individuals, do to bring about constructive change?

You've raised two questions: What's possible? And how can we deal with our inability as individuals to solve that problem?

For almost two decades, I've wrestled with recognizing my own limits. I can see the problem, but I can't solve it. I'm compelled to acknowledge that what I have to offer isn't the wave that will wash things clean. It's a drop in the bucket. That awareness has taught me the need for humility and the need for faith. I need humility to say, "I'm only one out of almost five billion people on this planet. I can't do it by myself." And I need faith to say, "Well, although I'm only one, there are almost five billion others. If I do my part, and if all the others who have the same divine spark in them will do what they can do, maybe it will all add up to what's necessary."

We need only reach into ourselves to put into the world the best that we can give. And just have faith that it will add up.

You mentioned in The Parable of the Tribes *that the challenge we face is to design systems that use power to disarm power. Will you elaborate on that?*

The United States Constitution is my favorite example. Of all the things in the United States, I think the Constitution, the whole concept of the Constitution, is the most remarkable. It is our greatest contribution to the species.

In the *Federalist Papers* (which Madison, Hamilton, and Jay wrote to persuade people to choose union voluntarily), Madison says, "If men were angels . . ." and then acknowledges, ". . . but we're not angels." From that premise he sets about to construct a system that doesn't depend on our being more than human.

The message of *The Parable of the Tribes* is humbling in that it says we haven't been masters of our own destiny. We've created civilization, but we've been its victim as much as its master. At the same time, that vision of what has happened also exonerates us. It says that the evil we see in history isn't a function of the evil in human nature. Because we're creative, we've developed the powers of gods. But we aren't gods, and we have to recognize that.

We need to set up a system with adequate checks and balances. We can't afford to have sovereign entities who can infringe upon their neighbors with impunity. I'm suspicious of having a single central world government, but we need some kind of world order, some kind of confederation of units that, individually, are powerless against the larger system. Without such an order, the worst among us can drive all of us toward their moral levels. Only in an anarchic state can someone like Hitler or Stalin terrorize hundreds of millions of people.

When a foreign body comes into the human body, the whole system mobilizes to keep that contaminant from spreading. But if you don't have a unified body, an infestation of a part can spread. Humanity has been fragmented in that way. We need to knit the whole of humanity into a single body so that when a contaminant appears—an individual like Hitler or a nation like Nazi Germany—we can deal with the threat and keep it from spreading.

In the Reagan years we heard the Soviet Union categorized as an evil empire. Do you think the Soviet Union is more responsible than the United States for the arms race?

There's plenty of responsibility to go around for the arms race. After the Soviet Union has been given its fair share, there's a great deal left over for the United States. Beyond that, the question of blame isn't useful. It would be better to ask how we'll transform the destructive and dangerous course of superpower relations into something better. The Soviets' system is more rigid than ours, and their history is more nightmarish. We shouldn't forget that they're human beings, just as we are. If they behave in ways we find offensive, such as shooting down an airliner over their territory, our outrage may be appropriate. But we should also understand how frightened those people must be if they're so extraordinarily threatened by a violation of their borders.

Our relations with Mexico and Canada show that we Americans have a more relaxed attitude about boundaries—and about relationships with people we don't control—than the Soviets historically have had. Their relationship with the Chinese has been filled with fear, mutual suspicion, and the threat of war.

The United States might do well, however, to emulate the Soviet Union by being more cautious, more consistent, and more prudent in international affairs. The Soviet Union isn't a reckless power. We tend to veer around; we've been inconsistent. We seem unable to proceed with a long-term view, which is what humanity requires of us. If the Soviet Union were more like us, we would probably be able to work out a more benign competition. Many of the ways in which we struggle for self-esteem are nonmilitary. The Soviets' sense of security, their sense of the nature of relationships among people, is based on force more than ours is. If you took away the role of their military, their position as a superpower would be greatly diminished. But that's who they are. Our task is not to fault them, or to make them like us, but to find creative ways to transform our relationship with them into one that isn't threatening.

The United States and the Soviet Union have important common interests, the most obvious of which is to avoid nuclear war. Given that common interest, all of our conflicting interests pale by comparison.

You write about the loss of wholeness during the history of civilization and suggest that the lack of wholeness is detrimental to our search for peace. What do you mean?

One form of wholeness—synergy—characterizes a system to the extent that each actor's efforts to promote its own well-being also enhance the well-being of others. Some relationships among people are synergistic, and others aren't. The struggle for power is based on a sense of scarcity. Each person thinks, "What others have threatens me, and if I want more, I must gain it at their expense." The relationship between lovers exemplifies another kind of interaction, in which giving and receiving are indistinguishable. We must organize human systems so that each participant, by trying to meet its own needs, enhances the rest of the system.

One of the problems of the international system is that the anarchy creates real insecurity. The insecurity inflames people's paranoia and suspicion, and that frame of mind makes people see only conflicting interests. We must see ourselves, fundamentally, as members of one species, as having common bonds. That experience is more important than our membership in various nationalities that make claims of superiority, or of territory, at each other's expense.

What's the relationship between the ideas you explore in The Parable of the Tribes *and the way nation-states deal with and suppress the threat of terrorism?*

Terrorism is a many-sided phenomenon. Open societies are more vulnerable to it than closed societies are. You don't hear about terrorism in the Soviet Union, where travel is difficult and searches are frequent. We've decided to have more of a police state at our airports, and we accept that because we want to prevent skyjackings. The problem of terrorism in open societies illustrates how, in a poorly controlled situation, an individual or a small group of people can have a disproportionate and negative effect. Sometimes the worst among us are able to foreclose our options. History often listens to those who wield power most ruthlessly.

In recent times, terrorism has become a means of waging war. Some states use terrorism covertly to wage war against other states without declaring war or necessarily inviting retaliation. The explosions that killed so many Americans in Lebanon were at least permitted, if not actually instigated, by sovereign states. Yet it's difficult to trace the connections and difficult to know how we would respond even if the connections were obvious. It's not as if some nation's air force had bombed American territory. In a world in which waging war has become suicidal, some nations have found new ways to achieve war's ends.

Have we simply been conditioned to believe that democracy is better than communism, socialism, and Marxism?

The issue is people's need to feel superior to one another. Why should it be difficult for us to accept that another nation has another way of being? We Americans tend to have a missionary attitude that everybody should be like us. We have a shallow understanding of our place in the spectrum of human possibilities. We tend to think that we just emerged spontaneously out of nature as Americans. Yet our way of looking at things, which makes a liberal society appropriate for us, is a complex artifact of several thousand years of history.

Soviet history, Chinese history, Indian history, Brazilian history—all histories—are different from ours. Even if we can legitimately point to problems in those societies, it's likely that what's best for those societies would differ from what's best for ours because of differing cultural values. That should be acceptable. We should delight in the diversity of humanity.

Being threatened by diversity, by people whose beliefs are different from ours or by people who look different from us, is a sign of our own insecurity about what we are. The more comfortable and at peace we become with ourselves, the more we'll celebrate diversity.

You asked about the various aspects of wholeness. One kind of wholeness we can seek as individuals entails coming to terms with ourselves. The Delphic oracle said, "Know thyself," to which I would add, "and accept what you know." Self-acceptance at the individual level spreads peace among individuals and nations. The more we're at peace within ourselves, the less we need an evil empire. Sometimes we seek an external focus of evil because we can't acknowledge the imperfections within ourselves.

I chose to answer the question about democracy in this way, rather than to say why I think democratic values are worthy of human aspiration (which I do). In the modern world, America's principal task now is less to spread democracy than to be able to embrace other cultures in a less judgmental and condescending fashion.

Those comments are related to what you call choosing life.

Yes. Within us and around us is a domain of sacredness. As far as we know, this planet is the only place in the universe that's alive. It may or may not be unique. But it is, at least, the realm of life entrusted to us. The film of life that envelops this planet is an order of mind-boggling complexity and beauty. The little piece of the life-force that courses through our nerves and veins, flowering into the human consciousness that can appreciate this creation, is also something of sacred beauty.

I wrestle between willingness and unwillingness to experience the magnitude of what's at stake, between ability and inability to allow myself to experience all the pain that living things suffer. We've been entrusted with something beautiful and mysterious. How will we deal with that responsibility? We can behave like a rhinoceros running through the Louvre, mindlessly scattering gems and trampling masterpieces. Or we can learn to tend and nourish this garden. In this creative species, life has embarked on a dangerous and wonderful experiment.

You speak of the pain that living things suffer. Was your more recent book, Out of Weakness: Healing the Wounds That Drive Us to War, *a natural outgrowth of* The Parable of the Tribes?

The Parable of the Tribes is about how choices have been taken from us. That's still the perspective in which I see what has happened to our species during the last ten thousand years. But one need only look at a newspaper to see that something else is also going on. Even from among the choices that are left, we seem unable to choose, consistently, the best and wisest of our options. People often seem drawn to create strife. I wanted to understand what happens within people that drives them to war. *The Parable of the Tribes* is about the system, the circumstances into which we've unwittingly plunged ourselves. The destructiveness of history is not to be understood in terms of human choice or human nature. But we've come out of that history, and we have to deal with where we are. We're wounded animals and somewhat crazy for it.

Think of it this way: Civilized peoples live in a state of more or less chronic insecurity. We brought ourselves out of the ordered regime of nature and plunged ourselves into this anarchic situation. Civilized societies must confront each other outside of any order. That's not the way life evolved over three and a half billion years, but it's what happens when a creature gets creative enough to step across that line. Out of the gift of our creativity have come the curses of anarchy and the constant struggle for power. Our survival as individuals, communities, and societies has been more or less continually at stake. That trauma indelibly imprints itself as a fundamental truth of our existence. We enshrine warriors as our heroes because they protect us. But the warrior spirit also endangers us. As you mentioned earlier, in a nuclear age we had better understand both elements of that paradox—the heroic and the mad, the strong and the wounded.

One observes political leaders posturing and positioning themselves, and it's sometimes as if they're acting out something personal in a public arena.

When we select our leaders, we choose from among people who have striven, with single-minded and obsessive devotion, to achieve a position of supremacy. They don't represent a random cross-section of the population. Also, our leaders are the people at that highly charged and dangerous boundary of what Hobbes mistakenly called "the state of nature." They're at the edge, looking into that disordered realm where no law holds the Hitlers in check. We have a not-altogether irrational desire to ensure that the individuals who represent us there can deal with the problems of power that inevitably arise in that realm.

You used the word "posturing," which suggests an element of pretense. That's at the core of the discussion in *Out of Weakness*. Some kinds of strength don't require posturing. Other kinds of strength involve pretending to be something we're not. That pretending, that posturing, fuels the excesses of the warrior spirit and makes us really dangerous animals in our wounded condition.

In some ways, we have to take responsibility for creating our leaders. It's almost as if we've put them on the ramparts so that we ourselves won't have to wrestle with the problems of that realm. Then we complain about the way they handle things.

One problematic aspect of leadership in America involves our willingness to pretend that untrue things are true. We collude with our leaders. The Reagan years were a period of collusion in a trance state—collusion with an effective actor in pretending that untrue things were true. To the extent that we demand that our leaders be something other than human beings with weaknesses and vulnerabilities as well as strengths, to that extent we're responsible for some of the pathologies we enact in the world.

I remember when, in 1982, President Reagan first used the term "evil empire." Perhaps that typified what you talk and write about.

People who are trying to run away from something in themselves like to have an evil empire for a focus of evil. The implication is that we're all good. It's comforting. We can avoid confronting our shortcomings and wrongdoings. Some Americans like to hear our leaders polarize the world in terms of good and evil and cast us in the role of the righteous. It's a dangerous posture.

What about our over-concern with personal and national security?

One shouldn't dismiss security as a goal. Security has value. The question is: In what does our security consist? At the material level, we're devouring the earth because we think security consists of meeting our merest wants and satisfying every lust.

Some of our spiritual leaders point to a better path. The warrior with his armor represents an effort to deny the weak and vulnerable self within. Jesus and Buddha, who offer open hands rather than fists, represent true strength. Buddha's stomach is full; Rambo's is like a scrub board. One kind of leader asserts the strength of defensiveness and, in many cases, denies vulnerability. The other kind of leader affirms the strength of accepting our vulnerable condition and facing it without fear. The courage of the warrior is important, but the courage of a Jesus or a Buddha is even more important. Similarly, at the material level, there's a way to find nourishment that's more fundamental than the ways we're usually encouraged to choose.

We're entitled to struggle, work, and pray for security. The issue is whether we're able to see the route to true security and have the courage to avoid trying to fill the void and calm our fears in counterproductive and ineffective ways.

Some leaders try to appear invulnerable. In Out of Weakness *you refer to Hitler as someone who felt invulnerable. You describe an incident when he was whistling an opera and whistled the wrong note.*

Somebody pointed it out to him, and he said, "It's not I who made the mistake. It's the composer who erred." Yes, there's the assumption of invulnerability, the insistence on perfection. It's a denial that we're flesh and blood. Stalin wasn't born with the name "Stalin." "Stalin" is Russian for "steel." He changed his name from his original Georgian name to deny flesh and blood. Those inflamed with that defensive passion want to encapsulate themselves in hard things that are impenetrable and can't be scratched.

Hitler also claimed to have nerves of steel. Max Planck reports that someone once suggested in Hitler's presence that Hitler was nervous. Hitler pounded on a desk, shouting, "Nervous! I have nerves of steel!" He worked himself into such a lather that, according to Planck, there was nothing the others could do but excuse themselves.

And then there's the "Star Wars" defense system, a poignant and contemporary example of the desire to deny the reality of our condition. I had the job, in 1983 and 1984, of going around the country and talking to the best thinkers I could find to explore our choices for ensuring security in an age of nuclear weapons.

You had an interesting encounter with someone you call "the General."

Yes. That was shortly after Ronald Reagan—without consulting the usual scientific, military, and other advisers—had launched a significant military initiative. He had fallen in love with the idea that technology would save us from the threat of the evil empire. Among the people I interviewed was the man I call "the General." He was one of the primary promoters of the "Star Wars" idea.

I called him, told him what the project was about, and requested an interview. He agreed to give me an hour, and I went to see him. We sat down, I asked him an open-ended question, and he launched into his prepared comments: Mutual assured destruction is intolerable; we need assured survival; the idea of deterrents is unacceptable because the Soviets are such monsters that they wouldn't mind absorbing tens of millions of deaths. He summarized various scenarios and stressed the importance of building the "Star Wars" defense system.

My goal with everybody I interviewed was to probe for underlying assumptions, so I began to explore some of the things he had said. On what basis did he conclude that the Soviets wouldn't mind fifty million of their own people being killed? If they launched the first strike, how many warheads would his system intercept? How many would that leave? And if five hundred warheads instead of two thousand fell on the United States, did that really change anything?

About ten minutes into the interview, he said, "The interview is over." I looked at my watch, I looked at him, and I said, "General, we've been talking for only ten minutes. You agreed to give me an hour." He said, "I've changed that." I said, "Could you explain why you've changed that?" He said, "I don't have to explain myself to you."

I thought for a second and said, "General, if you've concluded that I'm unsympathetic to your position, let me assure you that my feelings about these issues are not what I'm here about. I'm challenging everyone's position. The more convincingly you answer my challenges, the better I can represent your position to people who disagree with you."

He said, "Get out of my office."

I'm an American, and I've been brought up on athletics and cowboy movies. I felt my own warrior juices starting to move around. And then it came to me—because, after all, I've been trained to channel some energies into the head. I saw the connection: He could deny any position he found intolerable. It would be intolerable for him to admit being vulnerable to the Soviets, so he would deny any possibility of that being true. He didn't have to deal with the Soviets, he didn't have to deal with the facts, and he didn't have to deal with me. So I gathered my stuff, stood up, said, "Well, General, I see what you mean by good defenses."

There's a Sufi story that I think illustrates what the proponents of the "Star Wars" technology were doing. A man is working in a garden, and he sees Death come in. Death looks at him strangely, and the man trembles. "Oh, that's Death," he thinks, "and he's looking at me strangely. I'd better get out of here!"

He drops his tool, runs out the garden, and takes off down the road to Baghdad. Another gardener, who has watched the exchange, goes over to Death and says, "Why were you looking at him so strangely?" And Death says, "I was just surprised to see him here. I have an appointment with him tomorrow in Baghdad."

"Star Wars" was our way of running off to Baghdad for our appointment with Death. What we won't acknowledge as our own will possess us, and what we run from will catch us from behind.

Nobody seems to be talking seriously about an invulnerable astrodome anymore, but it was on the table in the mid-1980s. And it had the real and dangerous effect of being the principal obstacle to progress in talks between the two superpowers about strategic arms control. The IMF agreement was a small thing; "Star Wars" impeded a larger agreement. An illusion produced a very real effect.

Even more important: If we had built that system, we would have been more vulnerable to attack. The idea of deterrence is to structure weapons systems so that no matter how nervous either side becomes, neither has a motive to be the first to push the button. That's called stability, and it has been an important part of keeping the world relatively peaceful for more than four decades.

Nothing we could have built would have protected us from a first strike. The only possible advantage of the "Star Wars" technology—and the Soviets understood this—would have been its usefulness in protecting us against a retaliatory strike. The logical Soviet response to "Star Wars" would have been, "We'd better not let them strike first or we'll really be in trouble." If a crisis occurred, the Soviet Union would have something that generations of American strategic planners had sought to avoid: the incentive to use their weapons rather than lose them. They would feel the need to strike first, not because they wanted war, but out of fear.

"Star Wars," again, was like running to Baghdad. It involved denying the truth of our vulnerability, and it's a good metaphor for how the warrior condition can endanger the very things we're trying to protect.

Yet as we enter the 1990s, we're still spending billions of dollars on the Strategic Defense Initiative—"Star Wars."

So much of American politics is theater in which things have a symbolic property. "Star Wars" is like a branch cut from a large tree. The leaves are still green, with our billions, but the branch is severed from the source that made them green. In a while they'll wither.

In a more rational world, we would stop that funding more quickly. But in our symbolic situation George Bush can't, according to his way of conducting himself, openly admit the folly of the man on whose coattails he rode into office.

I'm struck by the number of politicians who continue to see defense and weapons systems as sacred cows. In Out of Weakness *you discuss the "wounded male." I think there's a connection in that, in a patriarchal system, so many males carry those wounds. It probably goes back to caveman days, when men had to kill mastodons for meat and defend the cave against all kinds of creatures. We don't always remember that times have changed. Instead of dealing with the deep wounds we carry, we project them externally. So we build up huge weapons systems as a defense even though, in fact, they're no defense at all.*

In the age of mastodons, men were probably less infected with pathologies than we are now. When power is uncontrolled in the world, the weak are ground up. Being weak invites victimization, and being vulnerable is the pathway to pain. People are afraid to show the world anything but strength. Victimization frequently passes from parents to children and from group to group as people try to push down that sense of being small and vulnerable.

Late in the Carter administration, I interviewed a man at the National Security Council who had models of U.S. and Soviet missiles. The Soviet missiles were much bigger, and he maintained that the United States was at a disadvantage. The Soviet missiles were bigger because the United States had developed a better fuel system, which enabled us to make smaller missiles. But the image in his mind was that the Soviets were twelve feet tall.

The wounded warrior always tries to hide his underlying feelings. Hitler and Stalin were severely abused as children. No matter how much they denied it, they could never stop feeling like wounded children.

Andy, you live in the Washington, D.C., area. I grew up there, surrounded by the monuments to our history—the Washington Monument, the Lincoln Memorial, the Jefferson Memorial. I remember, in high school, encountering Shelley's "Ozymandias" and realizing that those monuments would some-day be in ruins. I was pleased that you incorporated "Ozymandias" in Out of Weakness, *and I'd like to talk about its significance relative to conflict and war. Here's how it goes:*

OZYMANDIAS

I met a traveller from an antique land
Who said: Two vast and trunkless legs of stone
Stand in the desert . . . Near them, on the sand,
Half sunk, a shattered visage lies, whose frown,
And wrinkled lip, and sneer of cold command,
Tell that its sculptor well those passions read
Which yet survive, stamped on these lifeless things,
The hand that mocked them, and the heart that fed:
And on the pedestal these words appear:
"My name is Ozymandias, king of kings:
Look on my works, ye Mighty, and despair!"
Nothing beside remains. Round the decay
Of that colossal wreck, boundless and bare
The lone and level sands stretch far away.

Shelley realized, certainly, that we live in time, that change is inevitable, and that, although we sometimes think we're invulnerable, we're not. We don't know what will happen tomorrow, yet we act as if we do. Why did you use Shelley's poem in your book?

It captures an element of what happens when we try to deify ourselves, when we forget that we're creatures and not the creator. Hitler launched his thousand-year Reich, and a decade later it was in ruins. The denial of what we are leads to ruin. Hitler's plan for his master race required someone else to be vermin, and that led directly to his leaving his nation in rubble. Our spiritual teachers have taught us that the real path of life lies in embracing our condition and recognizing that we're flesh and blood. Life is not ours to keep, but a gift that flows along. We're not immortal, but if we let the flow come into us and flow out of us, the greater whole—of which we're a part—goes on.

I now live in California, where we name freeways and overpasses after politicians. As I drive on those freeways and see some name—the John Sturdly overpass, for example—I reflect that someday no one will know who John Sturdly was, and the overpass will lie crumbling in a field.

In *Out of Weakness* I often use the word "we" when I talk about monsters such as Hitler, Stalin, Pol Pot, and Idi Amin. At least in my case, I can look inside myself and see some of the elements that were so destructive in them—organized differently, I'd like to think. Those elements don't rule me; they don't possess me. Nevertheless, I must acknowledge their existence in me.

About the naming of overpasses, I must say that I get some gratification from knowing that a couple of books have my name on them. When I'm no longer here, the best that was in me will still exist to speak to anyone who might find meaning in these ideas.

That's preferable to an overpass, I think. I'd rather have a book as a memorial than a freeway overpass.

You and I are into the abstract rather than the concrete.

Or steel, as Stalin was. But still, the ideas of omnipotence and immortality are part of the myth that drives us, I think.

To the extent that we can find ourselves living in a world that really feeds us, we'll be able to embrace our mortality. But in a world where people suffer so many traumas—a world of walking wounded—death is terrifying. Hitler was infatuated with death long before he was the Führer. For those who bury a part of themselves because of the wounds they suffer, the ongoing pain of *that* death makes the prospect of confronting actual death terrifying. So we get into postures like that of Ozymandias.

What about narcissism and self-love?

Maybe it's human nature to view the treatment we receive from the world as a verdict on ourselves. For example, when we suffer a great misfortune—a flood, an earthquake, disease—we sometimes ask, "What did we do to deserve this?" As if what happens to us is a moral judgment.

As a consequence of the social-evolutionary process described in *The Parable of the Tribes*, tremendous victimization can continue for century after century. Peoples are conquered and humiliated; poison is incorporated into family structures; and other abuses take place when principles other than human needs govern civilized societies. In time we interpret all those messages to mean, "There's something wrong with me."

The more powerful that message is, the less we can acknowledge it. We compensate by identifying with a part of ourselves. Freud called this phenomenon "narcissism." The result is an identification with an ideal image—the great warrior, the Achilles, or the Hitler who knows better than the composer how the musical phrase should have gone. We do everything we can to suppress the stuff from below that represents our genuine experience of life.

Two stories from the Old Testament illustrate what we're discussing. In the first, Cain and Abel both make offerings to the Lord. Up to and including the time of his offering, Cain has done nothing to indicate anything is wrong with him. He's not a bad guy; he just makes an offering. His brother makes an offering, too. But nothing explains what happens next: The Lord looks with favor upon Abel's offering and with disfavor upon Cain's.

That tells us something about our experience of the cosmos. (In the story, God is the cosmos talking.) Wouldn't it be wonderful if we saw the cosmos as a place where two brothers make offerings to their heavenly Father or Mother and hear, "Thank you, boys. I really appreciate your gifts, and I love you"? We experience a cleavage in the cosmos, however, and that cleavage reflects a cleavage within the narcissistic structure. We are among the chosen, or we are among the rejected.

The story also shows what it feels like to be the rejected. The underlying feeling is of the core part of oneself that narcissism pushes down. Cain feels rage and slays his brother.

From generation to generation the children of Israel—my ancestors—have repeated the story of Cain and Abel. That early part of Genesis is, in fact, a meditation on the dynamic of the chosen and the rejected. The self-declared chosen people are telling themselves about that dynamic.

The story of Joseph and his brothers is also revealing. It begins with Joseph receiving a coat of many colors from his father. His father is Jacob, who, after his transformative experience by the campfire, becomes Israel. So the story literally is about the children of Israel. Joseph's eleven brothers look at him in his favored status and feel pretty much what Cain felt. They express their resentment to one another, throw him into a pit, and then sell him into slavery to a passing caravan.

The children of Israel tell the story from the point of view of Joseph, who goes on to do great things, eventually becoming the Pharaoh's right-hand man. He wields power. He arranges that there will be enough grain in a time of famine. It's a gratifying story for us, with our narcissistic injury, to hear.

The point to remember, however, is that the children of Israel are twelve. We identify with Joseph—that's the conscious part, the narcissistic image, the winner. But beneath the tip of that unconscious iceberg are eleven brothers who feel hurt, rejected, and enraged. That's the dynamic: Push down the eleven brothers, and their rage is always there waiting to come out. Any insult is a message from the world that "you ain't worth much." That underlying feeling threatens the precarious narcissistic structure. So the warrior with a narcissistic wound continually looks for aggravation. He needs to retaliate; he can't allow a challenge to pass.

It's almost as if we create the thing we're trying to overcome—the warrior attracts war.

Just as the paranoiac makes enemies. The truth, somehow, always pursues us.

We must be careful what we resist, because that's what we become?

Yes.

Andy, you wrote a story, a little essay, that national public radio broadcast a few years ago as a commentary. Would you share it here?

That was in 1985, about a week before the first Reagan-Gorbachev summit. We didn't know where things were heading, but the preceding four years had been a period of great anxiety. Many people feared that the superpowers were on a course to catastrophe. I never thought we were on the brink, but polls indicated that a high proportion of American young people anticipated nuclear war and didn't think they were going to be alive ten years later. I call the essay "To Live Free from the Grip of Terror."

I went to the Kennedy Center the other night. On the way in, I noticed that the huge bank of windows around the entrance, flanked by tall metal columns, formed a visual doorway sixty feet high. The place was designed at the height of the American Empire. We thought we were bigger than humans, so we built entrances for giants.

The occasion was a concert to celebrate the fortieth anniversary of the founding of the United Nations, with people from more than a hundred countries in attendance. Elliot Richardson spoke words of welcome, and spoke as well of the importance of nations resolving their differences by discussion rather than war. He was followed by a young black American diplomat. Beautiful in his elegance and eloquence. Beautiful too, standing as an embodiment of the genuine possibilities for human liberation. "We must," he said, "rekindle the hope that brought the United Nations forth out of the devastation of World War II. The hope for a new beginning for mankind."

Part of the concert was the Fifth Symphony by Shostakovich. I read over the program notes, and the story they told took my breath away. The symphony was written and first performed in the Soviet Union in 1937, at the height of the Stalin terror. Through his music, Shostakovich spoke to that unspoken terror. Spoke so deeply that many in that Leningrad audience wept.

The applause went on for an entire hour, our conductor, Rostropovich, was quoted as saying. People ran up and down until the small hours embracing and congratulating each other on having been there. They had understood, said Rostropovich, the symphony's "message of sorrow and suffering and isolation. Stretched on the rack of the inquisition, the victim tries to smile in his pain."

I was moved by the depth of the yearning of those Russians to live free from the grip of terror. I was moved to remember the obvious, that more than anything else the Russians are our fellow human beings. "It is those Russians who wept in Leningrad, and their children and their grandchildren, whom we are poised to vaporize by the millions," I thought. And it is they whose weapons stand ready to annihilate us.

We're all living now in an era over which terror rules. Our fear we have in common, yet we've allowed our fear to divide us. From fear of being vulnerable human beings, we make ourselves into nuclear giants. These giants hide their fear behind the fortifications on which they display their bluster and threat. Bigger than human, but less than human too.

The true high frontier lies not in an outer space waiting to be filled with still more weapons. It is in our inner space, where we are challenged to find the common humanity that can bridge over the walls we've built between us. As our leaders go to Geneva like those who first heard Shostakovich's symphony, we long to hear something that speaks to our common terror. We too would weep with relief as we ran out into the night to embrace each other.

I value that passage because it came to me as a gift. I sat in the auditorium, and the piece wrote itself. I went home and, a couple of days later, just wrote it down. I feel that I was given it, and it gives me pleasure to give it back.

It occurs to me as we talk about conflict and war that we need another way of being in the world. Certainly following the spiritual path is one way of doing that. Yet isn't there also the need to integrate the spiritual path into one's daily life, to be able to express it in all parts of life?

The challenge we face has two principal dimensions. One is the spiritual path, in our lives and within ourselves, and the other is the need to transform the whole global arena. We need to transform its organization, to create a structure in which power is controlled and human choice can govern our destiny—which it hasn't done since we stepped across that threshold ten thousand years ago.

We also have larger tasks. It's true that to remake the world, we must remake ourselves. There's a truth to that, but it's not sufficient truth. We also have to envision the limits of spiritual transformation in turning the world into the Face of God, or whatever language we choose that speaks to our deepest visions of what we, as a species, should be about.

Imagine that you're an early Christian. It's the first century A.D., you're being persecuted, and you're afraid that the persecutors will somehow snuff out the sacred fire you carry. An angel comes to you and says, "Be of good cheer. I bring you glad tidings. This man whom you have called the Son of God will be regarded as God by millions of people. The words you write down will one day be the sacred scriptures of the preeminent civilization on earth. Christians will go out and spread their ways and their vision across the whole of the planet."

You, that early Christian, would go to bed with peace of mind, envisioning a planet in which the words of the Lamb of God—who said to turn the other cheek, resist not evil, and love thy neighbor as thyself—will become the dominant determinants of how human beings live.

Imagine the shock, though, if that early Christian could see what has actually transpired. Everything our hypothetical angel promised him did come to pass. But it came to pass in a world in which power was still rampant. Only three centuries after that hypothetical conversation, the Cross was leading armies into battle. After another millennium, the civilization emerging out of the fragmented continent of Europe—where the powers contend ceaselessly for dominance—that "Christian" civilization was doing to its neighbors everything *but* what it would want to see done to itself.

We do need a spiritual transformation, but we also have to make the world a safe place to embody the spirit of a Christ or a Buddha or a Rabbi Hillel. We have to make a world of a different order, otherwise certain kinds of evils will continue to govern our destiny. That's a structural problem. We have to work at both ends at the same time. It's like a journey on both feet. If we move only one foot, we can move only a short distance. But if we free both feet, the movement of each one enables us to move further with the other.

The Dalai Lama has said that it's not enough to have prayer, that we need to conceive a plan for peace and pursue it actively. It's not enough to think it, or to want it. One has to pursue it.

The Dalai Lama has his feet on the ground. It's good to see divine energy flowing through someone that grounded.

Henryk Skolimowski

Eco-Mind &
Thinking Reverentially

WE'VE REACHED a stage in social evolution when it is imperative that we develop a larger view, to see the whole in order to better understand the parts. Our techno-scientific world-view has achieved much, but its limitations have become all too apparent. The house of cards upon which our energy and economic needs are built is but one result of this lack of vision. Decision-making within institutions has become a completely rational process affected by parochial pressures and the strain of expediency. No longer are human values a consideration, much less a part of the equation. Spirit has been removed. A vital piece of life is missing. Is it any wonder there is confusion, consternation, and chaos? We are in the midst of information abundance, yet there is a dearth of genuine wisdom. Henryk Skolimowski has put forward a new vision, and he calls it Eco-philosophy. It may just provide a positive response to the demands of our time.

MT: *Henryk, what is Eco-philosophy, and how does it differ from what we ordinarily interpret as traditional philosophy?*

HS: Eco-philosophy, as I see it, is a rational reconstruction of the human condition as we approach the twenty-first century. I emphasize the term "rational," for reason at large is not something to scorn. Indeed, I cannot see any reconstruction whatsoever to be accomplished through unreason. However, I do not identify reason and rationality with the precepts of narrow science, or with computer-like thinking. Reason and rationality are a glorious accomplishment of evolution, and for me reason encompasses it all, including all our sensitivities. The generic term for philosophy is *philosophia*, the love of wisdom, and this is what philosophy has been through millennia. It tries to aid us in the quest for meaning, in the quest for an understanding of not only the trivial everyday life, but also of this larger cosmos—its furniture, its intricacies, our connection with it on the physical level and all other levels as well.

Now in the twentieth century, as a result of specialization, all disciplines were forced to specialize. And even philosophy has done it. The idea of scientific philosophy arrived on the stage around 1910 with Bertrand Russell. Then the philosophers from the Vienna Circle in Vienna, in Austria, picked up the idea and pushed it to an extreme. Philosophy became a scrutiny of the structure of language and, in my opinion, was short-changed. Bit by bit, philosophy was made an inquiry into the nature of linguistic propositions. Philosophers became preoccupied, to the point of obsession, with how language works. Distinguished philosophers such as J.L. Austin started writing essays on "Ifs and Cans." If you think how much that is removed from the real quest of philosophy, then you realize that something bizarre has happened.

Nowadays, even analytical philosophers themselves are rather unhappy with the position they have been pushed into. They try to get out of it. Somehow, however, they are stuck. They try to get unstuck in a piecemeal way, while what we need is a total reconstruction, changing the whole mode of thinking, of perceiving and of valuing. It is here that Eco-philosophy comes into focus as a new cosmology, a new way of rethinking the multitude.

Instead of conceiving the universe as a clocklike mechanism, governed by deterministic laws, in which we are stuck as a little bolt or screw, we can assume that the universe is a *sanctuary* and we are its custodians—priests if you will. The mechanistic universe was based on the assumptions of the mechanistic nature of the cosmos. Eco-philosophy is based on the view that the nature of the universe is unfolding, evolutionary, and emergent. Because it's emergent, you don't know what will happen next. It is the glory and the beauty of evolution that it is creative, producing new variations—of which the human mind is one. Every new idea is a blossoming of creative evolution. A new philosophy is for me a manifestation of the ability of evolution to create through us. Put otherwise, a new creative conception of the cosmos is a response of evolution—through us!—to get unstuck. For if we are stuck, evolution is stuck. We have got locked in a cul-de-sac and now we are unlocking ourselves by creating new vistas through which we show that we have somewhere to go, and that evolution has somewhere to go.

This is a very short answer to what Eco-philosophy wants to accomplish. It wants to create a new cosmology within which we are at home in this universe and at peace with all creation.

Most of us, when we hear the term "philosophy," have a vision of musty books on library shelves. In our society, philosophy has been relegated mostly to the halls of academia. One doesn't find the philosophical view, or the philosophical approach, very much present in mainstream society or life. We don't often hear our politicians ask, "What are the philosophical implications of this particular piece of legislation?" That's just not part of the consideration. Why do you think this has happened in our society? Why have we come to this, where philosophy is no longer really present in the everyday, practical side of life?

It is in part the result of the growing specialization in the twentieth century. But it's also the result of a mistaken myth that the glory of the human condition lies in the improvement of our material lot and that, consequently, you have to bank on material progress, on technology and science.

Yet I want to point out to you that those very assumptions of material progress are philosophical assumptions par excellence. We may think that we have thrown philosophy out of the window, that we do not need it. But our pragmatic modes of operation, the ways we think what reality is, are all based on some philosophical assumptions. Usually they are rather crude assumptions in which the universe is conceived predominantly as material, and we are conceived as predominantly acquisitive creatures, or comfort creatures. Yet we know that the most glorious moments of our life and in the history of the human species are not the ones in which we live as comfort creatures. So to the degree to which present philosophy has cast us in the image of comfort creatures, it has put a philosophical straitjacket on our being. We are thus victims of a shallow philosophy.

True enough, a good deal of philosophy is contained in those dry books that gather dust on the shelves of our libraries. But in addition to those, there are some very exciting books on philosophy to which we return over and again. If you take the history of your own program, "New Dimensions," what I've been seeing over the years is a development of a new, exciting philosophy. Philosophers do not have the monopoly on creating new philosophy. New philosophy is emerging all the time. For philosophy has always been an in-depth reflection on the human condition. It will be alive as long as the human condition is alive, as long as we persist in being human. Thus I dare say that as long as we search for humanity in ourselves, as long as we search for freedom, we are not going to be confined by shallow philosophy which reduces us to comfort creatures.

In a sense, each of us is a philosopher?

Right. And if you examine in some depth those notions which assert, "We don't need philosophy, we are pragmatic, we are realistic," you find they are based on some philosophical notions. What is it to be "pragmatic"? It means to assume that economic gains are most important in life. Is that true? What is it to be "realistic"? There is a paradox here. What goes under "being realistic" is totally unrealistic nowadays. For we behave in a foolish, destructive, antiproductive way vis-a-vis ourselves, vis-a-vis the environment. And we call it "realistic." When you think about it, it is totally unrealistic.

Thus, we have to evolve a new concept of realism whereby we are less destructive to ourselves, to other beings, to the environment—or expressing it in positive terms—more life-enhancing. And this is another name for Eco-philosophy. It attempts to be life-enhancing. It attempts to show what kind of beliefs and values may help us in seeing ourselves more clearly as human beings, a very special kind of species, who have the responsibility for themselves, but also the responsibility for the planet and, if you will, for the rest of the cosmos.

Henryk, I remember Buckminster Fuller saying that more than seventy percent of the work force in America is devoted to non-life-support activities, activity in work-a-day America that really isn't oriented toward enhancing life. In a society based essentially on capitalism, with an orientation to the bottom line and profits, how would one integrate Eco-philosophy? I mean particularly society where the bottom line is paramount.

I would look at the situation the other way around. Not how one integrates Eco-philosophy into the existing structure—that concept would be a kiss of death for Eco-philosophy—but rather how one integrates the existing world and structure into Eco-philosophy.

You may think this to be ambitious, but we have to be ambitious in order to make sense of our life, in order to survive, in order to have a future. We are all searching desperately for a new lease on life, for structures both economic and political as well as human and ecological that are life-supporting—not only to our individual quest for meaning, but also that are life-supporting to the economy at large. What we are seeing is that the capitalistic structures simply do not work even in terms of capitalism itself. These structures desperately need a new lease on life.

I see capitalism as a cycle, a rather extravagant one, of Western civilization. It was one avenue to see how far we can explore the world and what kind of benefit we can accrue to ourselves individually if we say, "Everybody has carte blanche to do as he or she pleases." We have found that in the contingent world we can't do it, because if some pursue their avenue as they please—to the detriment of others—the whole boat begins to tilt sooner or later. And this is what is happening. So I see Eco-philosophy as an attempt to provide a new set of structures whereby existing practices, visions, and ways of interacting with each other can be renewed and translated in life-enhancing forms.

One of the principles of Eco-philosophy is frugality, which must not be mistaken as imposed poverty or abnegation. Frugality, for me, is a positive principle. Frugality is a precondition of inner beauty. You have to pause a little in order to realize that this is how the greatest works of art were created. When the artist imposes on himself severe limitations and out of the chunk of marble creates a marvelous sculpture, this is frugality in the best sense. With limited means creating wonderful ends: This is what frugality is about. This is partly in keeping with Buckminster Fuller's idea of doing more with less. This is what inventiveness and creativeness mean: with limited means creating rich and excellent ends. This is, incidentally, what the Norwegian eco-philosopher Arne Naess advocates: a life which is slender in means and rich in ends.

In the present society, it is just the reverse. We use enormously rich and versatile means, and achieve ends in no proportion to the investment. We have become a people who are developing means for other means which never translate into ends which we can acknowledge as life-enhancing, as adding to our life and as adding to the life of the planet. The other definition of frugality is that frugality is grace without waste. I think we don't have to apologize for using the term "grace," for it is part of the human condition.

On occasion I am asked to give a brief definition of Eco-philosophy. You cannot do it. You need ten to fifteen hours to do justice to the idea which seeks to redefine the lot. Eco-philosophy, like the Buddhist Eightfold Path, suggests that all things are interconnected. Right assumptions about the world lead to right beliefs, lead to right or correct thinking, lead to correct action, lead to right livelihood, and lead to right contemplation. Action is important, but only if it is based on right values and right visions. Otherwise it is blind action. Actually, we so often rush from one form of action to another form of action, thinking that this other form of action is our salvation, while the whole foundation of our action is unsound. Nowadays we have to re-think the whole lot. Another way of looking at the situation in which we are at present is to summarize it in the following way.

> Life is short.
> Art is long.
> Experience difficult.
> Truth is enticing to seek.
> Difficult to attain.
> The delights of being are many.
> The delights of becoming are infinite.

And the last phrase is one I want to emphasize. We are the creatures of becoming. This is the nature of evolution. This is the nature of all evolving societies. Unless we continually transcend, we petrify. The problem with our society and with our education is that we have gotten stuck in certain forms of being. And we petrify. Our present social structures and institutions are really interested in self-perpetuation and creating people in their own image. They want supporters which keep the system going. This is one of the reasons why in spite of the fact that we have a huge system of education, it doesn't help us in the quest of enlightenment. Our educational institutions are set to make us obedient ciphers, not to make us free people.

Seemingly another principle in life is resisting change, being comfortable with the status quo. When you speak of Eco-philosophy, one of the things that seems to be present is constant change. There's always an emergence of new thoughts, new ideas, new ways to think, new ways to do things—that can be very uncomfortable. What about that discomfort and working through it?

Well, it can be very uncomfortable. But living in changing time is always uncomfortable. However, if you live a life that is open and engaging, you always find a response to the unexpected. It is the unexpected, the new, that is the joy and delight of life. In the States, we try to immune ourselves from change because it means insecurity. This is one of our paradoxes: On one hand we say that we are the society that is changing, we are the society on the go; on the other hand, we have tried to create an economic structure of security through which we can be undisturbed. The two do not go together.

We need to go deeper into the nature of the human condition and how we conceive of what it is to be human. If you think that we are unfolding with evolution, that we are creative, you have to embrace change and discomfort, for it is a part of the beauty and agony of becoming. And you better persuade yourself that it is good, because it cannot be otherwise. So far as I can see, there is no way to make people comfortable and immune from change and pain unless they are in the grave.

Perhaps we can talk about how we can become more co-creative and over-come the negative view of the world which is so prevalent today. Optimism may be a biological necessity, and it's certainly a principle of Eco-philosophy. Henryk, as you were saying, we are co-creators with evolution and we're the determining factor as to what happens next. Also inherent in your remarks is the idea that somehow we need to celebrate life more than we're doing, that life is rich and full. But so often we're looking at the holes, noticing the gaps, and experiencing problems. When we look around us, we realize that we're in an environment permeated by a constant reinforcement of what's wrong with the world—the negative, the darker view. How does one break through this incredible reinforcement of the negative?

You are quite right when you say that optimism may be a biological necessity. And I would add that hope is not a prerogative of foolish people, but part of the ontological being of man in this world. Once you lose hope, you disintegrate as a human being. Well if so, why are we ridden with the plague of hopelessness, helplessness, and a kind of dreariness? Why do we not celebrate life, when in a sense life fully lived is life celebrated? There are many reasons, I'll just speak of two of them.

One is that the prevailing system of education develops above all the critical faculties, the skeptical faculties, nihilistic faculties. In order to be clever, you always try to puncture everything that is presented to you. You try to cut everything into bits and pieces. This doesn't develop an attitude of wholeness and celebration of life. The educational system says, "If you are clever, try to decompose and destroy everything." But there is a deeper reason still for this attitude of critical scrutiny, of dismembering everything, of showing how you can always cut. This deeper reason is the acceptance of the mechanistic world-view, which assumes that everything is made of discrete atoms which interact in a deterministic way; and which also assumes that the deeper you cut, the further you go. The tunnel/atomistic vision is inherent in our mechanistic world-view.

The other side of the coin is our inability to perceive holistically, in a connected and integrated way. Now, hope requires an affirmation of a meaningful universe which is one coherent whole. The mechanistic universe isolates, separates, detaches everything from everything else. Moreover, it is devoid of human meaning. Hence, we have to transcend mechanistic science to create the universe of hope. If you closely look at the mechanistic scheme, you realize that the celebration of life is not there. "It does not belong to the system," the system does not have the terminology for such things.

The hard-headed scientist may insist that this view of the universe is the right one. I say that his assumptions are myopic and are distorting the real picture of the universe. According to Eco-philosophy, we can choose a celebratory universe in which hope is one of its dimensions. Now which assumptions about the universe are right? There is no logical way of resolving the dilemma. So my response to the question of who is right, the pessimist or the optimist, is not to try to argue out the proposition on logical grounds. Rather, I would propose: Let's see what pessimism is doing to us, on one hand, and let's see what optimism and hope can do for us, on the other hand.

Why should we assume that the universe is dreary? Why not see that it bursts with new forms of life, it bursts in joy all the time? We need to embark on the universe that is a place for celebration, and we need to act upon our assumption. Only then we can see the strength and the power of this kind of universe. And to the extent that we are one of its most intricate forms, the universe celebrates itself through us. You cannot disprove logically such an assumption. Let us assume the universe helps us to dwell in it, for we are a part of this universe. There is nothing strange in the assumption that the universe is home for Man. Intuitively, this view is more convincing than the one which assumes that the universe is a hostile, indifferent, cold place in which we drift like helpless monads.

So what we are doing while developing Eco-philosophy is returning to a connected and hospitable conception of the cosmos, in which we are its right inhabitants and which is home for us. I should mention here that these ideas are developed more fully in my book, *Living Philosophy, Eco-Philosophy as a Living Tree*. (Penguin, 1991)

Many of our institutions, as they have evolved and become a part of our everyday life, have lost the original vision for which they may have been created. They may have been created with a sincere concern for solving a particular human problem, they may have been based on certain values and ethics, but it seems almost one of the principles of institutions that as they get larger and larger the values and ethics and similar concerns are almost pushed out of the everyday decision-making process.

Going back to my earlier question about corporations and living in a corporate society, how do those values and ethics come back into play? From what you were saying, one projection of the future may be that an institution—say, a corporation—might have a resident eco-philosopher to assess how profits and the bottom line may be directly related to that institution's concern with the future overall effect of what it is doing. I'd like to relate that to the importance of institutions once again showing a real concern with human values and with ethics—basically, a return to integrity as an important component in one's everyday functioning.

Well, again, integrity is something peculiarly human. It is not a property of the mechanistic universe. It is not a property of a corporation that makes profit. It is not something that you find in our economic accounting. It is only when you have the peculiar sense that without integrity you are not whole, you are not fully human, that you begin to inject into the system—whatever the system is—a new parameter, a new dimension. And it is at this point that you examine all institutions and realize that, somehow or other, almost each of them alienates itself from the purpose for which it has been originally created. This is part of the dialectics of life.

An institution—or any set of institutions—is created to provide for certain needs, certain requirements, social or individual, and usually it serves those needs for a while. But then once those needs are satisfied, we come to evolve new needs. The institution usually doesn't evolve to cater to these new needs, and it tries to respond in terms of the old needs. After a while, we find the institution quite antithetical to new needs that have evolved in response to life and in response to our own quest for going beyond, for transcendence. To that degree, every institution—whether we take a little civic institution in the city or an institution like the Catholic Church—has a tendency to get stuck and to respond to early needs rather than new evolving needs.

Well, it is the genius of a people or an institution that is able to adjust itself and change with changing needs. Most institutions do not do it. The bigger they are, the more clumsy and the more entrenched they become, and they try to translate our needs into what they can do for themselves. At that point, there is quite a chasm between what an institution is doing and what it ought to be doing if it were doing its right job. And this is what has happened, not only with institutions, but with technology at large.

Technology may be thought of as a form of institution for taking care of our needs. Each and all technologies were conceived for our good, for the betterment of our individual and social life. This is the purpose they served for quite a while. Then they became too big, too independent, too autonomous. And now they are perpetuating themselves and—if we can anthropomorphize a little—have the cheek of claiming us as an appendage to them. At this point it's pathological, it's really bizarre. An instrument has taken over. The sorcerer's apprentice has unlocked the secrets, unleashed the tremendous powers which it is unable to control.

There is something wrong in the process if it leads to consequences that are antithetical to the original purposes. Well, to that degree, we have to really change and scrap lots of institutions, including technology. I'm not saying that technology will have to just be thrown on the rubbish heap of history. But some of its forms that are antithetical to the ends of our life and that are threatening the whole planet, that become a major threat to the whole model of evolution—these have to be revised.

What the humans have done can be changed and undone. To that degree I am a kind of staunch optimist. This is a way of really empowering ourselves, by knowing that it all came as a result of certain visions, certain purposes, certain programs, and that we have to restructure our visions. We can have the courage to say, "We take our destiny into our hands again. We are not so helpless and powerless as we would be made by some institutions."

As to your suggestion that every major corporation might have a resident eco-philosopher to oversee its overall values and its positive contributions to life at large—it's an excellent one! I actually would love to be invited by some corporations as a resident eco-philosopher—and prove to them that it would be a good idea.

Henryk, I would like to relate what you were talking about to a pragmatic, real-life situation. If we look at the institution called health care, and if we look at where hospitals have come to and how we deliver medical services to people, we've reached a point of health care being a privilege and not a right. We're talking about excluding certain people from receiving adequate or the best health care. I think this is an example of an institution that has come to a place where the original vision that it was created for has been lost. Even though there is still a concern to take care of people, we're talking about ways that can only take care of a certain number of people—those who have the right kind of insurance and the right kind of support in order to take advantage of the services provided. What about that?

Health care is a very good example of institutions that somehow alienated themselves from what they were supposed to serve. Again, you cannot blame the institutions, the hospitals and doctors; there is the whole universe that has gone its own way and become uncaring to our well-being. And this is, again, a matter of in-depth perception, a matter of realizing what health care is about. Is it the maintenance of the machine, that maintains our spare parts? The more sophisticated the machine becomes, the more expensive spare parts become and the more difficult they become to replace. And the more sophisticated the process, the more costly the process, the more difficult it is to provide it to ordinary people.

So the right response is not to try to make the mending process via this mechanistic process less expensive, but to look at the larger picture. What is health care? It is the maintenance of our health. It is our health that is at stake. If you look at the problem of health as not only curing illness, but maintaining our well-being, you change the whole perspective on life, on health. And then you ask yourself what kind of institutions you need to have, what kind of health care you have to have in order to maintain health and keep it in the state of radiance, rather than how to stop this process of prohibitively expensive medical care that is bound to be more and more expensive as the scientific and technological process gets more and more sophisticated. And again, if you are locked in our system, there is no way out. So you have to get out of the system, and go to China.

I went there in 1976. What struck me is that China is a poor country without poor people. What struck me is that in spite of the fact that there are 800 million people there, everybody has basic health care. But it's based on a different principle than ours. And by Zeus, if China can do it, being such a poor country, we should be able to do it. But we'll be able to do it only if we change our perspective. And this perspective is really not the perspective on the medical machinery and how to improve it, but the perspective on life, health, and death. When we talk about institutions and how to cope with them, I think that the answer lies in changing the perspective of the people who run them, changing the entire vision, and saying to yourself: We can do it otherwise.

It occurs to me that the eco-philosophical view would encompass and accept death as being a part of life. One of the problems with modern health care is the constant emphasis on the prolongation of life at all costs. The lives of people who are essentially no longer functioning as living beings are prolonged with technology, thereby creating more occupation of hospital beds, and so on. To some extent, the medical establishment hasn't accepted death as a part of life.

Eco-philosophy tries to do that and tries to suggest that at a certain point the prolongation of certain biological functions is not the prolongation of life. It is just slow death which is already there which we try to prevent, although we know that we can't. And this requires, again, a deeper look into the human condition, rather than new strategy for how to make those people who are already partly departed survive on a kind of vegetative level.

One of the parts of Eco-philosophy is what I call eco-yoga. In addition to rethinking our principles, we have to go in our existential substratum through certain exercises that enable us to perceive the world and people in a new way. One of those principles is what I call reverential thinking. Once you start to think reverentially about other human beings, and about our relationship with ecology and the world, it does something to you. It really changes your perspective.

Part of this value vacuum, part of the problem with ethics, part of the problem with integrity, is that our attitudes and our thinking are so *irreverent*. This objective thinking is a kind of careless thinking. It's nihilist thinking, while life in its *modus operandi* is a very tender phenomenon. When we really take care of life, we take care of life on the basis of a certain reverence for it. I would like to reintroduce reverential thinking as a part of our *modus operandi*, as a part of our daily perception.

So, in addition to the courses I teach at the university, I go to a retreat, you may say, and I run two-week workshops at Arcosanti—which is Paolo Solari's city in the middle of the Arizona desert—in which we try to translate principles of Eco-philosophy into real-life situations. More recently, I have been offering workshops on Eco-philosophy and eco-yoga on the island of Thassos in northern Greece. To enact a new philosophy requires more than just thinking.

Reverential thinking is not thinking about reverence, it is *thinking reverentially*. And there is a difference. In order to think reverentially, you have to, in a sense, rewire your perception, rewire your assumptions. You have to stop thinking always in economic terms: How I can use this piece of land as a resource . . . How I can use this person to my purposes? Thinking reverentially is possible because we know that part of our life is lived reverentially, that is, when we care for those who are dear to us, when we are in love. Indeed, to be in love is to treat the other person reverentially.

So reverence is not an idealistic principle, but one that really is part of our state as human beings. I would wish to emphasize that this principle of reverence for life is something that will help us on our road to the future. Reverence for life is not high idealism but stark realism, if we are to have a humane future.

Henryk, when I first saw the title of your book, The Theater of the Mind, *what came to me was the drama that so often is a part of what our mind creates. I thought of how much "theater" we create, which in a sense takes us away from what our real purpose may be. I'd like you to comment on that.*

Well, for me life is a drama, the whole evolution is a drama, and indeed the mind is one of the most interesting theaters of all. I chose the title *The Theater of the Mind* quite deliberately in order get away from various scholarly and pedantic titles and the very scholarly, pedantic, and dry treatment of the subject. I think that we have been overwhelmed with the quantity of words, which has the effect of really numbing us. We often assume that the more knowledge we have the more enlightened we become, that the more words we can use the more knowledge we have.

I feel that often the opposite is true. We are inundated by the mountain of information and there is no enlightenment at the end. So I decided to structure the whole book in a different fashion—as a series of illuminations inspired very much by the *Upanishads*. It may be a bit presumptuous to say, but such was my purpose: to write a series of *Upanishads* for our times. *Upanishads* are those immortal stories about life and death, the meaning of the universe and the meaning of our own life. And in those *Upanishads*, the role of the mind is second to none.

In the West, we have made everything pedestrian. Everything is ground to a dry powder of concepts, including the very miracle of mind. I think it is time that we reach for this splendid glorious instrument of evolution, the mind that we have and that is so important for everything else, and give it due respect. But giving it due respect also means celebrating it, realizing that the joy of the universe is the joy of having a joyous mind.

I remember being really excited by a book I read in high school—a book by Will Durant entitled The Pleasures of Philosophy. *It excited me because here was an opportunity to explore ideas, to study ideas, to see how people thought and the ways they perceived the world around them. And yet what I saw of philosophy in school courses was often, as you say, pedantic. It was presented as taking dusty ideas out of the past and saying, okay, this is the way they thought and this is what you learn. It was not an evolutionary process. Ideas from the past were being dusted off and looked at in contemporary times, but philosophy wasn't a growing animal. In contrast, when I come in touch with your work, it's clear that you're evolving a philosophy that is both new and at the same time influenced by older and other philosophies. What are these influences? What has most influenced you to move in the direction of this new philosophy?*

One doesn't have to be pedantic in order to be profound. And indeed, when I look at the history of philosophy, the great philosophical systems, the great philosophers were those who had the courage to confront problems. When you read their texts, they are exciting although at times difficult. Philosophy for me is exciting because it tries to confront those ultimate questions which are always at the back of our minds.

I was converted to philosophy—or seduced to philosophy—by Plato in my teenage years in Poland. I read voluminously, almost everything. After reading great French writers such as Balzac, Maupassant, and others, I discovered the Greek writers. I read Sophocles,

Euripides, and then stumbled upon Plato, whom I first read as a poet. But the reading was so fascinating, and the kind of fiction—science fiction—he unveiled was so spellbinding that I couldn't recover from it. To this day, I don't know whether Plato was one of the greatest fiction writers or one of the greatest philosophers in his attempts to discover what reality is all about.

Of late, I am of the opinion that the greatest philosophical and metaphysical systems are as much created as they are discovered. By this I mean that by imposing a certain architecture on reality, we weave the whole reality around this architecture and then consider this reality as objective. While doing this, we forget that the original blueprint (to which reality conforms) is the human invention. And to that degree, all metaphysics and all reality is human invention!

You gather from those remarks that Plato was one of the greatest and most lasting influences on me. But then one had to move on. While studying in Poland, I got under the spell of analytical philosophy. At that time, Plato was called an old-fashioned metaphysician, a fuddy-duddy. One was encouraged to believe in semantic analysis, in logical calculus, in propositional calculus. The power of logic was supposed to be our salvation. There was a kind of messianic message behind analytical philosophy: If we get our language straight, if we get our mental hygiene right, then we'll be able to solve all problems. This myth prevailed until the 1950s. After that time, the leading minds, that had invented this myth, one after another renounced and recanted it.

However, lesser minds have never been able to do so. We are under the spell of those lesser minds who are perpetuating the myth that analysis is the only philosophy while completely forgetting what analytical philosophy was supposed to be about. It was supposed to be about getting the language clear and precise, so that we could tackle all the problems and solve them satisfactorily.

Present philosophy has become sharpening tools for sharpening tools. Because academic philosophy does not help us in understanding the world and ourselves, we turn away from it. However, we also are aware that because of the unprecedented problems that have emerged in the second half of the twentieth century—such as nuclear waste, the looming ecological catastrophe, and, last but not least, understanding the universe and matter brought about by the new advances of astrophysics and quantum physics—we cannot find solutions to our dilemmas in past philosophies.

Thus, we need to create a philosophy appropriate for our times and our problems. I am neither decrying all philosophy nor advocating a return to the past—be it Plato, the *Upanishads*, or some other mystical tradition. I am in favor of creating a new, comprehensive holistic philosophy suitable for the age of ecology which is dawning on us.

In The Theater of the Mind, *you wrote something that I had experienced in my own life, and that is the incredible similarity in the philosophies espoused by de Chardin and Sri Aurobindo. Though they were in some sense contemporary, they didn't know one another, and you make the connection between them. De Chardin was a Catholic, Sri Aurobindo was an Indian, came out of the Hindu system. How about that connection? What does it mean?*

Teilhard de Chardin was one of the great influences on me in recent times. I have been fascinated by his story of evolution as one of the most thrilling adventures of the human mind.

To try to reconstruct and shed light on such a phenomenon as total evolution is like holding the whole universe, from its inception, in one's palm. I've tried to puzzle out how Teilhard arrived at his system. When I discovered Sri Aurobindo, who arrived at a very similar system, I couldn't believe it. There is, of course, the theory that the *zeitgeist* has worked through both of them. *Zeitgeist* or not, I thought there must have been some influences.

So when I was at Pondicherry in southern India, where Sri Aurobindo Ashram is located, I finally got to some people who knew the entire opus of Aurobindo and also were aware of Bergson. One lady had done a doctorate dissertation at the Sorbonne on Bergson and Aurobindo. I said to myself, "Right, this must be the connection." I asked her point blank, "How much did Aurobindo learn from Bergson?" She said, "The influence is so great that I would not be able to distinguish one from the other."

We know, of course, that Teilhard was very greatly influenced by Bergson as well. So this is the connection. Bergson's influence is really tremendous, though not obvious.

You see, evolution goes on. And so does our evolution about the meaning and the significance of evolution. Darwin published his *Origin of the Species* in 1859. It was exactly the year in which Henri Bergson was born—1859. When Bergson was a mature man, about forty or forty-five, the whole impact of Darwin was already absorbed. So Bergson could really accept the idea but also look at it in a different way. This is what he did. He came up with the idea of *creative evolution*. He conceived of evolution not merely as a process of chance and necessity—as Monod and other Darwinists and neo-Darwinists tried to make us believe—but as something much more subtle, much more miraculous. In his work *Creative Evolution*, he put this point across, and it is from those views that both Aurobindo and Teilhard learned. Now, when we move into the second part of the twentieth century, the impact of Bergson is already more accepted. One of the evolutionary biologists, Theodosius Dobzhansky, said: As it was important in the nineteenth century to see the connection between the human species and other species—that we are brothers of chimpanzee and other apes and other animals—so it is equally important in the twentieth century to see what distinguishes us from lower forms of life. What I see as happening is that we are articulating the idea of evolution. And it is such an awesome, complex, and beautiful idea that we are far from fully understanding it.

My whole book, *The Theater of the Mind*, is a series of articulations of the idea of evolution. In a sense, it is a celebration of evolution through the dancing mind, through the theater of the mind.

Henryk, what about the idea of the super jump, the quantum jump that can occur from one thing to another? One often thinks of evolution as gradual, taking thousands of years. And yet throughout history we see this indication of the quantum jump. What about that?

Well, in a sense we are all waiting for this quantum leap of evolution that will carry us all to the realm of enlightenment whereby like pure angels we'll be able to solve all our problems. I think that this state may be a bit away from us still. However, I accept the idea that evolution does not progress smoothly from one stage to another. It is not like building a pyramid. Evolution is discontinuous process whereby after a discontinuity occurs there is a leap to a new level, and this you can trace in various ways.

Take the history of science. Until the second half of the twentieth century, the view prevailed that science is like a monolithic pyramid to which scientists, like masons, add one stone each. If you look at the picture of the evolution of science as presented nowadays by such people as Karl Popper and Thomas Kuhn, it is a different picture altogether. It is a dramatic picture, a discontinuous picture, reminding us more of a kind of Shakespearean stage in which main actors—basic theories—like kings in old tragedies are slain and new ones emerge. After a new paradigm emerges, the old paradigm is dethroned like an old dynasty.

This is also confirmed by psychologists, according to whom our own individual development does not proceed smoothly from year to year. At certain points, there are periods of tension which is so great that we do not know who we are any more. After the process of inner transformation, as it were, a new person has emerged. For instance, a teenager has become a young adult.

The Polish psychologist, Dombrowski, calls this process of inner transformation through pain "positive disintegration": Disintegration of an older personality occurs and a new personality emerges. The person has been able to reintegrate. Hence positive disintegration. But some do not make it. And hence the tragedy. This kind of process occurs not only once, but probably three or four times. We shed off the old skin in pain in order to acquire a new one. Thus we can see that in actual life evolution proceeds through continuous stages, but also through discontinuous ones.

A similar idea is also expressed, though in different terms, by Ilya Prigogine. He talks about dissipative structures which occur when an organism or environment is under such great stress that it is unable to bear it any more: There occurs a disintegration, after which there is a reintegration on a new level whereby the old tensions and stresses can be accommodated. This is another way of acknowledging that evolution is discontinuous. When unable to bear old stresses, forms of life reintegrate on a new level. I think those are different names for a very similar idea. A leap is made which is accompanied by pains and some trauma.

I am inclined to think that we as a civilization are going through a similar process. Hence so much tension and pain in societies and individuals. There is no way of knowing what will be the result of this leap. The nature of the emergent evolution is such that the new stage, the emerging stage, is unsimilar to the previous one. Let us hope that it will be a truly creative one and that it will enable us to find structures and solutions adequate to our present problems.

You mention that evolutionary change frequently involves pain and trauma. We can apply that to our own individual evolution as well, our own individual living of life and growing and evolving. Sometimes we go through painful times, traumatic times, and yet usually after that period is behind us we can see how it was a growing process. We can see how we went into that stage as one person and, out of the process of the pain and the trauma, we became another person. An evolutionary process took place there at an individual level.

Quite so. But it is much easier to see it after the fact than when we are in the period of transition and pain. Those periods are confusing, because we are in between two stages, in between two paradigms, as it were.

The point is that individual evolution happens in the same way as the macro evolution does. I think that is an interesting point to make, that personal evolution is the same as planetary evolution. And that would make the connection, too, that as we evolve so also will the planet and the cosmos evolve.

It is perhaps a thought to think of, but not to celebrate, that pain may be a precondition of growth. We do not want to acknowledge the idea while we are in the process of pain. But perhaps it is inevitable that real growth is accompanied by pain because it is the pain of transition from one state of being, within which we are comfortable, to another state of being. Becoming is always difficult.

There is a Buddhist prayer that actually asks for suffering because that is the way to growth, that is the way to enlightenment.

That is beautifully put.

Sometimes we need, and it can help us, to see our suffering in a different way and experience it.

Let us reflect deeper on our culture which so often tries to avoid suffering at all costs. The consequence is that avoiding suffering at all costs happens at the great cost of developing a kind of anesthesia, and this itself is a form of suffering. I would rather acknowledge the suffering as an instrument of vital growth than have the numbness that leads to atrophy and another form of suffering. To put it briefly: As long as we live, as long as we grow, as long as we become, we must not avoid suffering because this is how this universe is made. In the universe of angels it may be different, but in the universe of contingent human beings that is just the way it is.

I could be wrong about this, but my sense is that often, when we think of philosophy, we tend to see it as some kind of subject that gets studied. We go to books and study someone's philosophy, what they wrote, what they put out, maybe centuries ago, or more recently. It's a particular philosophy, and we study it. And somehow in that process we lose something of the value of philosophy. I'd like to hear you talk about how you see the relevance of philosophy to the living of our lives, even the relevance of the study of philosophy to how we live our life. Does philosophy have anything to do with what we are doing?

It has a great deal. One way of looking at philosophy is to consider it as the study of ideas of the past. Very respectable, very good for your general knowledge. But there is another way. You then look at philosophy and consider it as a form of life. Philosophy is a form of life itself. What we witness today is a separation of philosophy from life because in our atomized, analytical society everything is separated from everything else. No wonder culture atrophies.

In a society in which everything is separated and analyzed *ad nauseam*, philosophy is on one shelf and life is on another shelf—and indeed so often life is on a shelf. When I talk about the relevance of philosophy for life, I think I am not alone. In his book *Small Is Beautiful*, E.F. Schumacher emphasizes very strongly that the most important task for our times is not so much an economic reconstruction, although this is vital and necessary, but what he calls a metaphysical reconstruction or a religious reconstruction—looking deeper into our philosophical and metaphysical foundations and seeing what has gone wrong. In this sense philosophy is vital, because many of our problems stem from the fact that we started to look at the universe in too limited a way from the seventeenth century on. The metaphor of the universe as a clocklike mechanism has constricted not only the meaning of the universe and the meaning of cosmos for us, but also the meaning of our own life. We have somehow strangled ourselves.

So what I am trying to do in *Eco-philosophy* and other books is to look for alternative philosophical and metaphysical foundations. We have to realize that the mechanistic way is only one way and not the best one. It is pernicious nowadays. Although it has brought great material rewards, it is counterproductive in the long run. We have to create another matrix, another architecture around which we can weave reality and the cosmos. It must be an architecture of the cosmos within which our life can breathe, and thereby our philosophy will be life-enhancing. We need to establish a symbiotic relationship with the cosmos and other forms of life. This cannot be done within the mechanistic universe which splits and disintegrates everything in the mortuary of our analytical thinking.

Life-enhancing philosophy is one that tries to bring to bear such a conception of the universe which is home for Man. In it, we are part of the flowering of the great blossom of evolution. Within such a conception of the universe, we are not pitted against other forms of life and especially we are not pitted against each other.

On top of the mechanistic conception of the universe, we have grafted Social Darwinism, *"homo hominae lupus est,"* man is wolf to a man. And those two conceptions, which are philosophical *par excellence*, are working towards our own undoing.

What I am saying is the following. Our philosophical roots are not nourishing us any more. They are responsible for our plight. We'll have to change those roots, this whole foundation, so that it becomes again a tree that is nourishing us, that connects us with the universe, with other forms of life, and with our ultimate destiny which some call God. We cannot live in a shattered, meaningless universe. Human being craves for meaning and this meaning is part of our nature. So rethinking our foundations is not only an intellectual exercise, it is part of the quest for meaning. It is our existential necessity.

To that degree, I not only do not apologize for what I am doing. On the contrary, I think that I am a part of a new wave whereby life takes itself seriously again and wants to assert itself in meaningful forms—simply wants to flourish. *The Theater of the Mind* is homage paid to life, which not only crawls but has the capacity to fly.

Hearing what you are saying, it seems to me that a life-enhancing philosophy would go beyond the notion that there is only rational thinking and would include the intuitive process. Intuition so often gets excluded when philosophy is presented as a rational, linear, logical-mechanistic type of process.

In my conception of the mind in *The Theater of the Mind*, I distinguish three minds. The first I call analytical or discursive mind. The second I call the mind that is made of all the sensitivities that evolution has developed. Intuition, compassion, and aesthetic appreciation are included within the second mind. We can enjoy various aspects of the universe only insofar as we possess appropriate faculties. I call these faculties "appropriate sensitivities." Through them we elicit from the universe what is there. Among those faculties, intuition, insight, emotional responses are very important.

When we look at each other, straight eyes to eyes, we see much more than the eyes. We see the whole soul of the other person. We see in a sense the whole history of the person. We see the whole history of the species. This is not an exaggeration. Because eye-contacts are so important, because we have this sensitivity built into our eyes, built into our mind, we can carry on many conversations beyond mere words. We talk eye-to-eye.

In my "Mind 2," love is also included. Love as an evolutionary, and *existential*, phenomenon is both emotional and rational. As long as human beings are alive and are not crippled, love between two human beings is both beautiful and rational. We do not need to apologize for it. We need to celebrate it.

The scope of what I call Mind 2 includes all the sensitivities that evolution has ever evolved, from the first tropisms of an amoeba to the genius of Einstein. Mind 2 is the whole spectrum of these sensitivities. Within this spectrum, human life is lived. We need to evolve a new broadened concept of rationality which accounts for the whole spectrum, for the entire mind. We don't want to throw out rationality and become anti-rational or totally emotional. I insist that both rationality and emotions, insight and abstract reasons are capacities which evolution and human beings have evolved and which we enjoy.

All these sensitivities have to be incorporated into a larger symphony of life, plus those other faculties, sensitivities in *status nascendi*, which have not yet been fully articulated—as, for example, premonitions. As evolution is not completed, new sensitivies are being articulated. The "third eye" is perhaps this sensitivity which enables us to see beyond seeing. So often we do seem to be able to see beyond seeing. What is the phenomenon of extrasensory perception if not the phenomenon of seeing what our eyes cannot see?

There is a way of integrating all those developments—from the development of the first reactions of the amoeba to the development of faculties in mystics and in people with extrasensory perception—that makes sense within the spectrum of the sensitivities of evolution. It is for this whole spectrum that we have to create a new rationality. I think that we can do it. And we can rationally defend it. I myself refuse to be browbeaten by narrow rationalists who try to intimidate us by telling us that the searches beyond the empirical that extend to the mystical are not rational, and therefore are not worthy of human beings.

We need to salute evolution in all its flowering. We need to see its greatness in our capacity for compassion and in our capacity for abstract logic. The riches of evolution are immense. We have every right to participate in them because we are a flowering of evolution. We also have the responsibility to defend this participation as a rational process.

It occurs to me, Henryk, what could one do that is more important than exploring ideas and seeking wisdom? What else do people do?

I am glad that you have said it. We must be aware that exploring ideas and seeking wisdom have a great value. But we must not stop at this stage. We in the West have a great propensity to be little squirrels, to hold on to those great ideas and think that because we have read them all, accumulated them in our abstract coconut, these ideas themselves will make our life better, fuller, and more beautiful.

I think the second stage is to be able to translate those ideas into our lifestyles, and I think that in this process the Eastern philosophies are much better. We in the West are very long on theory and short on practice. In the East, I often feel, it is the other way around. They are very long on practice and often short on theory. In the West, you have the paradox that you cannot act upon the idea unless you understand it. So we create elaborate great theories and we try to convince ourselves that the theory is right. But in the end we do not do anything with it.

Henryk, you just struck a chord. I used to feel that, too, about the Eastern approach. When I first became exposed to Hindu philosophy, the Upanishads *and Vedanta, there was an emphasis on getting the* experience *of becoming one with the universe, as opposed to developing the philosophy behind that experience. Then I came in touch with the Tibetans. And it's really extraordinary. They emphasize the practice, but they have an incredible philosophy behind it. They have what seems to be an endless supply of literature and tradition. It's recorded in writing, and is the bedrock philosophy of their practice.*

Yes. I have envied Tibetan monks for their capacity to lead a connected life wherever fate and vicissitudes brought them. They seem to be able not only to survive, but to flourish in such a way that they become exemplars. We look at their lives and wonder how it is possible to have such a connected life in those very distressing and disintegrating times. It may be so because of their integrated philosophy, whereby general Buddhist philosophy is combined with rigorous practices and yogas which make this philosophy one's inner reality.

When I was commenting on the paradox of the Western mind, what I meant to suggest is that so often after we have learned the theory we say: "Well, now I know the theory, and the theory should work for me." And we stop at that. This is not really a living philosophy. I think that for the last three centuries we have over-emphasized the abstract quality of knowledge and the importance of ideas in one's mind at the expense of life as a living form. So many great minds, including the Buddha, said that the art of living is second to none. What is important, therefore, is to be able to find the ways whereby good ideas are interiorized, whereby they reach the level of our being, change our consciousness, and we become them.

For this reason, I have developed of late, as a parallel to my Eco-philosophy, what I call eco-yoga. At first when one hears the term, one thinks it's a bit of a joke. But it isn't, because no good ideas, no good principles, no wisdom that one accumulates in the abstract part of our brain is good enough unless it can inform you how to live. Unless it becomes living wisdom, it is not wisdom.

To find a way whereby a good idea is translated into the layers of your being is itself a creative act. For this reason, I have claimed that we have to make a radical transition in our culture from what I call the methodology of objectivity to the methodology of participation. The whole of life is participation, while methodology of objectivity in a sense denies this idea. Within our methodology of objectivity, everything is an object, set apart, put in the laboratory and cut with our analytical scalpels. In contrast, the methodology of participation is based on empathy, on understanding other forms of life in their own terms—on understanding the underlying unity of it all. It is a holistic one. It is one that requires that you take responsibility for all. If you are aware that you are a part of a greater whole, you have to take responsibility for this whole.

My eco-yoga is a part of this methodology of participation. It took us time to develop fully the methodology of objectivity to where it became enshrined in our schools of academia. So it may take us a considerable time for new insights to be transformed into new participatory strategies, whereby our research and our learning will be based on the idea of participation, empathy, compassion, rather than dissecting, objectivizing, and separating.

Sounds to me, Henryk, like a Western philosopher has taken on the nondualistic thinking of the East.

When you look at evolution holistically, you realize that it is one total process. You remember our friend Anaxagoras, who was Socrates' teacher. Anaxagoras claimed that all is mind. Then the history of philosophy developed along different avenues. But now when you look at how important mind is in co-creating with the universe in creating realities, it makes sense to say that at a certain point of analysis, mind becomes indistinguishable from reality itself. This conception I call Mind 3—to return to our earlier discussion—mind as coextensive with reality. The idea of mind, *nous*, in Anaxagoras, is so important that it is conceivable to think about the doctrine which I call "noetic monism," one which asserts that mind is inherently woven in every aspect of reality and every perception of it. Through this conception of mind, we can resolve many of the spurious dichotomies and various dualisms which we inherited from Descartes on. Our various activities—loving, doing logic, creating new worlds—are parts of the same mind. Doing different things, we are all parts of the same mind which functions in different capacities.

You're talking about what might be called universal mind, that we're plugged into.

Universal mind, that's right—of which we are aspects and which we articulate. I think that this idea of nondualism, Advaita in Hindu philosophy, can be now justified in a new rational way. Part of my rethinking concerning the nature and place of mind in the universe goes in this direction.

We have to simultaneously re-define three things: reality, knowledge, and the mind. By trying to understand one part of it, we simultaneously throw light on the other two parts. For each concept defines the other two. The conception of mind informs you what knowledge is and what reality is. Conversely, a given conception of knowledge immediately delineates for you the scope of the mind and of reality. It follows that if we start with a wrong concept of reality—for example, that it is some kind of clocklike mechanism that is detached from us—we immediately receive a distorted conception of knowledge, one that accentuates the accumulation of physical fact; we also receive a very screwed-up conception of mind as a Tabula Rasa, a blank sheet of paper on which experience writes. You can see that if you make one basic step that is wrong, the whole thing falls into pieces. This is what happens with Western culture and Western philosophy. We have to reconstruct it. You and I.

So you and I. And you're suggesting too that we have to take our minds, our little minds, and expand our notion of what our minds may be capable of.

Our little minds which, I put it to you, are not so little if we allow them to be as great as they potentially are.

Merlin Stone

When God Was a Woman

AT A TIME when our planet Earth is threatened with various destructive forces, people are discovering the Goddess of ancient times. Five thousand years ago, peoples of the earth revered the Mother of All Life. They envisioned a mother who had given birth to the cosmos and to the very first people in the world. The Creator was the first mother. She is the All that is: Immeasurable and incalculable, and deep like space itself, yet she is also the ground of being. From this wisdom we can begin to understand that we are not the stewards of nature, but an intrinsic part of the sacred wholeness of all nature. In this important time of transition from an age of materialism and accumulation into an age of intuitive and creative living, the Goddess has re-awakened.

During the past decade or so, a few point riders have been bringing forth the knowledge and wisdom of the long-buried Goddess energy. One of these pioneers is Merlin Stone, whose ground-breaking research and writing about the Goddess tradition has inspired many.

MT: Merlin, how did you choose the title of your book, When God Was a Woman?

MS: My original title was *The Paradise Papers*, which was meant to explain that it was an exposé of the story of Adam and Eve in the Garden of Eden. The book was first published in England under the title *The Paradise Papers: The Story of the Suppression of Women's Rites*. When it was later being prepared for publication in the United States, the editor decided that "When God was a woman"—which is a line in the book—was the most wonderful line. She thought that the title *When God Was a Woman* would draw many more people to the book in bookstores.

What prompted you to do the many years of research required to put that book together? What was the motivation?

I'm always being asked that question, and I wish I could give one brief and simple answer. I've explained many times that my motivation was, in part, politically feminist. I wanted everyone to know that ancient Goddess reverence has existed all over the world, in many different cultures. It was especially strong in the Near East and the Middle East, where we have incredible amounts of evidence—archaeological evidence from about 9000 B.C. to 3000 B.C., and written evidence from around 3000 B.C. on.

But, in fact, I'm not exactly sure what really drove me on. It was like a compulsion or an addiction. So much information was just being sort of dumped in my lap; things just kept coming up on their own that were begging to be put into the book. Looking back, I have the feeling that there was a female energy in the universe that wanted this information out, and that, as long as I was willing to cooperate as an instrument of that goal, I would be used in that way.

Before you published that book, there wasn't much information out about Goddess reverence. The interest in Gaia hadn't yet emerged, had it?

There was *no* information known by the general public. I had learned a little about it because of a personal interest. As a sculptor teaching art history, I was fascinated by ancient civilizations. I learned something about this tradition in the process of just poking around for exotic titles for my sculpture.

I think what finally made me decide to write a paper on it, though, was meeting several women who had doctorates—doctorates in theology, in anthropology, in sociology—who knew nothing about it. They not only knew nothing about it, but they said there was no evidence. And they really believed that. It was a rumor, they said, with no evidence to support it. But I knew there was evidence, because I'd read the various prayers to Ishtar and prayers to Isis.

So I started what was intended to be a ten-page paper. I was going to send it to these women and say, "Get on with it. I'm a sculptor; you're the scholars, so you do the work." But then I found myself constantly discovering new materials, constantly thinking, "Oh, well, there's just one more thing that maybe I should add here." As this process continued, I not only wrote *When God Was a Woman* but found all the material for *Ancient Mirrors of Womanhood* as well. So when I say that I was being "compulsive" and being "pushed along" and "pulled along," that's what I mean.

When I began to write that "ten-page paper," my radical feminist friends in Berkeley kept saying, "This has nothing to do with feminism. It's esoteric and ivory-tower. Why would you want to waste your energies on this?" Even then, I couldn't quite explain. It wasn't until I finally had all the material together that I realized how important it is for us to understand that the creator of all life—even of our planet and the heavens—has been envisioned as female, as mother.

Why had that memory, that tradition, been so long suppressed?

I have various thoughts about that. My initial thought was that historians had just sort of dumped it off the edge of "real time." I thought that because Goddess worship hadn't been taken seriously, historians had chosen to start ancient history later, with Homer. Most ancient history courses do start with that period, about the eighth century B.C.

But then I started to realize that there were huge libraries of written materials, all throughout the Near and Middle East, from around 2600 B.C. on. Writing was developed at around 3200 B.C. in the Jemdet Nasr period of Sumer, and by about 2600 B.C. there were many written tablets from this tradition. By 2000 B.C., there were huge libraries of legends, prayers, and so on. So my next thought—and perhaps it was a bit paranoid—was that this material had been suppressed because its content—Goddess reverence—had been considered unacceptable.

As I thought about it further, though, I realized that the suppression may also be very racially motivated. We think of Greece as the foundation of Western civilization, and Greek people are Caucasian. Many of the people of the Near and Middle East were darker people—third-world people we'd say today. And I wonder if this tradition was suppressed just because Western educators don't want to face the fact that civilization was initiated by other than Caucasian or lighter "white" people.

There must have been a large body of this knowledge in the Alexandrian library that was destroyed.

Well, since it was destroyed, we're not sure what was there. But that destruction came later, at about 300 A.D. I'm talking about two thousand years or more before that. In many places throughout the Near and Middle East, archaeologists have found massive libraries that held many tablets of prayers, legends, and other materials. In fact, one recent find is Ebla in northwestern Syria, near the Mediterranean. This area had always been considered to be one where early people didn't use writing. But when Ebla was discovered about twenty-five years ago, it had large libraries that held many legends and accounts. These are still being deciphered, but similar libraries were all over the Near and Middle East.

Christianity must have transformed the Goddess into the Virgin Mary, Mother of God. There's also the Sophia concept in Christianity, where the androgynous energy of male and female conveys something of the same idea. But somehow it did get changed.

 Geoffrey Ashe wrote a very interesting book called *The Virgin*. He talks about the various Goddess images as a prelude to Mariology. One fascinating aspect of studying ancient Goddess worship is that the images of Isis with Horus on her lap look, if you didn't know what they were, very much like statues of Mary and Jesus. This is evidence that a certain amount of that imagery was taken into Christianity from the Egyptian religion of Isis, which was very popular in Rome.

We also know that the religion of Kybele—some people say "Cybele"—came from Turkey (then Anatolia) to Rome. The Sibyl ordered it in during the time of the Carthaginian Wars, around 200 B.C. She asked that the small black stone of Kybele be brought from Anatolia to Rome. The idea was that the wars that were going on would not stop until this black stone was brought to Rome. So it was done. The stone came, and the wars stopped almost immediately. Then the religion of Kybele became a very major one in Rome.

In this religion, the son and consort (the same person) of Kybele was Attis. In the springtime, at the vernal equinox, an effigy of Attis was carried around on a tree and then buried. Three days later, Attis would arise from the dead, saying that he had died for the salvation of all people.

I found it very interesting that such rituals had existed in Rome long before the Christian period.

Very interesting. Even having died in the springtime, Easter.

Exactly. It was a big springtime festival. It was called the Megalesia. There's a lot about it in the classical Roman literature.

Did you have any idea, when the book was published, that it would have such a life of its own?

When I was writing it, I thought that maybe ten people in the world would bother to wade through all these unfamiliar names and places. This material was something that almost no one knew about. Even when it was taken by a publisher, who actually contacted me rather than me trying to contact a publisher—which is what completely assured me that this was out of my hands and being done anyway— I really felt that way.

I tried to make the book as coherent and as easy-reading as possible. I asked my daughter, who was about seventeen when I was finishing the book, to go through everything. She pointed out any word that she didn't understand, any sentence that she thought was too long; and I really tried to simplify it. But even then we had so many unfamiliar terms: Goddess places, Goddess names, and dates floating off backward into the B.C. periods that had always seemed like chronological vacuums. I really didn't think anybody would wade through it.

But I am amazed. Since the book came out in March of 1976, hundreds of thousands of copies have been sold. It's being used in many Women's Studies courses in universities and it's being treated as the original classic of Goddess reclamation. I'm very happy that the information about ancient Goddess reverence has become more familiar.

How did it affect your life—both the act of writing it and its longevity? Did it transform your life?

It certainly did. I think that it was the *writing* of the book, and the *re-*

searching, that really transformed my life. I genuinely felt that there was an energy that was moving me along, an energy that I learned to trust after a while.

I was not a trusting soul when I started this work. I thought I was in control of everything. But as the book developed, I started realizing how everything flowed along—whether or not I was trying to control it—for the best.

So I've just lived that way since 1970, when I started working on the book as a book—although I had been reading about ancient civilizations for many years. I've just been sort of following an understanding—an understanding that I'm being used, moved along, and that I will be as long as I'm willing to be. I don't feel that it's anything against my will. I have to be willing to be used in this way, and I always am. I have lived very, very differently than when I was teaching art at the university in Buffalo. It has become a much more beautiful and satisfying way to live.

Merlin, what you're saying now resonates with the whole idea of Goddess energy, of going with the flow. Perhaps you could talk a little bit about that.

The flow of energy of the Goddess is very much within, very much within our bodies. It can be experienced. It can be felt. Rather than constantly fighting uphill battles, feeling that the harder something is the more important it is, I've learned to flow when my body is filled with an excitement, an energy, a sense of this is fun, this is pleasure. That is the Goddess speaking to me, telling me what She wants me to do. I always know what I'm supposed to do next, because I get excited and energized by it.

It's rather funny, because you would think that if you followed that way of living you'd never get anything practical done—like shopping for groceries or washing the floor. But I'm always amazed: Invariably there will also be that moment when I actually *feel* like going shopping, or I actually *feel* like washing the floor. In the long run, everything gets done, and it gets done the way it ought to. And yet I always have a beautiful sense of swimming along in the flow, with things being there when I need them.

And I don't worry. I don't feel that I have to worry about what's going to happen tomorrow, because I know that the next step just keeps on appearing on my pathway. I often don't know exactly what it will be. But, looking back, I can see that it has always been the right thing.

Are you able to impart this kind of experience or knowledge to others? How might one go about following the path you've been following?

One of our major problems is that so many external injunctions were placed on us, when we were young children, by various authority figures and religious institutions and so on. We've been told that we're not good enough or have no talents. We've been told that we lack what's needed to effect meaningful change. We've developed various fears and have absorbed many obstacles.

My first concern in workshops that I give is to get in touch with those internalized obstacles. I want to help people realize that those things have come from the outside. We've internalized them, but they are not really us. Once we put them aside, or really question them and deal with them, then we simply listen to our own inner voice. It's clear, almost like a radio receiver, when we've gotten the static out of the way as much as possible. And that's tuning in to that voice of the Goddess, tuning in to that energy level.

It involves doing meditations, certain exercises, carrying on conversations, getting in touch with how to hear that voice, and learning how to know that it is the right voice. The right voice is one that's not scolding, one that does not make us feel guilty. It's a voice that encourages us to use the gifts that we've been given, to use them well, and to use them for a contribution to the world and to all life in the world.

I feel that last quality in particular is an important way to recognize it as the voice of the Goddess. It brings the feeling that every one of us is here for a very specific reason, or we wouldn't be here. We somehow lose our knowledge of what that reason is because of all the external injunctions. But once we can tune in to what excites us, what energizes us, what gives us pleasure, we realize what contribution we can make—whether through writing or music or healing or dance or philosophy or whatever it may be. We know that the gifts we came here with were given to us to be shared. This realization eliminates the feeling of "Oh, well, she's done it, or he's done it, so why should I bother?" It also puts an end to feeling competitive when someone else seems to be doing exactly what you're doing, because you see that no one gets the same mission. There are no two identical assignments.

Merlin, you were working as an art historian. You weren't an anthropologist or an archaeologist. You even knew some women anthropologists who said that you were all wet with this idea, right?

They didn't say that I was all wet, they just said that there was no evidence. But since I had already discovered a lot of the evidence in these various logs from excavations, and in translations of ancient tablets, I knew they were wrong. It wasn't even a matter of discussing it or arguing about it. The facts were there. And, of course, spending nearly five years in the archaeological library at Oxford, and traveling to the excavations of sacred sites and museums in the Near and Middle East and Europe, confirmed what I had been saying.

Your experience could be typical of almost any specialized field in our culture. Authority figures may be saying one thing, and yet the truth may be very different.

In *The Time Falling Bodies Take to Light*, William Irwin Thompson mentioned how all new ideas seem to come from outside the specialized field. And there's a reason for that. When you're in a field, to some degree you are brainwashed to believe that what you are told at a university is all there is to know. For example, if you're assured by your professors that there isn't any evidence, you won't bother looking for it. But if you're coming in from a fresh point of view and don't know that there isn't any evidence, you will look for it. I wasn't told that there wasn't any evidence until after I knew that there was. So I was able to do what people who had been trained in those areas didn't even think to do, because of what they'd been told.

That insight is a good one for all of us to reflect on. Somehow the system in force tends to inhibit real creativity. We have to get past that when we're exploring a new area that could be a good one for our creative development.

There are two things that come up all the time when people have an idea. Either they are told, "Oh, nobody else has ever done that, so obviously it isn't a good idea," or they're told, "Everyone is doing that, so that's sort of silly to do." It's amazing how most people will respond to any new idea from one of these two points of view: If it isn't being done, it's not worth doing; and if everybody's doing it, it's not worth doing! There's so seldom an encourager, someone who says, "If that's what excites you, then obviously that's exactly what you're supposed to be doing—as long as it's something real to you and to life, something that won't hurt, but will contribute to life in the world."

There are many "tracks" laid out today, particularly in the United States.

The emphasis now, for example, is on going to college. And then inside the colleges, students choose particular tracks to move on that will bring money and success. There are all kinds of tracks. In many ways, they may be chan-nels for creativity, but they're not necessarily channels to realize one's full potential. Even though they may be "creative," they may not be the channel of one's own destiny.

It's unfortunate that, since the early eighties, there's been an incred-ible fear provoked that "if you don't do it now, and don't do it in a hurry, and don't move right in on it from the time you're fourteen and a half, then there won't be enough room for you; you are going to be left out." Young people have been raised on fears of this kind, which is exactly the opposite of what I was saying about trusting the flow. So they jump in. And very often, years later, they realize that it's not at all what they wanted to do; it's something their parents suggested or something some teacher suggested.

This is a real problem. Paranoia and fear make it difficult for people to get in touch with what they really would like to do.

The fact is that many of us who have lived a while have had many different careers. You have, I have. We go through different cycles.

Exactly. I was having a conversation a while ago with a woman who told me that she has had two different careers. She had been a teacher and is now an editor. I mentioned that I had been an art teacher and sculptor, and now I'm a writer. Then she said, "But I really want to be a choreographer; that's my secret fantasy." And I said, "Well, I have a secret fantasy too: I would love to be a dancer. So when you become a choreographer, would you write a part for a little old lady?" [laugh-ter]

She promised she would.

Great.

Merlin, as we explore the importance of the Goddess in everyday life, could you give examples of how we can use Goddess energy from moment to moment in our daily lives? I was particularly interested in what you discov-ered about Taoism.

Yes, of course. There's a big discussion within the women's spiritual-ity movement about whether Goddess is transcendent or immanent. When She is thought of as transcendent, people think of Her as up in the heavens, floating around on a cloud or sitting on a big throne—you know, very much the way many people see a male God. Most women say that the Goddess is immanent, meaning that She is within us. But every time I tried to deal with that concept of Goddess as within, I kept getting an image of a little lady behind my sternum, which didn't quite feel right either.

I started to realize that, for me, Goddess is the flow of life-energy, the all-organic process we mean when we say "Mother Nature." And it became as simple as that: Goddess to me is Mother Nature. All the life-energy, the life nurturing forces, the cycles of birth and life and decay are what the Goddess is about. Mary Daly says that "God is not a noun, God is a verb." And that makes a lot of sense. So once I really got in touch with my own feeling that Goddess isn't some lady up on top of the clouds, or some specific image of a woman, I realized that it's that sense of nurturing, nourishing—maternal, in a sense—female energy that makes life continue in its cycles and in its flow. That's what I mean when I say Goddess.

I've always been very interested in Taoism. I read constantly in the *Tao Te Ching*—whenever I feel that I need some centering or that I need to get back in touch with that feeling of flowing. So I was thrilled to read a paper by a woman named Ellen Marie Chen, a Chinese scholar who works with the original Chinese materials. She wrote a paper on the fact that the *Tao Te Ching* is a remnant of, or was derived from, the worship of the Great Mother in ancient China.

When I was doing *Ancient Mirrors of Womanhood*, I wanted to include Goddess imagery from all over the world—not just from the Greeks or the Romans or the Celts. So I was gathering material from all cultures, and I realized that the Tao itself is a Goddess-related concept, a Goddess philosophy. Taoist writings are constantly talking about Mother Nature and the matrix. So I tucked Mother-Nature-as-Tao into *Ancient Mirrors of Womanhood* as a Goddess image.

One of the feelings that I get so strongly from the Chinese concept of Goddess, where there is no scripture such as the Bible or the Koran, is that all nature is the Scripture of the Goddess. I feel that if we learn how to read nature by *really* looking at it and understanding it as a process—as the flow of the river, as the tiny leaf that becomes a big leaf that eventually discolors and falls off the tree and then becomes compost at the roots so that the tree can continue to grow—if we begin to understand, with our whole beings, the continual organic process of all nature, then we can read nature as a scripture. It will always give us the right answer to any question.

One of the exercises that I do in the workshops is a good example of what I mean by this. Before the workshop, I ask each person to bring with them one natural object, something they might have found along the way, at home, or—if we're out in the country—something they might have picked up the day before. Then, in the workshop, I ask each person to think of a particular problem they have, a decision they have to make, or a particular obstacle that they might be having in their lives. I tell them to ask the natural object they have brought how to solve the problem. I tell them to ask its *process* what answer it has for their particular question or their particular problem. This involves much more than just the way the object looks, which is only part of it.

Then I ask them to put this answer into the form of a poem or a song or some choreography or a drawing, or whatever they feel like they want to use as a means of expression. It's amazing how every single time, every single woman—whether or not she thinks of herself as a poet or writer or dancer or whatever—will come up with the most incredibly beautiful and clear answer from whatever object she has picked.

Nature is always talking about growth. It's always talking about change, ways of movement, ways things will develop and deal with obstacles, showing how water will flow around a boulder rather than smack into it all the time. We can see in nature all the answers to everything we need to know.

Do men ever come to your workshops, Merlin?

A lot of men do come to the lectures. Most of my workshops are just for women, but every once in a while I have workshops that are mixed. Sometimes the men are wonderful. Sometimes they really get what we're saying and really flow along with it.

But I have had situations, especially at lectures, where that was not the case. It seems to happen when I have a question-and-answer period. For some reason—I don't quite understand why this is—but for some reason, one man out of the ten or so men there seems to need to have the attention of the entire group. He seems to need to engage me in what feels more like a battle than a conversation.

There may be fifty or a hundred people in the room. The women, for the most part, are aware that everyone else might want a turn to ask a question. But this one man is oblivious that there might be other people who would like some time, and he just takes over. It always puzzles me that a man like this can be so oblivious to what others in the room might want or need.

I think this is changing; I hope it's changing. I've known some wonderful, wonderful men who seem to really understand this flow, this cooperation, this sense of sympathy and empathy that, to me, is what the Goddess is so much about—our sense of connection and our oneness in the world. But unfortunately, men in our society often have been trained to feel that they must be separate, that they must stand out.

Don't you think men got that from their mothers?

[laughs] No, I think they got it from society. Society led them to believe that they aren't anybody unless they're putting on that tough stance, that stag-fight type of attitude. It's unfortunate not only because they end up having to lock horns in stag-fights with other men, but also because at this point most women don't find that style particularly interesting either. Most of the women I know are much more interested in very gentle men, sensitive men who don't just "help" with the dishes or "help" with the baby, but actually see the dishes and the baby as part of their own lives as well. It's changing, and, I think, definitely changing for the better.

It's important to emphasize that the Goddess energy is not just in or only available to women. It's in and available to men as well.

Definitely. A lot of the groups are mixed. Most of my mail does come from women, but about ten percent of it now comes from men. When the book first came out, I might have received one letter a year from a man, and all the rest were from women. More and more men are entering into Goddess reclamation. They're willing to learn, willing to open up, willing to go ahead without having all the answers right in the beginning. They're learning to trust and not feel that they have to control everything, which I think is even harder for a man to do than for a woman.

At least since the industrial revolution, men have been raised with certain fixed ideas about what they're supposed to do. The ideas my parents and my grandparents had are very different than the ones I hold now about what a man should do. And I think that many men would say the same thing. We have to overcome a lot of conditioning, a lot of training.

It seems as if men in those earlier generations felt that they weren't going to be considered masculine if they didn't follow those particular ways of being. But now we understand that a lot of women feel that it's more *masculine* for men to be sensitive and gentle, and that it's really false when a certain macho attitude is put on: "I don't do dishes" or "I don't diaper babies" or this kind of thing. There really is a tremendous change happening in our society. People have become people.

It's better for everyone when a man and a woman who get together can feel that they're friends who are sharing these experiences, and can just do things as they seem right to those particular people. That's much better than having to feel, "Well, that's your job, and that's my job," according to automatic gender assignments.

Because of your work and the work of others exploring the Goddess, there's a whole new generation of mothers who have a different view of the world. That will certainly have an effect on male-female stereotypes.

Right. And also the fact that more fathers are there when the babies are born.

To me, it's very simple: Men and women are people. All we have to do is simply act like people: deal with each other lovingly, relate to each other in cooperative rather than competitive ways, sympathize and empathize with the needs of one another—whether it be our lover, our husband, our wife, our children, or whoever. Each of us is struggling and working, trying to do the best we can. If we simply see each other that way, we can be loving in each of these relationships. We can try to help, to encourage the development of the potential of each person around us.

That's all we really need to do. That, to me, is what love is all about. It's not clinging and it's not pushing or pulling. It's really caring about each person's development, about the flowering of each person's potential. When we do that, then there isn't any need for stereotypes. We don't have to be this or be that. We simply have to be. And to love. The rest of it takes care of itself.

One of the goddesses that's very important to us today is Gaia, the earth goddess. We live in a time when the earth is seriously threatened by many destructive forces. We're facing a major environmental crisis all over the world. Perhaps you could talk a little bit about the relevance of the Goddess to some of the things we're facing on planet Earth.

Well, when we understand that the Goddess *is* life energy, *is* Mother Nature, we realize that the entire planet, the entire universe, is involved in this. It's not just in our town or in our neighborhood. We're all so interconnected that everything we do has an impact on everything else.

One of the major concerns now within women's spirituality is the preservation of the planet. We're trying to develop a sense not only of *planetary consciousness* but also of *planetary conscience*. This will make us aware of what's happening to all other races of people, to all other species of animals, to the trees, to the rivers, and to all else that has suffered from our ignorance.

One of the things that always struck me, when archaeologists would ridicule the ancient Goddess reverence as being so many "nature cults," was that it wouldn't be so bad if we had a few nature cults today. It would be even better if we all believed in nature cults! If dumping chemicals in a river were considered as blasphemy, instead of being considered simply as pollution, maybe people would stop doing it. The preservation of the planet and the growth of our consciousness depend upon realizing that to hurt—whether it's to hurt plants or to hurt other animals or to hurt other people because they're different—is to go against the feeling of the flow of the Goddess, against the life-nurturing and the life-nourishing ways.

I suppose there are many ways to think of this philosophically in terms of Goddess religion. In my own personal way, seeing the Goddess as the flow of life, I see us as a bridge in the flow of evolution. I see that we are all bridges in evolution, and that *we* create the future. Each one of us acts or doesn't act, and that creates the future.

So, as a bridge, having children—and now having four grandchildren—I realize that it is essential for us to wake up to Goddess consciousness. We have to realize that all nature is sacred. And we have to realize that if we don't preserve the planet, those children and grandchildren, and their children and grandchildren, will not have a home.

Earth is our home. Whether or not they want to build space colonies, we can't think of Earth as something to use up and toss away like so many other things in our toss-away society. We really have to wake up and think about this planet as our home, and as the home for our children and our children's children, because that is the Goddess energy. It is that life-energy. If we destroy life on the planet, we destroy our home; we destroy our Mother.

This issue has become a really important one for many, many women involved with Goddess reverence and women's spirituality. We have to help people realize that every time they throw a plastic bag somewhere or in any way do destruction to our home, it's as bad as dumping garbage in the middle of their own living room.

It amazes me that people still throw stuff out of their car windows onto the highway. When you drive down the freeway here in California, you often see row after row of big orange bags that are used by crews hired to pick up the trash. We have to have full-time crews picking up the trash that people throw out of their cars.

Much of that comes from a lack of aesthetics with regard to natural beauty. Would the same people who toss a beer can or a Coke bottle or whatever, in the midst of something so beautiful, dump their garbage on the Mona Lisa or on some other beautiful painting? It's as if certain people don't have the sense of aesthetics to appreciate the natural beauty of our entire planet, so they don't hesitate to destroy it.

This thoughtlessness is also tied in with the incredible consumerism of this country and Europe. We supposedly need so much to make ourselves happy, and there's never enough. No matter how much people have, they seem to want more and more. And, of course, the more we consume, the more garbage we create.

My feeling is that when people really tune in to this understanding of Goddess as flow, and follow that excitement and that energy level of pleasure, they don't need as much. I've always found myself needing incredibly little, because I usually feel wonderful about my life, about what I'm doing, and about what's going on with people.

People who need so many of these consumer items are the ones who are truly unhappy. They have much more than they actually need, but they're still not satisfied. And they never will be satisfied, because material things are not the way to gain satisfaction. In the process, they're using up our resources and creating this incredible pile of garbage.

It seems that we are driven to distraction, with lots of distractions to drive us.

Exactly. And this process also creates paranoia. If you've created a huge pile of belongings, then you start worrying about who's going to come and take them away, or bomb us so we don't have them. And this just creates more and more trouble. We are not taught that it might be fun to share, or that other people might need a little bit if we have so much. We keep piling it up even though we're not really satisfied by it, but we don't want anyone else to have it either.

The excess baggage not only weighs us down, it also limits our creativity.

That's really true. It becomes a burden instead of a pleasure. People seem to think they're going to find satisfaction and contentment in a shop at the mall, and that's definitely not where it is. It's right inside, in our hearts, in our ability to feel loved and to give love. When we have that, we don't need all the other paraphernalia.

So here we are in this moment, creating the future, Merlin. How are you creating your future? What lies in store for you?

Well, in a way, I don't create it. It's more that it sort of happens to me, as I explained. But what Goddess seems to be tossing in my lap at the moment is a play I'm working on about the Sibyl of Delphi, the Pythian priestess of the ancient oracle at Delphi. Delphi is where the voice of Gaia was heard, before Apollo. So the priestesses were literally hearing "The Voice of Earth," which is the name of the play.

Parts of this play were envisioned by Olympia Dukakis—the woman who won an Oscar as a supporting actress, the cousin of Michael Dukakis. She has had some incredible visions. We're working on this play together, and I'm very excited about it. The Goddess has just sort of dumped it on us, and we're willing. We're ready to go, and it's very, very exciting. So I know it's the right thing to be doing.

David Bohm

Creativity, Natural Philosophy, and Science

WE LIVE IN an age when science is accepted as the key to progress and the betterment of life. Clearly, the world of science impacts all of us who live in contemporary society. However, science has become increasingly specialized and fragmented, so that its viewpoint necessarily precludes seeing the whole context.

Life in the nuclear or computer age is not as gloriously beneficial to human society as was once promised. The abstractions of science have replaced the creative process where ideas, new territories, and probing questions can be explored in depth. In earlier times, science was intimately engaged in natural philosophy, and ideas were its lifeblood.

David Bohm, a preeminent scientist and physicist, suggests that a renewal of science is possible, and that such a reformation can lead to a deeper understanding of society, the human mind, the nature of creativity, indeed, of life itself. David Bohm is considered one of the world's foremost theoretical physicists. His book *Causality and Chance in Modern Physics* has become a classic in the field of quantum mechanics and is widely used at universities, as are his books on quantum theory and relativity. For more than two decades he enjoyed a close association with J. Krishnamurti, the late world-renowned religious philosopher with whom he deeply explored questions of mutual interest.

MT: *David, how did science get onto the track of becoming specialized and frag-*
mented? How did that happen?

DB: It happened gradually, over the past few centuries. In early days,
scientists regarded themselves as natural philosophers; that is, they
were interested in the whole of existence. They were pursuing this
interest through science, but they were also interested in broader
questions. There was however a gradual increase of specialization,
concentrating more on techniques and on the development of very
complex apparatus and highly organized institutions for carrying out
research, which is now expensive and requires many people to work
together. It has to be organized hierarchically, and so on. Also, a lot of
the work became more and more abstract, and it became less clear
how this approach would be connected to philosophical conceptions.

At the same time, there developed a kind of philosophical point of
view called "positivism" or "operationalism,"—this was in the early
1920s or thereabouts—which was in a certain way against philosophy, or against metaphysics, as these people called it. The main point
of science was supposed to be to organize the facts in a logical way
and to make predictions. With the development of technology along
these lines, the interest in broad ideas gradually decreased.

The philosophical component is what science really began with, though, isn't
it? In the days of Pythagoras, wasn't natural philosophy really the lifeblood,
the foundation, of science?

Yes. It began as inseparable from philosophy, and even inseparable
from art and other activities. Yet the whole of our more modern civilization has been characterized by a constant breaking-up into parts,
into fragments which don't have much to do with each other. Science
has gone this way, too. Not only has it isolated itself from other areas
of life, but also within itself science has broken up into many parts
which are only distantly related.

What I thought was the interesting point that you and David Peat made in
Science, Order and Creativity *is the importance that mathematics has as-*
sumed in science. It seems that if you can't come up with a mathematical
formula for an idea, then it's not regarded as a good idea. The pursuit of ideas

has kind of been lost in the name of mathematics.

This is especially so in physics. In other sciences it is less so. Although perhaps their ideals are similar to those in physics, other sciences haven't managed to realize them yet. Biology is one example. But in physics, the emphasis now is on mathematics.

In ancient Greece, there was a group of people called Pythagoreans who believed that number was the essence of reality. For example, they understood harmony mathematically as the ratio of length of strings. They thought everything could be done in that sort of way. But this emphasis became really common with the advent of relativity and quantum theory, where it didn't seem to be possible to get a clear physical picture of what these theories meant. People like Sir James Jeans and Werner Heisenberg and others said that mathematics is the essence of reality and that imagination merely displays the meaning of the mathematics. This idea gradually spread, as people taught it that way, and now students who go through this kind of education think that it is only natural and that anything without an equation is not very significant. If they do admit that there is any use for thought that's not mathematical, it is only if such thought leads to some mathematics.

So if you come up with an idea, and you're unable to come to a set of equations making it possible to provide its proof through scientific experiment fairly quickly, then it's not an idea worth pursuing.

That has been a common notion. But there's another interesting development in physics in connection with what's called "string theory," where they allow free mathematical speculation. They admit that it might take twenty or thirty years before such a theory could be tested experimentally. Nevertheless, they feel that if you have such a body of mathematics, then there's something definite to work on even though you can't compare with an experiment.

So the way people are doing physics is constantly changing. But what has remained fairly constant has been the general tendency to regard mathematics as the essence of what is being talked about.

This tendency has also affected the way that physicists communicate with one another, not to mention scientists in general. It has had an effect on the language employed in communicating scientific concepts and ideas, hasn't it?

Yes. The language is primarily geared to the mathematics. You do use an informal language, but mainly to talk about the equations. The equations, as it were, come between you and reality, and you talk about the equations which, in turn, are in some way about the reality. But the equations have a kind of intrinsic structure which makes many people in physics feel confident that this is a better language for talking about things than ordinary language is.

You made a reference to an obscure philosopher—at least to me he was obscure, maybe he's better known to others—named Korzybski, who pointed out that words are never the thing. Could you talk a little bit about that?

You're referring to Alfred Korzybski, who published a lot in the 1920s and who was moderately well known at that time. He wrote quite a bit, but the statement that sums up his view is that whatever we say anything is, it isn't.

This may sound paradoxical, but he's saying that what we're talking about is not made of words and even the *meaning*s of the words are not an exact representation of the reality. They may be similar, but reality always goes beyond. Reality has more in it than we can say, and also in some ways it's different. This is to say, our ideas are neither a complete representation of reality nor are they absolutely correct. I think this a very important point, because there's a tendency to believe that at least someday we're going to arrive at a complete and absolutely correct set of ideas—say, about physics, for example.

If you just stay at it long enough.

Yes. There's a very well known physicist called Steven Hawking, for example, who said that physics will be finished in perhaps thirty or forty years and after that theoretical physicists could be replaced with computers. I don't know whether he was talking tongue-in-cheek or whether he meant it, but it's a kind of thought that's fairly common.

An interesting example which you mentioned in the book was the dialogues that occurred between Niels Bohr and Albert Einstein. You spoke of how these two geniuses and idea generators, who started out as friends, eventually became alienated from one another—largely because each focused on his own particular perspective. They weren't able to bridge a gap that separated them.

This example shows the importance of fixed ways of thinking. Einstein and Bohr were two of the leading theoretical physicists of this century. They began as very close friends, very interested in physics, with a tremendous amount in common. But they disagreed on a philosophical point about how to answer the question "What is the criterion for truth in science? What sort of theory will you allow?"

Einstein wanted to say that eventually we'd get an idea which was in unambiguous correspondence with reality. There would be an objective reality in which the observer wouldn't play a very big part. He would be there, but not as fundamentally important. But Bohr developed a view in which the observer plays a key part; the thing observed and the observer were inseparable. To Einstein, Bohr's proposition seemed inadmissible as a fundamental scientific theory. He called Bohr's view a "tranquilizer philosophy." And Bohr felt that Einstein was now turning, in a reactionary way, against similar ideas he had himself developed in relativity theory.

They talked about this for many years, and they came up with arguments and counterarguments. But gradually they had nothing more to say to each other. Each one asserted his own position and defended it against the other. They got nowhere, and after a while they probably got tired of going on with it and just drifted apart.

Some years later, Bohr was invited to Princeton, where Einstein worked at the Institute for Advanced Study. A mathematician, Herman Weyl, thought that they really ought to meet again, so he arranged a party and invited both men and their students. At that party, each one stayed at an opposite end of the room with his own students, and they didn't meet. They really had nothing to say to each other.

Here are two people who have two fundamentally different values about what constitutes truth, and they can't really meet. When they did talk in the past, they argued about the scientific content; but that was not really the point at issue, you see. Their argument was not really meeting their philosophical disagreement.

David, I think that most of us amateur scientists, as it were, think of mathematics as a very linear and very ordered process. You spent a great deal of time, certainly in the book Science, Order and Creativity, *looking at order. Can you talk a little bit about order, and what it is from your perspective?*

Order is a very fundamental notion, so fundamental that it's implicit in everything we do. We can't define order, because even in defining it we are using order—the order of language and thought and so on. In the book, David Peat and I discuss the order of society as a vast thing. There was a change of order from the Middle Ages, for example, to modern times. The old order was based on the notion of some eternal notion of truth. The order which replaced it was called, when it came into being after the Middle Ages, "the new secular order," which emphasized time and development and so on. That change in society was a vast thing. In the book, we show the significance of order for our whole life.

For example, you have the order of points on a line, the order of words, the order of a geometric figure, the order of music, the order of thought. The meaning of thought depends on its order. Everything depends on order. One of the most elementary features of order is just dividing everything into categories, distinguishing human beings from animals, the sheep, the goats, and so on. This appears in all the creation myths, that the earliest form of order was just dividing things up—putting things together that belonged together, and keeping them apart from the others. But that's a very elementary notion of order.

We develop a more organized notion of order by thinking of points on a line. One could think of a line, say a straight line, and break it up into equal segments. Now each segment is similar to the next, but each is different in its position. The differences are similar, however, and that makes the order—right? And if you'll imagine that each segment bends a little bit, that the same bend exists in each one, you could form a curve. Again you have similar differences. With this idea of similar differences, you can get a more precise notion of order.

This idea reminds me of the story that you cited about how Helen Keller was taught language. Tell us about that.

Yes. That illustrates order. When Helen Keller's teacher, Ann Sullivan, came, she saw what she later called "a wild animal" who had very little relationship to other people. But what she did was to play a certain game with this child. The game was to make Helen touch various objects and then Ann would scratch the object's name on Helen's hand. They played this game for a long time, with no success. Though for the child it was something of a game, she couldn't see the point of it.

Then one very fortunate day—whether it was an accident or not we don't know, but probably not entirely—Ann touched the child's hand to water in a bucket and scratched the word "water." This was in the morning. In the afternoon, she touched the child's hand to running water and again scratched the word "water." And then the child had a tremendous insight, which was that this was one substance—*water*. You see, the puzzling thing for her was that the same name was scratched for two experiences that, without vision, are so different as standing water and running water. And this gave the insight that these two were different forms of one substance, water, and that the thing scratched on her hand, which was always the same, was the symbol of all water. Then she suddenly had another insight: Everything has a name! which tied up with the whole game that she'd been playing.

After that, she was able to start using and learning words faster. In a day or two, she was making sentences. Soon she was *communicating*, and her whole character changed from this wild animal to a very cultured person. She went to the university, wrote books, and so on. So you can see that order was involved there, the order of the concept. She needed the concept of water to put it all in order, to distinguish water from other substances and to connect them up so that she could relate them.

Speaking of order, there's a new branch of science emerging called "chaos theory." One would think chaos is the opposite of order. What is your view of chaos?

My view of chaos is that it's an infinitely complex order. People used to think of chaos as disorder, or lack of order. And many people still think that way, calling it randomness. But it has been shown mathematically that you can make curves that are more and more complex.

If we were making similar differences, there are curves where one difference is enough to tell what's going to happen. Sometimes you need two or three or four; eventually it would become infinite—it would be an infinitely complex curve.

You could imagine, for example, rolling a ball down an incline. If it were a flat incline, the descending ball would follow a very simple order. But suppose the path were a very complex shape of hills and valleys and saddle points and obstacles. The slightest shift of the ball would make it go to a very different place. Imagine an extremely irregular path, so that you would need an infinity of elements to describe it, to determine it. This would eventually become what we call "chaotic." But it's still determinate. And therefore chaos, I say, is a determinate but an infinitely complex order.

The image of the water washing on the beach, for example, may look chaotic; but there are all sorts of sub-orders in it, like swirls and currents. Eventually these sub-orders get more and more complex, and you lose track of the order altogether. You call it randomness. But there's always, I say, some order.

The mind, what you call the "brain mind," starts reeling when you start going into the levels of order that may exist in watching an ocean wave crash to the shore. Somehow it's almost too much.

It is too much for us to grasp. But logically and abstractly we can think it's still ordered, right? Maybe with very good instruments—computers and so on—we could even demonstrate the order. But the point is that we have to free our minds from the idea that order is always just a simple thing that we could grasp. If we go back to Korzybski, we'd say that whatever we say order is, it isn't. It's always more than what we say, as well as different.

So there will be order within chaos.

Yes. Chaos is a kind of order.

What about randomness?

Randomness is a form of chaos which has certain properties. People have argued a long time about how to define randomness. One idea is that you don't find any regular sub-orders in it. The ocean wave crashing on the shore looks complicated, but you see little bits that are ordered, like swirls and currents. Now, in a random distribution there aren't any such bits that can be seen. For example, people generate random distributions by computers. That's a determinate generation, but there are no visible sub-orders. However, there may be average properties. If you shoot a gun at a target, the pattern of results is never exactly the same. It varies with the distribution of shots. This distribution has no visible sub-order, but it averages near the target, with a certain spread.

If one could get to the secret of randomness, one might become a big winner in the lottery!

Well, perhaps there is no secret, really. There is a story of some mathematicians who went to Las Vegas and played a roulette wheel. Such a wheel is supposed to be random. But probably it's not a perfect wheel and, from time to time, little bits change on the bearing. So it's slightly off random one moment, but then later a little bit more breaks off the bearing in a slightly different way. By observing the sequence of results carefully, they were able to win. They won many thousands of dollars until the management became suspicious and told them to stop. And the management then bought a better roulette wheel with better bearings.

So, in order to have a random roulette wheel, you need perfect bearings—right? There are always small deviations from randomness, but they change in such a chaotic way that unless you're very observant you can't use them. Eventually it gets too complex to be able to follow it.

There's a poet-essayist in the United States, Wendell Berry, who writes wonderful essays and is a Kentucky hill farmer. I recall him writing something like "randomness is the scientist's way of describing the mystery."

Yes. Randomness is a kind of order. If it is mysterious, that is because it is an infinite order—which, however, we have come to call disorder. It would take an infinitely deep view to see all randomness as order. Since we don't have that deep view, we can conveniently call it randomness. However, it's confused to call it disorder, because there is always some order. One "random order" can always be distinguished from another one. So I say that it's not clear to talk of disorder or lack of order. It's not true, for example, to say cancer is disorder. It's an order that's not compatible with the life of the human being.

Would you relate that in the same way to, say, mental disorder? Would you say that in some way there's an order there?

Yes. Shakespeare spoke of "a method in madness." It's the order of what we call disorder. If there were no order in this disorder, then medicine would have no hope.

David, since we've been talking about order, this might be a good opportunity, for you to give us a description of your theory of wholeness and the implicate order. And I think one good way, if I might be so bold as to make the suggestion, is to do it as was done in the book—with the experiment with the ink in the viscous fluid. Perhaps you could describe that.

Well, this is the implicate or enfolded order. The example I gave was to consider two concentric cylinders with the inner cylinder held fixed while the outer one is turned slowly and regularly. In between the two, we place a viscous fluid, which may be glycerine, and we put a droplet of insoluble ink into that glycerine.

Now if you imagine a small element of glycerine which contains that ink droplet, then the outer parts—the parts with a larger radii—move faster than the parts of smaller radii, so that droplet is drawn out into a very fine thread as we turn. The ink droplet becomes a thread and eventually becomes invisible, right? At that stage, you could say that it doesn't seem to be there. It seems to have no order. You would almost think it was distributed at random.

But now reverse the motion. Turn the outer cylinder backwards slowly. It's important that the fluid be viscous, or else it will diffuse and this won't work. But if you turn the outer cylinder back slowly, every element of fluid will retrace its path. Finally it all gathers together in a droplet again, and the ink droplet suddenly emerges into visibility, after which it spreads out again.

When the ink droplet was spread out, you would have said that it had no order. Nevertheless, there was a hidden order in there which meant that it would re-form an ink drop and not something else. I call that "the enfolded order." I say that the ink droplet is enfolded into the glycerine and that it is unfolded by reversing the procedure. The word "implicate" means "enfolded" and "explicate" means "unfolded," so I can call it the "implicate order."

How would we relate that to the thinking process, and to consciousness?

The implicate order is present in many places, and it does seem to be present in consciousness. For example, we may say that one thought implies another, that one thought is implicit in another which has the same root. People wouldn't use the word "enfolded" except for the feeling that one thought enfolds another, that we have a series of thoughts, and one enfolds the next. They unfold, you see, rather like the ink droplet. When we have this thought we're not aware of the next thought, but in some sense we feel it's there, right? Very much as the ink droplet was there in the glycerine, the next thought gets unfolded. And then the next thought gets unfolded. And that, in turn, lets the next thought get unfolded. So it's as if you had a series of ink drops that were unfolding.

So, in some sense, there's a source that we can't really identify, but we know it's there.

Yes, well, at least we're assuming that it's there. We're using it to try to understand. As in science, you make an assumption and then see if it will shed light on the whole process.

What if you used many ink drops?

Well, you could put in one ink drop, turn it *n* times, and then put in the next one and turn it *n* times again. The first one would then be enfolded 2*n* times. If then you do the same with another one, the first would be enfolded 3*n* times. After a long time you would have a whole bunch enfolded, but each drop would be different because it was enfolded a different number of times. They would all look the same, but you could demonstrate the difference. As you turned the cylinder back, one would unfold, then another, then another.

Now, suppose that they were put in in slightly different positions. Then they would also unfold in slightly different positions. If you did it rapidly, you would apparently see a particle crossing the space. But in reality it was always the whole, unfolding and folding back— right? So this would be a view of wholeness in which the parts appear as an abstraction due to our perception, because we only perceive the ink when it's fairly concentrated.

You spent many years doing dialogues and mutual explorations with Krishnamurti. When you talk about your idea of wholeness and the implicate order, Krishnamurti's views of the thinking process and what he called the "knowing beyond the mind-brain" come to my mind. I'd like to hear you talk about the significance of those dialogues, from your perspective.

They're related in some way to what I said about the implicate order. In fact, the idea of the implicate order was inspired to some extent by considering what Krishnamurti was saying—as well as by other things.

I think Krishnamurti meant that the order of thought is wrong and that this is one of the basic reasons why human society is not working—why there's so much trouble. He said that thought arises from memory, that it's a response of memory. But in memory it's rather like it is with the ink drop. You're not conscious of your memory, right? But when something happens, the memory responds to unfold as a thought. This then stirs up the memory to make another such thought, and so on. There is therefore a thought-process similar to what he's talking about. But he's also talking about getting beyond that. He spoke of a movement of the mind which is not conditioned by memory, which would not get into the difficulties that thought gets into. This movement would bring thought to order, to a rational order. Let's put it that way, although thought is always in some kind of order. If the mind were silent, then it would not get into the incoherent order that we have been calling disorder. It would instead go into a coherent order.

Now I'd like to make the connection, as you did in the book, of this process to creativity itself. We generally think that somehow creativity comes out of thinking, when indeed that may not be the case.

Yes. We were just talking of Krishnamurti, who emphasized—and I think he's right—that creativity does not come out of thinking, though thinking may be an instrument that helps express creativity. He's not saying that thinking is always wrong, but rather that in certain areas it goes into a wrong order.

Now I want, first of all, to make a distinction between thinking and thought. Thought is the past participle of "to think." It means "what has been thought." Thinking thus becomes thought. Now, we usually assume that when we've finished thinking, it's gone. But it isn't. It goes into this implicate order as a kind of program, and it responds as thought—which affects everything, not only what you think, but also what you see.

If you're prejudiced, for example, if you think somebody is no good or is your enemy, you see him that way. If you or somebody else has thought that a long time ago, it's still affecting you years later. That kind of thought is mechanical and not creative. A great deal of our thought is of that nature. It can often be destructive.

Now beyond that, there is a perception, a much deeper perception, which I say is the source of creativity. I would like to compare this mental situation to a stream. The stream is actually in the implicate order. But let us first think of an ordinary stream. You can go from the source, all the way down, in a boat, for example. But you can see the stream all at once, let's say, from way up in the air, and then you understand without time how it all works. If there is something floating on the stream, you can see it floating down with the passing of time. But at any moment, you can see the whole stream from the source all the way down. And if there's pollution there, you can see where it's coming in—say, at the source—and where somebody is trying to get it out further down the stream.

Similarly, I say the whole mind is in a kind of stream with a source, and thought is fairly far downstream. That stream, however, is not in space; there's no space that it's moving in. As I have already said, it's in the implicate order. Do you see what I mean? It's everywhere, but it has different degrees of subtlety. Getting closer to the source leads you to a more subtle process of the mind.

And any part of the stream might give you a view into the whole stream, almost like a hologram?

Yes. Every part of the stream gives you a view into the whole. But by being open to it, you are led to the source. Every part comes ultimately from the source. You can also use the image of a tree going out into its branches. The branches seem to be separate, but that's a result of abstraction. Thought abstracts them as separate, though they're all coming from this one source, the trunk or the roots. And similarly there's some kind of origin to the whole mental process which is infinitely subtle and from which, I say, creativity comes—or intelligence, or whatever you want to call it.

So if we, to take your metaphor, are caught downstream in thought—and that's where we are, basically, living out the patterns that we create in our life around thinking and thought—then we never really get an opportunity to truly be in the part of the stream where real creativity can take place.

Yes. The source of creativity is far more subtle and requires awareness and attention, which are more subtle mental processes than thought—particularly attention. Attention is extremely subtle and has no fixed form. We can put our attention into the thought which is far downstream, or we can put it into something subtler and much further upstream.

You used your stream metaphor to describe different creative approaches. You said some artists or musicians perceive the whole stream at once. For example, Mozart saw a whole composition in his mind and then wrote it out. Other composers seemed to develop a composition in parts, a little at a time. Still others, such as Bach, wrote a composition part-by-part, but had a sense for the whole as they did so.

Yes. It seems fairly well established that Mozart was able to see a whole composition at once, in some way, I think, in the implicate order. And then he would write it out the very first time, without revisions. Beethoven, in contrast, had to rework his themes over and over again. But he was always working from the source, even as he reworked it. An artist who works on something again and again isn't necessarily doing it mechanically, because he may be reworking it from that creative source.

To take another example from the stream—which I think is an excellent metaphor—if you're in the lower part of the stream, in thought, then you have a particular way of perceiving what you're experiencing. You used the example of how sometimes, when you first hear dissonant music, it doesn't sound like there's any order to it. We can't understand it until we can get the context by moving from downstream to a little further upstream.

Yes. That's very interesting. Mozart used new combinations of notes which were thought to be dissonant, but people were able to move upstream and see the harmony in them. Thus, thought, musical thought of a certain period, would lead you to expect harmony in a certain form. Then if you just arbitrarily go out of the form, you will get chaos; but there's a way of going out that leads to subtler harmony.

When new forms of visual art such as impressionism appeared, they produced violent reactions among the viewers. Many said, "This is rubbish." But they were still seeing it through the old thought of what art should be. Gradually people learned that the viewer must also make a creative step into that stream, further upstream, to see this new form of art.

What seems to me significant here is that you, as a scientist and a physicist, are coming up with a scientific definition and view of how we actually perceive the world and think, and of how we may be more creative or more destructive depending on what part of the stream we're in.

My interest in science has always been part of a larger interest, which includes a view of natural philosophy and extends even beyond nature into human beings in society. I regard that as all one. I think that such an unrestricted context for creativity is essential for order. If we are not creative in this way, we are going to be destructive because our order will become so limited and rigid and mechanical that it no longer fits the reality.

We can see many institutions around us where that kind of rigidity has occurred.

Yes. We don't need any further examples. Also we can see individual human beings who become rigid and mechanical and not only uncreative but also destructive.

Maybe we can talk a little bit about how we can get upstream instead of being downstream. As someone who has been studying the whole river, the implicate order, for many, many years, you are better qualified than anyone I can think of to give us some suggestions about how to do that.

Well, here you have to say that going upstream means moving toward creativity and away from the mechanical repetitiveness. Therefore it would not be appropriate to give a mechanical prescription of how to get upstream, because it's a constantly dynamic, changing stream. It will never be the same—not only for yourself, but for other people. I can make a kind of map of what I've seen, but then it may be a bit different from your perspective as well as next time for me. You can get an idea in this way, but it's not an exact set of prescriptions.

Now, I think it depends, first of all, on seeing the value of getting upstream. Nobody will try it unless he or she can see it's important. But if you do see the value of it, then you can also see some of the negative features that tend to stop you. For example, the attitude of rewards and punishments will stop you if you're not genuinely interested in the creative act but only want whatever the reward is, which has nothing to do with the act. This attitude will tend to take you off track. So first you have to be interested in it for its own sake.

Then you have to look further into things that are keeping you out of it, such as repetitive patterns of thought, and become aware of your assumptions. A great many discoveries in science were made by people getting free of certain assumptions that are commonly held. You have to be sensitive to such assumptions.

It's hard to give a prescription for how to do that. But one feature which Krishnamurti emphasized very much, and which I think is really crucial, is *attention*—attention not only towards the outside but also towards the inside, to the factors that are getting in the way. For example, there is the kind of feeling inside of being stuck on certain ideas, the kind of sense of security and insecurity. Moving into a new area will make you feel insecure, perhaps, and staying in the old area may make you feel secure, but this may be an illusion.

Now you have to pay attention to such factors. And attention is a very subtle thing. I could compare it to sort of scanning. It has been shown that the eye, for example, scans objects in picking them up. It may be thought that whatever is inside the brain—thought, feeling, perception, you know, sensory perception—is somehow being scanned from a higher, more subtle level to bring it to a whole. We could call this attention, going to more and more subtle levels, leading you up the stream. It depends on the quality of attention, you see. This attention will bring you far up the stream, which is the source of creativity.

This notion has been more common in Eastern philosophy than in the West. For example, there's meditation. I've been told that in ancient India an artist would spend several days getting into the right frame of mind, by meditating, before he would attempt to start doing anything. And I think there's something in that.

In our society, and I think this permeates the West, we seem to think that if we're going to learn to be creative we should go to a seminar about it. In a sense what has happened is that the sense of there being a formula, the mathematical formula, has also penetrated the process of how we think creativity happens. We think that we can learn a formula about the way creativity works, or how to do something in a certain way.

But in response to my query about how can we get upstream you said, "There is no mechanical answer to that, because it'll be different for everyone." And it's recognizing that paradox, as it were, and being willing to hang out with it, that allows us to be in the creative space.

Yes. The principal barrier to creativity is the mechanical process, which has its use, but which has become part of us. Instead of just being used by us, it has come to dominate us and our whole psyche. And we have to be aware of this mechanicalness that we're stuck in.

So this is what Krishnamurti meant when he said, "Thinking is the problem."

Yes. Thinking tends to become mechanical. There is a kind of thinking that is not, when it comes from the source, when it's being used by the source. But when we just churn over old thoughts and patterns and formulae and so on, it will be mechanical. It will handle a certain range of problems and so on, but it will not be really creative.

The last few pages of the book that you wrote with David Peat emphasize the importance of dialogue. If I can paraphrase a little bit, "Dialogue can loosen the collective social/cultural rigidity that holds all of us in its grip." What did you mean by that?

We are held rigidly by thoughts and assumptions circulating around that we are not conscious of. For example, consider prejudice against people of a certain race. Very often a child will pick that up without even being told, just by the way people behave, implying that all people of that race are no good. And the minute the child sees one of these people, he'll see them through this prejudice. He's being held rigidly. The same sort of prejudice, the same sort of prejudgments, arise in all sorts of ideas about science, about art, about politics, and about everything. These ideas operate tacitly, subliminally. So you don't know you've got them.

Now, the point of a dialogue is that it's not just an exchange or just a trade-off, a way to negotiate points. Rather, it is important to have the attitude, the spirit, to look at assumptions—our own as well as other people's—and suspend them, examine them. It's often very hard, you see. If you have a prejudice, you'll find a tremendous resistance to examining the assumptions underlying it. But if we take the spirit of such dialogue seriously enough, then our assumptions will often be revealed by somebody else. And we can also see theirs.

So every time you see a mistake of that kind, whether it's yours or somebody else's, everybody gains. It's not a case of somebody winning and somebody losing. The purpose of a dialogue isn't to get your point across or to win. The point is that we are exploring these assumptions together, and we all gain by seeing them and getting free of them. This process will develop a spirit of fellowship and friendship. If people will sustain this kind of dialogue, I think that the whole state of mind of the culture can alter. But, of course, we don't have much of that yet.

Ram Dass

Sacred Odyssey: Seeking Freedom

THE YEAR WAS 1969, and I, like many others, had been through a healthy dose of Eastern mysticism. I picked up the paper one day in San Francisco, and read an article about a Harvard psychologist who had gone to India and returned with a new view of himself and the world. Thus began my personal, enriching encounter with Ram Dass, aka Richard Alpert, who has become a legend in his own time.

From the early 1960s, when he actively researched consciousness expansion at Harvard with Tim Leary, Aldous Huxley and others, to his journey to India where he was given his name, Ram Dass, "servant of God," by his guru, Neem Karoli Baba—which led to his writing of the now-classic *Be Here Now*—he has become a major contributor to the integration of Eastern spirituality with Western philosophy and psychology through books, lectures and tapes. He is the author of *Journey of Awakening*, *Miracle of Love*, and *The Only Dance There Is*, as well as co-author, with Stephen Levine of *Grist for the Mill*, and co-author, with Paul Gorman, of *How Can I Help? Stories and Reflections of Service*. He is also co-founder and a board member of Seva Foundation.

MT: *We first got together for an interview in 1974, and we've been coming to-gether ever since, here and there, from time to time. It has been an interest-ing journey through those years for many of us. In many ways you have reflected that journey back to other people, like myself and others, in the sense that you've been so open with your process and your path, and you've gone through a number of different cycles yourself, as we all have. And I think that the value of that has been enormous. I just want to acknowledge you for the value of what you've provided to many, many people, because you've been so open with your process.*

RD: Well, I've really seen myself as a mouthpiece for a process we're all going through, and that was the way I protected myself from getting caught in being somebody who knows. I've really had the mindset of being part of a group of people on a journey together, and we just keep exchanging map readings and anecdotes about what we've been going through. Clearly the value of truth in such a dialogue is, as Gandhi said in his autobiography, *Experiments in Truth*, that "truth is that which sets you free." So I've really been practicing learning how to be truthful about human beings. And to do that publicly is very interesting.

It's amazing to see people do that privately, much less do it publicly!

I understand, I understand. But when you see how much it opens the heart to be that vulnerable and to be that open, and how much it invites—I can't tell you how many letters I get from people saying, "Thank you for sharing that somewhat embarrassing issue," or "Thank you for that truth," or, really most interestingly, the letters that keep saying, "Thank you for being so human." Those are the ones that surprise me, you know—the fact that we *should* thank each other for being human. Because when we are on public projection, when we're public media, we're so often trying to be, if we're not careful, some image we imagine we should be rather than what we experience ourselves to be, and it's very interesting to get over that process of trying to be bigger than life, better than life. I did a book about my guru, a thousand stories about Neem Karoli Baba called *Miracle of Love*. In it I describe various sexual things he did, and I got so much flak from that, because holy people aren't supposed to exist below the waist, you know? I mean, it's not acceptable to be fully human. And I think the joy of looking at all the saints and seeing that they're all neurotic as can be is very refreshing [laughter].

I recall a talk that you gave to the transpersonal conference—I guess it was the summer of 1988—where you talked about all the things you had done over the years, just about as much as anybody has done, I'm sure, and then wound up saying you hadn't gotten rid of one neurosis!

Yes. But the beautiful part of that image is, I say that initially my neuroses were huge monsters that would scare me all the time, and now they're like little schmoos I invite in for tea: "Oh, hello, sexual perversity, come on in! Haven't seen you in weeks!"

The idea of seeing it that way is different from how our society has elevated neurosis to an art form, you know, and to a major identity for people. You can join a 12-step program for any neurosis you want now, which defines your existence in membership in terms of a class that has that pathology.

There are 12-step programs for 12-step programs.

Yes! [laughter] That's an interesting phenomenon, you know, because it's giving people family surrogates in safe ways. They're sharing whatever the thing is that bothers them most. They're finding others who have that same thing. And that's wonderfully liberating. The only thing it doesn't liberate you of is the definition of yourself that makes you a member of that group. So the whole process of the self-destructing of a method is, to me, very critical. Every method's a trap that you have to get trapped by for it to work—but at the end it should be like those little instructions in the television show: "This tape will self-destruct in five seconds."

That's always the paradox. You have to go through the suffering to get to the other side. Somehow you have to experience the pain.

But then they say, "When you arrive at the other shore, don't portage. Leave the boat that you used to cross the river; don't carry it with you." So you don't have to end up a meditator, or a 12-stepper, or an ex-alcoholic; you're free of identity. You don't have an identity. You're whatever you need to be.

So what are you these days?

I don't know. I really don't know, and that's kind of fun. I observe who I appear to be from situation to situation. If I do a benefit for Children of War or a nuclear free zone, I'm sort of a liberal, thinking, person caring about peace or ecology. If I hold the hand of a person with AIDS as they're dying, I'm both a yogi working on death and somebody who is playing the role of priest, almost, or a priest and a healer. If I'm at the Seva board meeting, I'm having fiduciary responsibility and making decisions about building intra-ocular lens factories in southern India to deal with blindness. And I love it. I just keep moving in and out. I've started to write short stories now, and it turns out I might be a writer, and that all this was preparation for me to be a writer [laughs]. It's funny not to have any idea who you are.

I'm not nurturing anything. There's nowhere to go with me. Gandhi's line is so profound in my life, it's like a mantra: "My life is my message." And it keeps changing all the time. Next year I'm going to be sixty. I thought, I've been doing the same gig for twenty-five years. Maybe that should be a critical point. I thought, well, what would I do? I thought, well, a few years ago I went to Burma to meditate for a couple of months. Maybe I should take a year to go to an island with a lover, and just paint and write poetry and make love, and lie in the water, and lie in the sun, and heal my whole Jewish, middle-class righteous thing, because I'm so busy doing good now.

I love doing good, but I can see the subtle trap of it. I mean, I see the subtle trap of, you know, "How good he is! He's gooder than practically anybody." And that isn't interesting enough. I want to be free. I don't want to be anything in particular. Because, you see, what can you really offer to your fellow human being to alleviate suffering? It's your own freedom. And if you're not free, subtly you're entrapping them, all the time.

I've been preparing for a tour, and I've been asking myself, "If you're going to speak to sixty, eighty thousand people—and that's a tremendous grace, to be able to do that—what are you going to share? What is it you really have to say?" And I can feel that I'm, in my own life, dealing with these incredible changes that are occurring in every facet of existence. I'm dealing with changes—the political changes, the economic changes, the ecological changes, social, cultural changes in terms of mores and values and societal structures, and it's just change everywhere.

I saw that what I've cultivated over these years, in terms of spiritual practices, leaves me in a position to respond to change without fear and contraction. And that may be the interesting thing to share. In a time of accelerated change, the society needs the kind of work many of us have done on ourselves, to bring grace and equanimity and compassion and discriminative wisdom to changing circumstances. Many things may change. We've lost our economic hegemony as a country, you know, a lot of things have changed. There's a need for what we can do to smooth the evolutionary process so that it doesn't have that violent edge of fear—because most people, when they face change, get frightened. And when they get frightened, they get unpredictable and often violent.

When I read all the stuff in order to get myself up to speed on nuclear waste and water pollution and the AIDS epidemic, and on and on, I could feel this kind of heaviness build in me. And I realized what was missing. What I felt missing was the balance of the *dharma*, of the timeless quality of the dharma, of the sense of perfection, of the unfolding, of the faith in the spirit. And so I realized I had to put the books away and re-center into my meditation, into my love of my guru, into my spiritual dance, till I could find that balance, because that's what I have to offer. It's that balancing act, not the Pollyanna-ish part, and not the other part, the Cassandra or whatever that other part is.

Some people have predicted that the 1990s will bring the coming-together of the spiritual, political, and environmental movements. Do you think that's true?

Well, the environmental issues, first of all, are unitive, because they occur to rich and poor and to everybody. To that extent, they force that kind of consciousness which involves new paradigms for living life.

Politics has a lot of inertia in it. It's the last to fall, because people don't give up their power lightly. And when you go from these vertical political structures into networking and horizontal structures and so on, that's a tremendous threat to the existing power structure. I mean, I can see with Eastern Europe, as exciting as that is, it's as if the United States won, but it doesn't feel like a winner because it feels frightened by the fact that it won, because the implications are more than it bargained for, because its power is jeopardized by the winning. Which is great. I mean, it's an absolutely wonderful moment. And it has such spiritual potential to it.

I will do my best to help those things come together gently, but I have no prognostications about how it will come out. Those of us who are growing, and using everything to grow, will grow. Those people who are identifying themselves with something external to themselves, something which changes, are going to get increasingly frightened.

As the power-structure changes, as people come into power who were from the 1960s and so on—as they become forty, fifty, fifty-five years old, that age range—what can be called upon in them is a resonance with the ideals which they touched in the 1960s, and then put back away because they weren't functional for their need to support their children and do what they needed to do. But these ideals are still in there. And that's part of what I would like to be doing, resonating with that quality in people that brings that forth—to make it figure rather than ground.

President Havel of Czechoslovakia, when he spoke in Congress, said, "What is needed is a new kind of consciousness." I thought, "That is being said in Congress, by a president of a country?" And my heart was just singing from that.

Yes, that was quite remarkable. And also, some of the things that Gorbachev has said—

Oh, he's extraordinary.

—have been remarkable as well.

Absolutely remarkable. Just for a head of state to admit an error is so refreshing.

Ram Dass, I'm reluctant to get into this, but I think I need to, just because so many listeners wonder about it. There's a term that we don't use much around New Dimensions—it's "New Age"—because the term is so amorphous and hard to define. It's difficult to really understand what that means, because it means so much to so many different people. And yet with Time *and* Newsweek *putting the term on their covers and stressing channeling, psychic phenomena, crystals, and that kind of thing, I'd like to get your appraisal of what you think the New Age is, and what value it may have, if any.*

For the past thirty years, there have been very profound inroads into the nature of reality as the culture defines it. You could say that there has been an increasing appreciation of the relative nature of reality, which allowed not only the reality that is known to the physical senses but also realities known to the intuition, to altered states of consciousness, dream states, and so on, to be real.

It has certainly been around for a long time—I mean, this is not anything new. But there was a major shift, in the 1960s, in seeing realities in a relative way, which freed people from the kind of vertical power-structures, from investing institutions with such solidity. People started to see that an institution is only relatively real, within a certain social structural framework. And so there were large numbers of people who began to experiment with doing things differently.

I think that sexual freedom, women's rights, gay rights—a lot of those issues—came alive because people stopped being afraid of these monolithic institutions and structures. And minstrels like Dylan and the Grateful Dead and the Rolling Stones and so on slowly carried these values into the culture. So what I see now when I travel through the country is the response to an understanding of relative reality in mainstream America. Polls show a tremendous increase in people's acknowledgement and acceptance of reincarnation, for example, and in the numbers of people who meditate. In science and psychology, the day of behaviorism as an out-and-out dominant value system has now given way. The idea that the mind is a causal influence on the body is a major shift in psychology.

These shifts are all new to us. They are requiring some profound shifts in the culture—a profound shift in the meaning of education, a profound shift in "What is the quality of the good life?" We are being forced to come to terms with the fact that a society based on consumerism to offset unemployment, with the GNP as the only criterion of the success of the culture, is much too narrow a definition, a bottom line, for the society. The myths we've been functioning under ended up seeming impoverished. I mean, people can almost sense that a Donald Trump is a loser as well as a winner. There's some recognition in society that the game isn't quite as simple as it was portrayed for us to grow up with.

That's all part of a shifting set of metaphors, myths, and paradigms of a culture. That's very much what the New Age is about, it seems to me, in its essence. It's a shifting perceptual vantage point about who the individual is, what a social structure is, what nation-states are, what a quality life is, and what the relationship to nature should be. These are all part of it.

Obviously, the minute a concept gains some kind of visibility in a society, then people will start to exploit it for their own ends, and the power people will try to subsume it under something that will keep them in control. But the nice thing about what I see going on is that it does empower individuals.

I don't mean to be presumptuous, but I think that what we did in the early 1960s empowered people to be active in the anti-Vietnam movement. The anti-Vietnam movement which ended that war forced the world to see the power of individual indignation about a moral error. That led, at some level, because of the interrelationship of all things, to Tienanmen Square, and that fellow standing in front of the tank. From there it's a short jump to Eastern Europe and the house of cards falling.

Now, that all has something to do with the individual human spirit speaking up and feeling empowered. And that is all new. I don't know if you want to narrow it down to something hip called the "New Age," but there are new qualities, there are windows of opportunity for consciousness at this time, which you could see as evolutionary, or you could see as a passing pendulum show. And they'll all go under again, you know, into something more material, because we are at the same moment trying to export our kind of Pepsi-Cola mentality, saying that our kind of democracy is the democracy that the world wants. But I think it isn't the kind of democracy that the world wants, actually.

I've read what a number of people like Ken Wilber and David Spengler have said about it, so I can hear that it is a concept worthy of continuing thought. It can't be used for arrogance or elitism, though, because the New Age has existed through all time, also. From where I sit in relation to spiritual awakening, throughout history there are always people awakening and there are always a lot of people asleep, and nothing much is happening at all. And I live in that realm of reality as well.

There has been a lot of criticism, mostly from establishment circles, of the quest for spiritual fulfillment as being kind of a negation of the world, a negation of the problems of the world.

That's missing the point completely. It's missing the point. It is true that, from an external point of view, people did start to turn inward because they began to see, as C.S. Lewis says, "You don't see the center because it's all center." And that awareness that "we're the center" of the change occurs within each human being.

When you see people trying to bring about peace with violence in their hearts, and you realize the interdependence of all things, of all people, and of all being, you realize that peace just doesn't come about that way. So a lot of people have awakened to the fact that they have a lot of inner work to do. And those are the people who can bring to social institutions and social change the qualities that are necessary for those institutions to realize the objectives that they've set for themselves. The peace movement activists have a lot of work to do on themselves, to be peaceful human beings.

A government that is interested in the well-being of beings has got to examine its own fears about inequality in economics, and its own greed, and its own insecurities, because an insecure person's fear feeds into the world's fear. And fear is the root cause of bombs and of inequality in the distribution of resources. I mean, think what it costs our human hearts to deny the fact that there are people starving while we have more than enough—the cost is incredible. And we can't afford it, we really can't afford it. Because we end up being starved.

In a talk Krishnamurti gave at the U.N. about a year before he died, somebody asked him, "Well, if I were living peacefully in a hut on the border of Pakistan and it was invaded, what do I do if I'm a peaceful person?" And Krishnamurti said, "Sir! Live peacefully for twenty years and then ask me that question!"

I was in the audience that day.

Were you? Do you remember that?

Yes, I do remember that.

It was great. It was wonderful. Again, the experience is so important.

Yes, but was he peaceful when he said that?

"Sir!"

Yeah, "Sir!" [laughter]

I was also reflecting on the Dalai Lama as somewhat of a model. Although he speaks of himself as "a simple Buddhist monk," he's really a remarkable human being who demonstrates peacefulness in action.

Yes. He's a beautiful, beautiful model for us of a human being facing incredible adversity and yet managing to keep joy, to keep equanimity, and to keep discriminating wisdom so that he knows just how to use each energy situation—not in an exploitive way, but in an abundant way, to bring forth all the possibilities. I've been very touched by him, by the quality of his being. And he just says to people, "Be a good person; just be a good person." He said, "It will liberate so much energy in you." And that's such a simple instruction. [laughter]

It cuts through all the stuff, doesn't it?

Doesn't it, indeed! I have a great video of him brushing his teeth. He's just brushing his teeth and brushing his teeth, and then he starts to giggle, and he has such a good time with the fact that a television camera is showing him brushing his teeth! He's delighting in the whole meta-game of it. He's a sweetie.

We so often tend, in our imagination, to put figures like the Dalai Lama on a pedestal. But when you get to see someone like the Dalai Lama in an ordinary situation—living their ordinary life, you know, just like another human being—it's so wonderful!

I understand, I understand. I love just the humanness, the fun of all of this. A magazine came out recently, *Omni* magazine, with an article called "Masters of the Universe" I was one of the masters, along with the Dalai Lama, and a number of other beings. My guru, fortunately, wasn't there. I mean, the whole thing was so embarrassing. People started giving me "Master of the Universe" toys [laughter]. And none of us could do anything but just delight in the absolutely bizarre humor of the situation.

It does seem to be a time of extremes of one form or another. It's almost like the blacks get blacker and the whites get whiter.

That's interesting. I don't experience that so much, certainly not in my life. In my life there are all shades of rainbow colors all the time. Maybe I'm not very realistic, maybe I'm not very connected, because I'm seeing less and less of that in my own life. I mean, I'm having a hard time with the kind of discriminative mind that says, "This is different from that."

When I look at a human being, it's just a fellow human being. It's not a black or a white or an old or a young or a sick or a healthy—I mean, sitting with a person with cancer, a person with AIDS, to me they're just a fellow being who has taken an interesting incarnation, you know? And all their self-pity and anger and fear and all that—I mean, my heart breaks for them, and at the same moment, how interesting, how curious. It's like sitting at the edge of the mystery. And that's probably something that has changed in me a lot over the years, my delight in the mystery. Just sitting at the edge of death and life and the uncertainty of it all.

It's a very thin thread when you realize that the breath is all that sustains life, really. It's pretty amazing.

Yes. I spent months in Burma, just following the breath from three in the morning until eleven at night, sitting in a little cell, breathing in, breathing out, watching that thin thread of existence, and then seeing the whole world kind of envelope back in or turn back in on itself, until it was just the breath. And then the universe starts again.

I think we undersell our potential as human beings so, so much. We don't even know how to get ourselves out of the predicament we've gotten ourselves into. To me, meditation is such an exciting thing. You know, I think of all the exciting things I've done—I mean, I've done really wild stuff in my life. But when I think of it all, the exploration of my own mind is by far the most exciting—it's like climbing Mt. Everest. It's just so far out to see the way your mind creates your universe, and to keep pulling the awareness back, and back, and back, until it rests in its own being.

It changes the way in which you are in the world, finally. I can just hear those lines, "One does nothing, and nothing is left undone." Or, "Truth waits for eyes unclouded by longing." Lines like that. So it's a taste of the quality of equanimity in the midst of the dramas of life.

You know, you don't even think it's anything special, after you cultivate that. And how you know that it's special is because of people's reactions to you, when they say, "Thank you. Thank you for being. You know, this was a delight." And you realize, and you listen, and you have to get over the ego part of it saying, "Oh, no, thank you,"—that's just a kind of courtesy. And you listen, and you hear they're really saying that.

There's a great story that we published again in *How Can I Help?* It was about the Dalai Lama's physician, who went to Yale Medical School to do grand rounds. He just took the pulses of this woman— he just stood there for about twenty minutes over her bed, holding her wrist. He got all done, and he got up to walk out—and he'd never said a word to the woman—and she leaned up and said, "Thank you, doctor." He turned, and for a moment they were together. Then he left.

That "Thank you" came from such a genuine place, because they had shared a space together. And all he had done was to hold her wrist. I think we have so much to offer each other that isn't the commodity we think we're exchanging, and we keep shortchanging what the dance is about.

Part of it requires one to slow down, to really take time to slow the pace, because we do live in a society, particularly in the United States, where the pace is fast.

Yes. Our whole relation to time is a very interesting one. Ultimately, of course, we're trying to arrive at our awareness being not in time, having nothing to do with life and death, and then dancing in the dance of time, the linearity of time. For example, when you and Justine go and live in the woods with nature, that's realigning your being with a different kind of time-frame. I remember when my folks bought a farm, and my mother went up and she hugged this big tree and said, "This is mine." Now she's dead, and the tree is still there. The tree hardly noticed—except maybe the sweetness of the moment, maybe the tree spirit noticed that—but the tree just has such wisdom, and the rocks have such wisdom. There's such a different time dimension.

I love to go out in the desert and camp, because it looks at first as if nothing's happening, and then you see it's all alive, but just changing so slowly.

There is a resurgence of interest in shamanism, and I don't think it's just people wanting to be like Indians. It's really kind of a grass-roots movement that seems to be taking place all over, people just getting together in groups and drumming and talking. Shamans, of course, were able to talk to the animals and communicate with nature. We've lost that, and we need to recover it.

Well we've gotten caught in "More is better." And there is the trap: the idea that if we cram more into life, it will be richer. If you not only do this and this but also that and that—even though you are tired—if you push yourself a little bit, then you will have a richer life. But actually what you're doing is impoverishing each moment, because you are living it *in* time rather than *out* of time. The richness of life is that which is lived so in the moment that it's out of time. That's not a contradiction, either. Like when I drive anywhere—I'm going from point A to point B, but as the buses say in their ads, "Getting there is half the fun!" [laughs] Really, when I'm driving across the Golden Gate Bridge, or driving through an industrial section or anywhere, it's "Wow! Look at all this! Look at all this!" And this is the moment.

So I do think we tend to have the opportunity, through media and advertising, to have our desires fanned, to enjoy the feeling that we have so much available to us. It's a stage where we think that because so much is available, if we accrue more of it, it's better. There is a point you get to where you see that more experiences don't change anything any more. You've looked at the sunset, you've swum in the river, you've beaten the drum, you've flown in the jet, you've done this and done that, and then you see. And what's awesome is to meet simple people who already have that realization, so they don't yearn for the jet or the BMW or the this or the that, and then you find a person who's content.

"Contentment" is a word that we hardly hear in our culture. We hardly hear it. We don't show pictures on the cover of *Time* of people who are content.

Interesting word, "contentment"—"content."

Yes. They have enough. They stopped collecting.

We are great collectors.

Aren't we? "Look at my pictures of life. Look at my whole butterfly collection." Those experiences.

Both psychic and material collectors.

Exactly. Until you see the Hochman line, "Your coming and going is nowhere but where you are." Like, I'm on a tour of thirty-eight cities, for two and a half months; almost every other day I get on an airplane, go to an airport, go to a motel—and if I've got my game down, nothing's happening at all. That's all happening on one level, and on another level I'm just sitting here watching it, like watching movies. "Oh, here comes an airport! Ah, Toledo! Hello!"

Like one long roller-coaster ride.

With you just sitting here: Nothing ever happens again. The realization that nothing's ever going to happen robs life of the romanticism and the melodrama—"Will the earth survive or won't it," all of that. It's interesting to be in the world and not of the world, to play with those levels. That's the fun of life, simultaneously being conscious on many levels.

I remember someone—this was years ago—asking Swami Chinmayananda,

"What will happen if there's a nuclear explosion and the world comes to an end?" He said, "Wouldn't it be wonderful? We could all go together and we'll have such a marvelous time." It's a totally different perspective on the scene.

Liberation for everybody. But until then, you do your best to relieve suffering. The high point of my life for the past eleven years now has been the Seva Foundation. What makes it high is that we're not only attempting to do good, but to do it well—which is not so easy, by the way. It's easy to do good; it's hard to do good well. Working with a group of people to do something to relieve suffering is great fun because it becomes like a *satsang* or a *sangha* around service, in which we hold each other responsible for being conscious in the way we do it.

Could you briefly describe what Seva does?

Seva is a Sanskrit word which means "to serve." The Seva Foundation is an organization that started out working with the blind in Nepal and India—doing cataract surgery, setting up structures so the Nepalese would become self-sufficient in eye care. Then we went into Guatemala, to the villages where people have suffered extreme violence and many of their family have been murdered, to help these people rebuild their lives. We work with Guatemalan refugees in Mexico. We work with American Indians in the Dakotas with some of their problems like fetal alcohol syndrome. We've also been working with the homeless in New York.

We're an organization that has three criteria. One is that we want to do something to relieve the suffering in the world. The second is that we want to grow in the process of doing it, because we understand that we are among the instruments for that relief of suffering. And the third, as Wavy Gravy the clown, who is a member of our board, insists, "We're going to have fun doing it." Those are the three criteria.

And what I've learned—it took me five years to learn it—is that the collective wisdom of the group is wiser than me. I've had to surrender many times to the group, and it has been very healing for me to realize I'm part of a family of service. We at Seva see we're just part of a league of this incredible quality of compassion that's emerging in the culture. I won't put anybody out of it, including "a thousand points of light" and all that stuff. It's all part of an emerging compassion.

The eight years of Reagan and that kind of not-caring quality of our society offended all of us in some deep way, and there's something emerging now which is an antidote to all of that. To me, Seva is a very exciting social institution attempting to do that consciously.

It's interesting for me—one who has been an inner worker—to get into social and political action, to feel the juices of frustration and anger and hurt and all arise, and then to start to work with them. It has brought me very close to Gandhi and Martin Luther King and people like that because, for us, the instruments of service, the means, and the end are so much of a piece, so much of a piece. The fact that the Guatemalan widows and the Nepalese doctors and the Indian doctors are all our family means that we start to respect them and to listen to "What do they want?" and not to "What do we want for them?" It overrides our paternalistic "know-best" attitude and we really hear what "appropriate technology" means. And, God, that's just a lesson a day in this business. I'll tell you, it's incredible.

It sounds like a rich experience for you.

Oh, boy, it is so rich, so rich. I wouldn't miss a meeting. I find myself, for example, up in the highlands in Guatemala, looking at women who have watched their husbands and sons be murdered. They have nothing, I mean nothing. They're eating tortillas and salt, and their babies have vitamin deficiencies. Just being with them, looking in their eyes and seeing the dignity of these Mayan Indian women, and their tenacity—like those little flowers that live in the rocks, you know, they're just living on—my human spirit is being fed by the very existence of these people. And then I just want to say—you know, this is my folly—"What can I do for you?"

It's interesting where compassion arises, because it can arise out of righteousness, or guilt, or fear, or anything. But the line in Buddhism is that "out of emptiness arises compassion." And when you've looked at suffering without blinking—death and AIDS and children starving to death and all of it, in India and Bangladesh and Africa and all—when you've looked at it straight on, you almost regurgitate as you open to the suffering and embrace it. And then in a way you become dead to it—to a certain kind of romanticizing quality in it. Then, out of that, comes a quality of compassion that is quite extraordinary. Because then you *are* compassion, you're not somebody doing a compassionate act. It's a different quality; you turn into the thing itself.

You know, in the early 1960s, in the first psychedelic session I ever had, I saw the experience of unity; I felt interconnected with the world. It has taken me thirty years to learn how to live with what I saw at that moment, and I'm still doing it. That's what I think our business is, that's what the "New Age" thing is, that's what East and West, all that stuff, is.

It really comes down to the basics—how to get along today in life with your friends and neighbors and family.

Yes. And how you honor the deepest truth you know. How you live as if that were true. I mean, I kid a lot about "We're all one, but it's my television set." And I think we have to play with those edges all the time: How do we live with those different realities? How do we integrate them? I think each person has to re-examine all the stuff in their life all the time. I don't think you can say, "Well, I solved that one," because as your consciousness changes, each thing comes up all over again. It's all a fresh, new issue.

Joe Campbell used to say, "Follow your bliss." A lot of people think that's just happiness, you know, great, "follow your bliss." But when you follow your bliss, the journey may take you downward into the depths of your own psyche.

It's interesting. I'll go into a meditation scene that's fierce, hard, demanding—they beat me, even—and it's blissful. And that wasn't what most people thought Campbell meant by that.

What insights might you provide other than what we've talked about so far, as we're racing towards the third millennium?

I'm hearing the way in which the inner work we do on ourselves—to free ourselves from our identification with our attachments and our aversions—is finding its way into the manifestation of how we live in the world, how we use resources, how we relate to each other, what we do from moment to moment. And the experiences of what we do in the world become continuous grist for the mill of deepening our awakening inside.

So I'm seeing a way in which a whole group of us are emerging, who see life as this incredible curriculum in which we live richly and passionately as a way of awakening to the deepest truths of our being. I no longer feel a renunciation in the sense of pushing away the physical, material plane. I want to see its grace and its beauty, and live with it with joy. But I guess I realize that my consciousness, and our consciousness, has now spread to include all of us, and there just aren't any "thems" left for us. It's all "us" now.

And it is unacceptable that a child is going hungry at this moment when there is so much abundance in the world. It is just unacceptable to my heart. Each of us has before us, in the littlest circle we live in, and in expanding circles, the opportunity to be a participant in the changing of the processes of justice and equity in the world, so that the human heart can be happy on earth. Burke said, "The worst mistake is to do nothing because you can only do a little." And Gandhi said, "What you do may seem very insignificant, but it's very important that you do it." And each of us starts to do that—in the way we recycle our plastics or glass; in the way we go to a town meeting and speak out; in the way we write a letter to a congressman or a senator; in the way we take a bag to the grocery store to save a rain forest; in the way we vote; in the way we make love, not lust; in the way we listen to our children as fellow human beings, and on and on and on and on. Each act becomes an act that has in it equanimity, love, discriminating wisdom, and compassion.

We're all hearing that now—not *all* of us, but a lot of us are hearing it, and this is our job. The transformative process is our job, so that we are not ruled by fear, but by love.

Rupert Sheldrake

The Past Is Present

IN 1981, a firestorm of debate was created by the emergence of a revolutionary new hypothesis that challenged the pillars of modern scientific orthodoxy. The groundbreaking theory of formative causation first appeared in a book entitled *A New Science of Life* by Rupert Sheldrake.

According to Sheldrake's radical and exciting alternative to the mechanistic world-view, each kind of natural system is shaped by its own field. There is, for example, an insulin field, a swallow field, a rabbit field, and so on. Thus, a lily of today is linked to a nineteenth-century lily by more than shared DNA. Indeed, the past is brought to the present not just by inheritance, but by heretofore unimagined non-material influences. In short, nature has a memory for the shape of things, be they rabbits or molecules or myths.

Unlike conventional scientists, Sheldrake argues that the answer to the question of shape in nature lies not in a better understanding of the machinery of nature but in the idea, endorsed by the recent revolution in cosmology, that the cosmos is not a machine at all; it is rather more like a growing and developing organism. Nature has habits that, like all habits, can change over time. This possibility points to a radical new understanding not only of nature but of life, matter, and mind.

MT: Rupert, what led you to first start questioning Darwin's theory of evolution?

RS: What I'm questioning isn't so much Darwin's theory of evolution as the neo-Darwinian theory of evolution. The idea of evolution is really something I deeply believe in and find the best way of looking at things. The problem with neo-Darwinism, the present orthodoxy in biology, is that it has narrowed down Darwin's vision—which was already somewhat more narrow than it need have been—and has focused only on material inheritance, material influences of organisms. And where I've re-read Darwin, I've found that Darwin himself was extremely interested in the power of habit. He believed that organisms inherited habits, that their forms and their development are shaped by habit. Darwin, in a word, was basically a Lamarckian when it came to thinking in terms of the power of habit in evolution. I find myself very much in sympathy with that aspect of Darwin's work, but it's a side of Darwin that's very much forgotten today.

Who was Lamarck?

Lamarck was an early nineteenth-century French evolutionary philosopher. He preceded Darwin by fifty years or more in thinking of evolution. His idea of evolution was that it happens by the habits of things. Giraffes run out of food; they stretch out to eat the leaves off trees; and through the habit of stretching out to eat trees' leaves, their necks get longer, they get stretched. And therefore there's a tendency for them to get longer in subsequent generations. So the elongation of the neck of the giraffe is through the habit of stretching, repeated over many generations.

Now Darwin believed that, too. It's an idea that's ridiculed in modern biology, where the approved idea is that the only way they got longer necks was by pure chance mutations. Just by chance, even though they liked eating the leaves of trees, they got a longer neck. And then the ones that by chance had longer necks survived better. I mean, that has a certain plausibility to it. It may be part of the truth. But Darwin and Lamarck emphasized the importance of habit in evolution. And in that I think they were correct. I just think that they didn't go far enough. I think that habit is not just an important principle in the evolution of life, but that it may be at the very root of the evolution of nature as a whole.

In the early stages of your book, The Presence of the Past, *you also pointed out very well that we're all coming from a conditioning and a history and an acculturation to a certain way of viewing the world, one that involves not only Darwinian views but also ones preceding Darwin—Plato, Descartes, and Newton, for example. Perhaps you could talk a little bit about where science has come from, where it is now, and why morphogenesis may have a place.*

My whole approach, which is evolutionary and also pays attention to the power of habit, means that we have to look at the development of science in the same way. Thomas S. Kuhn's idea of scientific paradigms, which are shared models of reality, shows that science can easily fall into ruts of habit and that the assumptions scientists make tend to become habitual. And when assumptions become habitual, they usually become unconscious also.

The interesting thing is that in the science we inherited from the last century, we inherited two conflicting habits of thought about nature. One is the evolutionary idea: We believe that human society has evolved, technology evolves, science evolves, and the whole of life evolves. Well, this is obviously a highly plausible view that I myself and many other people find the best way of looking at things. But we've also inherited another view from physics—a tradition of thought rooted in ancient Greece, in Plato and Pythagoras—that the universe is basically changeless, that it's made up of a constant amount of material energy, governed by eternal laws.

So we've grown up with a dual view of the world. In biology and in human affairs we've thought of evolution as a developmental process, going on in time. In relation to cosmology, until 1966 there was the idea that the universe was not evolving at all. It was eternal, and it was governed by eternal laws, laws of nature. If anything, it was running down. And the two visions seemed to be in conflict. A few people pointed this out, but most people just thought in one way in one context and another way in the other.

The big change in physics took place in 1966 when most physicists became convinced that the universe had in fact begun with a Big Bang about fifteen billion years ago, and that it has been growing and expanding ever since. So we now have the idea that the whole of nature is evolving—not just life on earth, not just in human affairs, but there's a cosmic evolutionary process going on, of which evolution on the earth and the evolution of human society is part. Previously it was a kind of momentary fluctuation in an eternal universe. It didn't mean anything because the basis of reality was changeless.

We don't hear much nowadays about the heat death and the running-down of the universe; it's not that kind of universe at all. It's not a machine that's running down, it's an evolutionary universe. When we recognize the implications of this, they lead to a completely different view of nature. But the effects of this revolution are slow in dawning on physicists, and it has been only in the last few years that they've begun to consider the evolution of fields. Physics is now in a ferment of activity, because the evolutionary concepts have finally taken hold, and at last an evolutionary physics is beginning to develop.

Where do you think that might lead?

Well, I think it's leading already to the idea that the fields of nature evolve, and that matter itself has a history and has evolved. There haven't always been hydrogen atoms, or iron atoms, or zinc atoms; all these things came into being in time. Even the atoms have evolved, and certainly molecules and chemicals have evolved. So if we think of the whole of nature as evolving, then the old idea that everything's governed by eternal laws is obviously thrown into question. Because if the laws are eternal, and if the universe came into being ten or fifteen billion years ago, what about the laws of nature? Where were they all before the Big Bang? Indeed, how could they have been anywhere? There was nowhere to be, no universe before the Big Bang.

Now, if they all existed before the Big Bang—all the laws that govern the growth of embryos, the crystallization of salt, and the behavior of hydrogen atoms—if they were all there before any of the things they govern existed, then obviously we're talking about a metaphysical or even theological assumption. One can believe that if one wants, but this is the basis of apparent "hard-nosed," orthodox, common-sense physics. And the minute you think about it, you realize that this isn't an orthodox, hard-nosed, anti-metaphysical assumption at all; it's a profoundly metaphysical way of thinking, which may not be justified. It's a hangover from an older metaphysic which has been implicit and habitual in science. It's now hanging over an abyss, like in those cartoons when one person is chasing another: They go over the edge of a cliff and go on running, and it's a long time before they realize there's nothing underneath, and then they plummet down.

Well, this assumption is rather like that—it's hanging over an abyss right now. The old world-view it depends upon has been taken away. And it's only just becoming clear that this is the case. So what I'm suggesting is that the laws of nature may not all be fixed in advance. If we have an evolutionary universe, if nature evolves, then why not think of the laws of nature as evolving too?

After all, the whole idea of the laws of nature is based on a political metaphor with human laws. The idea of the laws of nature came from the idea that God is the Lord of the universe and He fixed the eternal laws that govern everything. This is how the seventeenth-century scientists thought of it. It's a political metaphor, based on human laws. But if we actually look at the source of the metaphor, human laws, we find that they're not eternal.

American laws, British laws—in fact all laws—have actually evolved in time. In the American and British system we have common law, which evolves through precedent as new circumstances arise. It's a truly evolutionary system of law. So if we want to keep on with the law metaphor, then we might do better to think of the universe as governed by natural common law, rather than by a Napoleonic code that was all there at the outset.

But I'm suggesting that the law metaphor isn't really a good one. It suggests an external law-giver, whereas with the idea of the universe as a developing organism, it might be more appropriate to think of habits growing up within the universe. Even at the inorganic level, such as in the crystallization of salt, these regularities may depend on habits—deep-seated habits, but habits all the same.

Rupert, you came across a number of experiments that went on during the 1920s, 1930s, and 1940s, that seemed to support the idea of morphic resonance and morphogenetic fields. Could you describe a couple of those?

The most interesting ones were in the realm of behavior. One of them concerns experiments with rats, experiments that started at Harvard and were continued in Australia and in Scotland. The rats were trained to escape from a water maze, and over the course of ten years, new generations did it quicker and quicker, until they were doing it ten times faster than the original rats. At first it was thought that because the rats had been descended from trained rats, it was some kind of Lamarckian inheritance. In other words, it was thought to be the inheritance of acquired characters: they had somehow inherited the ability from their parents through genetic modification. However, it was then found that this improvement was showing up all over the world. It was showing up in rats that *weren't* descended from trained parents, in all rats of the same breed.

Clearly the change couldn't be due to genetic modification, but the results simply didn't make sense in terms of ordinary biology. So they were never followed up. That example I describe in detail in *A New Science of Life*. But since writing that, I've discovered several more examples in the archives of rat psychology. One of them consists of some experiments done at Berkeley by a scientist called Tryon. He was trying to breed bright and dull strains of rats, training them in a maze with an automatic release so that the rats were handled as little as possible, given as little influence of the experimenter as possible—an automatic maze.

He found that the descendants of bright parents got brighter and brighter, as you might expect. And he had thought that the dullest and dimmest parents in each generation would produce offspring that would be duller and duller. But actually, they got brighter and brighter too. They weren't as bright as the bright strain, but he was amazed to see the dull strain getting brighter and brighter as time went on. He hadn't expected anything like that. He reported it in his published papers. And again, this anomaly was simply left at that; no one was ever able to explain it. But the idea that it happened just because he was getting better at doing the experiment is not a very plausible suggestion, because the whole experiment was done so automatically.

Then there are evolutionary cases where this sort of thing seems to have been going on in the wild. The best documented example is the spread of stealing milk by birds in Britain, particularly by a species called the blue tit. (It's a curious thing—the bird is called a tit, and it steals milk.) Blue tits, starting in the early 1920s in southern England, in Southampton, discovered that they could tear the tops off bottles and then drink the cream at the top of the milk.

In Britain, as you probably know, we have milk delivered every day to the doorstep, fresh milk. We use the milk; we put the old bottles out; then they are collected and recycled. This system has been going on since the beginning of the century, and it's still going on.

We used to have that in America, too.

Well, the blue tits learned how to steal the cream from the top of the bottles. They didn't always get away with it—there were a few cases where drowned blue tits were found headfirst at the top of the bottle of milk. But the habit was on the whole successful; it spread locally. Then, after a year or two, it turned up somewhere else, over a hundred miles away.

It's interesting—the blue tit doesn't fly more than fifteen miles.

Not more than fifteen miles. So they couldn't have been the same tits. They're home-loving birds; they move very little. But the habit turned up further away. And then it turned up in other places in Britain.

Fortunately, amateur bird-watchers in Britain got onto this one very early. A whole network of observers was set up, and the spread of this habit was carefully documented—which is why it's one of the few examples where behavioural evolution has been carefully studied on a nationwide basis.

The habit spread faster and faster. It turned up in more locations, and it was clear from the increasing number of independent discoveries that there was an accelerating rate of spread, both locally, by imitation, and non-locally by new birds discovering it. Then it started turning up in Holland and in Sweden and in Denmark. By 1947, in Britain, it was universal.

And then what happened? Of course, the war came, and the milk wasn't being delivered.

Well, the Dutch case is the most interesting. In Britain, milk deliveries continued. But in Holland, owing to the German occupation, the milk was no longer delivered. What's interesting is that blue tits normally live no more than three years, and it was eight years before milk began to be delivered again in Holland. In 1948, the milk started coming to the doorsteps once more. The fascinating thing is that what had taken a couple of decades to build up in Holland before, by independent discovery and local spread, now took place in a matter of months, all over Holland. Within a very short time blue tits were again discovering that they could steal milk. So the Dutch evidence, because of this long break, is even more impressive than the English evidence for the spread of this habit.

That brings to mind some sort of communication system that's totally mysterious.

Well, that's the idea, you see. I'm suggesting that there's a kind of habit or collective memory inherent in the species. This isn't inherited in the genes. The blue tits that learned how to do it in other parts of Britain were not descended from the original ones that had learned it; it was nothing to do with DNA. It was a kind of tuning-in to the experience of the previous birds. That's the basis of the hypothesis I'm suggesting. And this case, the best documented, seems to suggest that something funny was going on that fits very well with this whole idea.

Soon after the publishing of your first book, A New Science of Life, *where you first postulated the theory of morphogenesis and morphic resonance and formative causation, the Tarrytown Center in New York offered a prize for the best three confirming experiments. And then those prizes were awarded in 1986. Perhaps you can describe the success of those experiments.*

All three winning experiments, selected by an international panel of judges, were in the realm of human learning. All of them suggested that it's easier to learn things that other people have learned before. Again, I would suggest that this is through a kind of collective memory, through morphic resonance. The idea is, of course, very similar to Jung's idea of the collective unconscious, which is a similar idea of a collective memory. But these were actual experiments designed to test for this effect.

The experiment that was done by Gary Schwartz, a professor of psychology at Yale, and which won one of the first prizes, was with Hebrew words from the Old Testament. This was in a way the most elaborate of the experiments, but perhaps the most interesting, so I'll describe it. It's a little bit subtle, so I'll have to go slowly to explain what he did.

He took twenty-four common words and twenty-four rare words from the Old Testament, three-letter words written in Hebrew. The experiment was done only with written words; there was no speaking, no sound. The script was in Hebrew. So the experiment had to do with pattern recognition of written words in Hebrew.

Schwartz had twenty-four common and twenty-four rare words, making forty-eight words altogether. For each of these words he then made a false, scrambled word by rearranging the three letters to give a meaningless word. In English, for example, "cat," c-a-t, is a word, but "t-c-a" is not a word, although it has the same three letters. So he made anagrams—meaningless, scrambled words—of each of these words. That gave him ninety-six three-letter words, half of them real, the other half false. He then jumbled them all up in a random order, and he assembled subjects who didn't know Hebrew.

The subjects were shown one word at a time, projected on a screen. They didn't know that some words were real and some were false. They were just told that these were Hebrew words. They were asked to guess the meaning of the word in English, by writing down the first English word that came into their head. After guessing it, they were asked to estimate, on a naught-to-four scale, how confident they felt in their guess—four meaning very confident, naught meaning pure guessing.

So Schwartz ran these words past them, one by one, in silence. The subjects were just looking at the visual pattern of the written word and trying to guess what it meant. Now when he looked at the results, a few of the people had actually got correct guesses in some cases. This could have been very interesting indeed, but to be on the safe and cautious side he discounted those subjects altogether on the grounds that they may conceivably have known some Hebrew, even though they said they didn't—you know, for example, by seeing words written up on synagogues in the Bronx or something.

So he took only those who had guessed wrong in every single case, which was the great majority of these student subjects. Then he looked at the confidence ratings. And this is where the interesting thing came in. With the real words, people were more confident about their guesses than with the false words. This showed up highly significantly over subjects, over words, and over experiments. And what's more, this confidence they felt was greater with the common words than with the rare words. It was twice as strong, this confidence effect, with the common than with the rare words.

Now Schwartz thought that this might be because through morphic resonance there's a kind of collective memory of these patterns, so that the word is seen as a kind of *gestalt*, or a whole, or a pattern. Maybe when people looked at these they somehow resonated with millions of Jews and Hebrew scholars over the centuries who had seen and read these words, and this gave them a sense of familiarity, an unconscious sense of familiarity that showed up in the confidence rating.

What's more, Schwartz even proved that this was an unconscious effect. In the next step of the experiment, he ran all ninety-six words past the subjects again. This time he told them that half the words were real and half were false, and he asked them to guess which were which. When they were asked to do consciously what they already had done unconsciously, they couldn't do it. The results were purely random. So he called this an "unconscious pattern recognition effect." And for him the most plausible explanation was that this was indeed an example of morphic resonance. So here's a rather subtle experiment, done by a highly competent psychologist at Yale, which does suggest that something of this kind is actually going on.

Rupert, continuing the application of formative causation and morphic resonance to human beings, could you talk a little bit about the nature of memory, and how we remember, and the relevance of that process to this theory?

The whole theory consists of the idea that there's an inherent memory in nature, that things are as they are because they were as they were. The basis of this memory is a process of morphic resonance, a connection through or across time and space, based on similarity.

Now when you come to looking at our own memory, it turns out that this theory has a lot to say about the possible nature of memory, because each of us is more similar to ourselves in the past than we are to anyone else. In general, the most specific resonance acting on a given organism in the present is from the past of the same organism. The most specific resonance acting on my present is from my past. Now, if there's a resonance between one's own present and one's own past, and this resonance is the carrier of pattern and form and patterns of behavior and so on—as I'm suggesting in this general theory—then this could be the basis of memory. It could be that we remember because we tune in to our own pasts by morphic resonance, and this tuning-in means we can access the past. The past in a sense becomes present through morphic resonance, without its needing to be stored inside the brain.

One of the useful metaphors that you have made compares the brain to a television set, or a radio set. Could you bring that metaphor in at this point?

The usual idea is that all the memories are stored inside the brain. People think of the brain as being something like a tape recorder, storing everything within it. If you think about this, since you can remember so many things—facts, words, ways of doing things, incidents from the past—the brain would have to have an enormous storage capacity if this were the case. Now, no one has been able to figure out how the brain does store memories. People have looked for memory traces, the alleged physical traces that storage is based on, and after decades of research have failed again and again to find them.

I think this is possibly because they're not there. There may be a very simple explanation for these repeated failures. If we think instead in terms of the brain picking up memories, tuning in like a radio set tunes in, this idea makes several things clear. First of all, it's not necessary for radio sets to store what is listened to. Our speaking over radio isn't stored in people's radios; there's no permanent trace of my words or yours through a radio set. The radio set can tune in to other programs, and each of them can go through it without being stored in it.

The second point is, this approach also enables us to understand how damage to the brain can lead to loss of memory. Many people think that memories must be in the brain, because if you damage the brain, you can get memory loss. We all know this. It's also true that in many cases of brain damage the memories can return again later. So how do you get loss of memory through damage? Well, it's easier to understand when you think of the radio set.

If I damage your radio set so that you can no longer receive FM but you can still get medium-wave, for example, this wouldn't prove that all the FM programs were stored inside the bit of the set I damaged. It might look like that, though, if you didn't know how a radio worked. If I took some components out and all the FM programs disappeared, and then I put those components back in and they all reappeared, you might easily think that all the voices and all the music you heard on those stations, those programs, were actually stored inside those components. But of course you'd be wrong.

Now, when people are thinking about brains, they say, "Well, you damage this tissue here, you lose these memories—therefore the memories are stored in the damaged tissue." This, when you think about it, is not a logical argument. It doesn't at all prove what they think it proves.

There's a similar line of reasoning which people use, based on Penfield's work on stimulating brains. Wilder Penfield was a Canadian neurosurgeon who found that by stimulating part of the brains of epileptic patients—the temporal lobes of the cortex—during brain operations, he could evoke vivid memory flashes of things that had happened years before. He had first thought that this meant that he was stimulating the memory cortex. He later actually abandoned this and came to the conclusion that the stimulation was simply enabling people to retrieve or recall the memories.

This can also be discussed in terms of the radio set analogy. If I stimulated the tuning knob by jolting it, or put some wires inside the tuning circuit and passed electric currents through it, I could get the radio to jump onto a different program. But of course this wouldn't prove that the sounds and voices you heard on the other program were stored inside the bit that had been stimulated. And no more does the stimulation of the brain, and the resulting evocation of memories, prove that the memories are stored there.

Some people claim to have memories of past lives. Using your analogy, could this be explained as simply a tuning-in to the morphogenetic fields of past energies, rather than an identity with the person whose life is remembered?

Yes. If we have this tuning-in model for memory, then the obvious question is "Well, if we tune in to ourselves, why don't we tune in to other people?" I think that, in fact, we do tune in to millions of other people, as a kind of background collective memory on which we're drawing the whole time, and into which we're contributing. That's like the idea of the collective unconscious. But if we tuned in to a specific person in the past, for whatever reason, and if this person were now dead, then we would actually be accessing the memories of somebody in the past through a tuning-in process.

There's quite good evidence that at least some young children, in cases studied by Ian Stevenson and others, can remember previous lives. These are very unusual cases, but nevertheless the evidence in these detailed case studies is quite good that they're remembering things from people who have died previously. And this is usually taken to be evidence for reincarnation. People say, "Well, if they can remember this previous life, then they must be that person, reincarnated."

What I'm suggesting is that they may be accessing the memories of those people by morphic resonance. That leaves open the question of whether or not they *are* that person, and an answer partly depends on what you mean by "person." If you say that by definition a person is someone who has a continuity of memory, then simply by a verbal definition you turn them into that person.

But you could take a different, more liberal view of the person and say, "Well, having the memories doesn't necessarily prove you're that person. All it proves is that you're accessing the memories of that person; it doesn't prove you *are* them." So it enables this data and the evidence for memories of previous lives to be thought about in a different way from the usual ones.

*It also brings to mind how important the process of ritual is, and the impor-
tance of initiation ceremonies. You also stress that a ritual which has been
carried on for many generations actually carries with it a certain energy that
we can plug in to as we perform it.*

Yes, this is another of the things that flow from the theory. It's a logical consequence of the theory, and it has extremely interesting implications. Because I say that similar patterns of activity resonate with
past similar patterns, this leads us to think about ritual in this context.
The fascinating thing is that all societies have rituals. There are religious rituals, like the feast of the Passover, done every year by Jews,
recalling the first Passover in Egypt, and the Christian Holy Communion, which is a re-enactment of the Last Supper of Jesus and his
disciples. These have gone on for centuries. The Last Supper that
Holy Communion re-enacts was, of course, taking place at the time
of the Passover, so it is linked into that even more ancient ritual. And
then there are secular rituals, like the American Thanksgiving dinner,
performed every year by Americans, going right back to the first
Thanksgiving dinner in New England.

So there are rituals everywhere, in both religious and secular con-
texts. And the interesting thing about rituals all over the world is that
they tend to be very conservative. People feel that for the ritual to
work, it must be done the same way it was done before. This conservative tendency is present in the gestures, the movements, the context, the food, the kinds of things that people say, and often, of course,
involves conservative ritual languages like Sanskrit in the Brahmanic
rituals of India. It's believed that you have to use the ancient words
because only the ancient words have the power that causes the ritual
to be effective.

And rituals are thought to be effective when they do indeed connect people in some way with the previous performers of them, right
back to the first time they were done. They're done in order to link up,
to remember, to reconnect with predecessors, with the ancestors. This
is why people do them. And they say that, by doing them, they're
making this kind of connection through time. They're in some sense
bringing the past into the present.

Now, with the idea of morphic resonance, the idea that similar
patterns of activity do indeed resonate through time, rituals may be
doing just what people think they're doing—reconnecting, bringing
the past into the present. And they may be reconnecting the present
performance of the ritual not only with the original one, but with all

the people who've done it over the preceding years. If you change the ritual, and especially if it's changed radically, then it may no longer tune in so effectively.

I think this may explain why people feel, without being able to say why, that rituals should be done the same way they've been done before. Whenever people try to change rituals, it's always extremely controversial. The people who oppose change usually just say, "We ought to do it that way because that's the way it was done before." For people who are keen on change, that never seems a very strong argument, but it may be stronger than it's usually credited with being.

I think of the radical changes that occurred in the Catholic Mass. It's now performed all over the world in the vernacular language of where the Mass is taking place. These changes are still very controversial.

I think the changes are controversial for just these reasons. The Latin Mass had a kind of resonance, as people I think would rightly say, which the vernacular ones don't have. Now, of course, there may be good reasons for reform, and rituals have to change now and then. I mean, all rituals had beginnings; it's not as if they've been going on since the beginning of the universe. So there's scope for liturgical reform. It's possible that something can be gained and a whole new pattern can develop when new liturgical forms grow up. But the controversy, I think, arises because people feel that something has been lost, something that connected them with the past.

The same kind of controversy is still going on in the Anglican Church, where the English language, of course, was adopted in the sixteenth century, with the Reformation. The traditional language of the Church of England, in the Book of Common Prayer, is Elizabethan English. Even when the Book of Common Prayer was formally published, in the seventeenth century, the form of its language was archaic; it was the language of a century earlier. The liturgical reform movement has tried to replace that with modern English, but many people don't like the modern form. They say it has no poetry, no resonance; it doesn't have the same feel, the quality, the timelessness, the feeling of connection that the older language gives. I experience that myself when going to Anglican services, and I personally much prefer the Book of Common Prayer to the new, modern English liturgy. But I daresay the modern English one will acquire a certain resonance as time goes on and people get used to it. These kinds of issues, though, are always controversial, and I think the morphic resonance idea helps us to see why.

Morphic resonance certainly explains the strength of some ideas of prayer, to carry your religious metaphor further. I'm thinking of the saying, "Take Christ into your heart." There's an essential resonance with who Christ was, who Jesus was, the kind of life he lived, and the energy that we plug in to when we pray in that way.

I think it's very interesting that many religious traditions have the metaphor of the path, or the way. There's the Eightfold Way of Buddhism, the path of Christianity, the path of the masters in some forms of Hinduism. By adopting a certain path, by tuning in, as it were, to that pattern or pathway of activity, the founder of the path—Christ in Christianity, Buddha in Buddhism—in some sense becomes present in your life. And not only do these founders become present, but so also do all those who followed the path after them. In Christianity there's the Communion of Saints, in Buddhism there's the *sangha*, the community. In Hinduism and Buddhism, in general, there is what they usually call the tradition or the lineage.

In all these cases it's believed that there is an influence from all these predecessors, and that there's, as it were, a field—what I would call a morphic field of this religious path—into which the believer or the follower of the path tunes, through the appropriate rituals, ceremonies, initiations, and so on. The following of this path is stabilized and facilitated by the morphic resonance from all those who have followed it before.

Rupert, what fascinates me about your theory is that it really supports the idea that the universe and we as inhabitants of the universe are evolving and changing. It supports the mystery of creativity by showing that there's room for new ways, new perceptions, new ideas, new organisms to emerge. Can you speak to that?

Well, this theory certainly fits very well with the evolutionary perception of a development of new forms and the openness, indeed, of the universe. The idea that everything's fixed in advance by fixed laws is much more restrictive, whereas I think this view shows there's a tremendous openness in things.

The principle of habit through morphic resonance shows how new patterns or forms can be stabilized once they come into being. If there weren't such a principle, then we'd have a chaos of creativity and nothing would ever last. So although it does allow new things to spread faster than current theories would allow, this principle of morphic resonance is a conservative principle.

When we come to the question of "How do new things happen at all, in the first place?" then we have to recognize—everyone has to recognize—some kind of creative principle in the universe. Different theories of creativity think of the creative principle in different terms, and no one really knows for sure how it works. Creativity is a mystery.

There are two main approaches I find myself being drawn to. One is the idea that creativity wells up from below, that it is a bottom-up process. The other is that it comes down from above, it's a top-down process.

The bottom-up process includes the standard materialist idea that creativity is due to chance, just arises from chance fluctuations of matter. It also fits with the idea that creativity comes up from the earth, from the darkness, from the unconscious, out of the womb of the unformed. These are various metaphors and ways of thinking about creativity from the bottom up.

The top-down theories say that creativity descends into us; it comes from higher planes, higher levels, some would say even from other planets, different regions of the cosmos, higher beings. And many would say, ultimately, from God.

Of course, there are those who would say that it's a mixture of both, that there are both top-down and bottom-up processes. And I think that's the view that I'd take myself.

There is a new competition, as it were, and a new prize being offered for new experiments. Perhaps you can describe that for us, Rupert.

Well, this hypothesis of the habits of nature lends itself to predictions which differ from the standard ones, right across the board—in chemistry, biochemistry, molecular biology, developmental biology, psychology, and animal behavior. In all these areas, it is possible for the theory to be tested. Over the last few years, discussions have thrown up all sorts of quite simple ways it can be tested.

It turns out that many of these tests are within the capacity of students. Since students in most universities have to do projects, the idea arose of asking them if they'd like to test for morphic resonance. It's an opportunity for students to do extremely original, groundbreaking research that could change our view of nature. And many of these experiments can be done on extremely small budgets—fifty dollars' worth of equipment or chemicals, or even less. So this provides a way in which students can test something and be at the very forefront of scientific exploration.

I don't know any other kind of scientific theory where it's within the capacity of students to do this kind of ground-breaking work. I even think that the breakthrough, if and when it comes, is most likely to come from students. More mature professors and researchers tend to be more conservative in their ways, and less likely to want to test for it.

So, to help this process along, the Institute of Noetic Sciences in Sausalito, California is offering a prize for student projects on morphic resonance. Results will be judged in three categories: pre-university, undergraduate, and postgraduate. Entries will be judged by an international panel of scientists, and the winners will receive cash prizes. Thousands of dollars must be won. [See address below to write for specific information on this program.]

Rupert, what do you see your own future being? Do you see more work in supporting and stabilizing the theory? What are you going to be doing?

Well, I'm quite occupied with trying to organize research on this. We now have had some funding made available by private individuals. It's obviously too radical, so far, to be funded by standard government agencies. With these funds, we're commissioning research and giving grants for research in universities. Some have already started, and I'm closely involved with this ongoing research project. So that's a major part of my future activities. The other thing I'm doing is working on a new book where I look at the way in which nature seems to be coming alive in so many ways. It will be about the rebirth of nature. (*The Rebirth of Nature* is to be published by Bantam Books in early 1991.)

Sheldrake Prize
Institute for Noetic Sciences
475 Gate 5 Road, Suite 300
Sausalito, CA 94965

Joan Halifax

Way of the Warrior

DURING CONTEMPORARY times we are witness to the most highly developed technology the world has ever seen, and yet our civilization, our culture, is in chaos. Hundreds of living species are endangered while others have become extinct in the past two decades. We have created more than two tons of TNT explosive power for every man, woman, and child on the planet. We continue to exploit limited forms of energy while allowing the sun, an unlimited source of energy, to go virtually unused. The streets of most urban areas are unsafe at night. Jails are overcrowded and violence is commonplace. Computers and sophisticated communications have given us access to more information and data than ever before in history. We are glutted with data and yet there is a shortage of wisdom.

In older and more primitive cultures, the shaman—the medicine man or medicine woman—was the keeper of the vision, the person responsible for restoring the tribal members to their original selves where access to wisdom lay outside the mind. Perhaps the warrior's way of the shaman holds answers for us even today, enabling us to take our passions and apply them to peace instead of destruction. Joan Halifax has specialized for most of her life in studying shamanic practices and traditions throughout the world. She has led pilgrimages to sacred and remote areas to explore the rituals, art, and architecture of ancient peoples. She is the founder and director of the Ojai Foundation, located in Ojai, California.

MT: *Joan, what is "the warrior's way?"*

JH: I'd like to start with an old story from Japan. It's a story of a great Samurai who went to the temple of a very famous Zen master. He went because he wanted to understand the difference between heaven and hell. He entered the temple, approached the Zen master, bowed very respectfully, and said, "Sir, can you tell me what is the difference between heaven and hell?" The Zen master stood up very correctly in front of the great Samurai and said, "Well, quite frankly, sir, I think you're too dull to understand the difference between heaven and hell."

Well, the Samurai began to take umbrage, began to experience a little anger, and he said, "Do you know to whom you are speaking?" And the Zen master said, "Of course, I know to whom I am speaking. But I think it would be too difficult for you to understand this distinction." Well, by this time the Samurai was in an absolute rage. Then the Zen master said, "And that thing hanging by your waist, you think that's a sword? Well, I tell you, that thing is as dull as a butter knife, rather like your mind."

At this point, Michael, the Samurai raised the sword over his head as if to strike the Zen master dead. The Zen master pointed toward the sword and said, "Sir, *that* is hell." The Samurai understood immediately. He bowed in absolute respect. The Zen master said, "And sir, that is heaven."

What is the warrior's way? The warrior's way is to recognize that everything is sacred. All of life and death. The warrior's way excludes nothing. The warrior's way recognizes that the worst has already happened, so there is nothing to do but enter directly into life.

When we look in the Oxford English Dictionary, we discover, interestingly enough, that the word war comes from the Old English word which means confusion. And it is precisely this confusion that we're addressing when we talk about the warrior. Because it is the warrior, the true warrior, who understands the location of the battlefield. The battlefield is not somewhere outside of us, but it's within. So the warrior's way leads toward the interior.

Now, why would shamans and warriors be related? It's very, very simple. It is the shaman who goes through an extraordinary psychomental crisis, a crisis of proportions which is not uncommon in the lives of most human beings. The problem with people today, however, is that we refuse to acknowledge that the crisis is upon us and we don't take advantage of an extraordinary opportunity for transformation.

One of the reasons that I became very interested in shamanism was because a crisis of that sort happened in my own life. I looked for a model in culture and in history for something that I perceived was happening not only to me but to many many other Western individuals. And I found that model to be the shaman: one who goes through a powerful transformation process; one who is wounded, who goes through the wound door, and exits self-healed. It was such an individual, the shaman, who brought the sacred view to the Paleolithic culture. That is, the locus of the mystery was the individual. That individual, the shaman, awakened to a greater understanding of the sacredness of all life, including ordinary life.

We're seeing, oddly enough, that the shaman is extant with us on the planet today. The forms of the Paleolithic period, of our ancestors of thousands and thousands of years ago, with regards to the sacred view still lives side by side with us. We can turn on our radio and hear them speak. We can turn on our televisions and see the faces of wise old ones. We can get on a airplane and then into a jeep and then into a canoe and, literally in a matter of hours, walk into a culture that is *so* different from ours. We can sit at the feet of an elder, a great elder, and listen to wisdom that can affect our lives deeply—and perhaps even affect the destiny of this planet.

Today there is a great sense of despair and helplessness arising because war is seen as an inevitability. Well, it *is*, from one point of view. And that is with regards to our inner experience. However, we do not have to be in a state of tremendous spiritual confusion. Thanks to Carlos Castaneda, Michael Harner, Barbara Meirhoff, and many anthropologists and individuals who have gone into the field in a good and humble way, the model of the shaman is being brought into the awareness of Western culture. It's entering intimately into the lives of millions of people through books, through the media, and through direct contact with these teachers.

This development is very timely. It's like the past and the present and the future become one. And this is precisely the dance of the shaman warrior. There is a quality of atemporality, of timelessness, which the shaman brings into play. In other words, all memory is activated when the shaman is in an altered state of consciousness, or in an ordinary state of consciousness. Memory is completely engaged in an individual who has a totally integrated mind/body. He or she is able to move into the future or into the past, or go into the deep present, and it's one thing.

Take, for example, Don José Matsua, an extraordinary old ritual shaman. When he went to New York City, though he had never seen snow, though he had never been in a city before, he walked with great ease. He understood that the city is also a dream. It's like the dream that he dreams at night, that he masters and dances with and asks questions of. It's like the dream he dreams when he has eaten peyote. And it's like the dream he dreams when he's awake. In his corn field, or in his village, or in New York City, he understands that it's all *bardo*, all qualities of dreaming. All the senses are involved, the mind is involved, and he understands that his job is basically to dance the dream awake. His job is to dance it awake so that we can all awaken within the dream simultaneously.

Do we have anyone in our society, currently, who fulfills the role of the shaman?

We have many such people. However, in Western culture, consciousness has been defined in terms of the lowest common denominator—"normal." But for the shaman, consciousness is greatly expanded. It includes transpersonal experience, psychodynamic experience, conscious awareness, subconscious experience, access to the unconscious, and total access to transpersonal content. So individuals who have shamanic potential are frequently hospitalized and defined as crazy, because part of the process of the realization of the shamanic potential is a totally disordering experience.

Of normal consciousness.

Yes, of so-called normal consciousness. But we're in a very peculiar situation. During the 1960s, we saw a great disordering of the social field through the psychedelic movement. During the 1970s, that disordering began to move toward psychosis. We saw the beginnings of a positive definition of going through an experience of being crazy. So in the 1980s there are all kinds of set-ups in which to go crazy.

Now, I'll give you a simple comparison. In the Huichol culture, there are many shamans. It's not just one of every five hundred people. It would be more like one of every five people. Among the Kung bushmen, *all* men have this power.

Are shamans always men?

Oh, no. For the Kung bushmen it is, in fact, the men who dance that role. But among the Mapuche in South America, only women do it. We do have a sexually biased notion with regards to who are shamans. Men did most of the field research in the early twentieth century, and they didn't tell us that there are so many women who are shamans. But I would say that it is equally divided. In fact, many secret societies have, at their secret center, a women's society which is like the driver's wheel of the men's secret society. This is true in Africa as well as on Turtle Island. You find, for example, that the shield carriers, the actual transmitters of the sacred content, are the grandmothers.

We are just beginning to understand these forms. Men and women in their forties who have digested their personal histories adequately, and who have come to realize that they're living in a cultural construct called Western culture, can now look with a sense of clarity and a sense of the relative view into other cultures. And, more than look, they can walk in. They can change focus and dance that dance. So there's a much deeper quality of engagement with regards to our investigation. It's an investigation not for the university and not for the publisher, but it has to do with our survival.

Survival seems to be an important consideration these days.

It's the ultimate consideration, if we look at survival in terms of quality. I'm not so interested in survival with an absence of quality. Many years ago, I worked with dying people. During the course of that work, I became acutely aware of the absence of quality with regard to human life and human death.

As we speak, I'm thinking of a situation that's very close to me now. A friend was just in a car accident and has sustained a crushed skull. I visited her in the intensive care unit on the night of the accident, and we don't know what her situation will be. There is no absence of compassion on the part of the doctors or the nurses. I don't want to fault the health care professionals. But I do want to complain about the setting. The setting was so ghastly that I thought, well, I hope I never end up in one of these.

What is the setting?

It's in a big hospital. There you are with a light glaring overhead, with the sound of people rushing around, with the chaos of new patients being admitted in disastrous conditions. It was a reminder to me of the disregard for the presence of consciousness when it doesn't appear to be present—either at the moment of death or in a crisis situation or in coma, which is a situation of apparent unconsciousness which persists over a long period of time.

So, what I'm going for, as we reach the end of the twentieth century, is survival with quality. But how can we get there? Again, we turn to the roles of the shaman and the warrior and we look at methods for reaching a situation of inner quality. Until you've attained that quality on the inward plane, it's not so interesting to try to create external quality. And this is one of our biggest problems.

As Krishnamurti said so beautifully in the book, *The Only Revolution*, the only revolution is the revolution within. The only war that has *meaning* is the inner war. It is absurd to pursue any fight outside of one's soul.

I frequently think of this in terms of the process of fission. When an atom is split, an immense amount of energy is released. When the mind is split—in terms of psychological process, we call that schizophrenia—an incredible amount of psychosocial energy is released. When the smallest social unit—that is, the marriage, the dyad—is split, an immense amount of social energy is released. And of course, countries split against other countries and we are divided from nature.

We're at the stage of ultimate division, the absolute dismemberment, and ours are very extraordinary times. What I would call the absolute irritant is upon us. We're at a moment where the entire planet is affected by the act of one individual.

When I was in the civil rights movement many years ago, I knew that one person could make a difference in that movement by doing very ordinary things. We would sit and have lunch with a person of another color, for example, in a place where that person wasn't supposed to have lunch; one person could make a difference through a very very simple act. A very simple act can change the destiny of this planet, turn it in a difficult direction or in a direction of absolute magnificence.

This is why, for me, the warrior is of such interest today. But by warrior I don't mean soldier. The soldier has no inner authority. The soldier has to take orders from an external authority. The warrior, on the other hand, operates from a position of totally realized inner authority.

But what are the enemies of the warrior, if we want to realize inner authority? I'd like to talk about that, because somehow I feel that if we don't dance totally with our warrior we're going to have a lot of soldiers to dance with. We will lose our sense of authority and will be at the level of effect instead of being at the level of cause.

The four enemies of the warrior are the four enemies which afflict any human being, as a matter of fact. I'd like to talk about this from the perspective of the medicine wheel teachings which come from Turtle Island, that is, come from *our* world. But I also want to speak about this in terms of Buddhism, because in the Mahayana world— that is, the world that we know in Zen and in Tibetan Buddhism— there is a role which we know as the Bodhisattva.

The Bodhisattva is a developed human being whose voluntary return to the earth is motivated by the impulse to save all sentient beings from suffering, to work for the good of all sentient beings. *Bodhi,* like the Buddha, means "awake" or "awakening," and *sattva* means "being." So Bodhisattva means one who is awakened, or an awakened being. But if you search around in the Sanskrit you find, interestingly enough, that in fact the word means "warrior." So an awakening warrior is a bodhisattva—one whose mandate is to save all sentient beings from suffering. The true warrior dances with the enemies in an absolutely magnificent and impeccable manner and transforms them into allies. The idea is not to conquer, in fact, but is to transform poisons into nectar.

The four enemies of the warrior are the enemies of our own life as simple, humble, human beings in the everyday world. We can keep them in our lives as enemies and be overcome constantly by them, or we can engage directly in dance with them, encounter them absolutely. If we do engage them absolutely, we can transform them from obstacles into gateways, from poisons into nectar—into that essence which gives us eternally awakened consciousness. To say it another way, our encounter with them can become an experience of absolute enlightenment. What can be the experience of *destruction* becomes the absolute experience of *instruction.* Instruction here means basically going within and being taught by the things that we most want to flee from.

In the medicine wheel teaching, the first enemy is located in the South, the direction of trust and innocence. It is the enemy called Fear. It is the enemy that is associated with bringing our personal history to the level of conscious awareness. We can do this by going crazy, or through ceremonial examination, or through many psychotherapeutic techniques. It's a very necessary aspect of self-understanding of self-awareness.

As Chögyam Trungpa Rinpoche says in *Shambhala: The Sacred Path of the Warrior*, "A warrior is one who has the courage to face himself." This is a very simple first step. But it is extremely difficult, because we live constantly in the illusion of our own mythology and the self-entertainment we derive from it. When one finally transforms one's personal history into something that is accessible and acceptable—accepting our shadow-nature, dancing with our monsters—the first quality of the warrior arises. That quality is the attitude of Humility.

Truly facing one's personal history is like eating humble pie for most individuals. One of the points of doing that is so that true compassion can develop. If we have no compassion for our own lives, how can we experience compassion for another?

Now let's move north in the medicine wheel. This is the direction associated with wisdom and logic. This is the direction we know as mind. In terms of the temporal aspect, the time aspect, we're dealing with the future because the mind's shape shifts the future. Well, we have a very interesting enemy in the North, Michael, one that afflicts people like me and you in a dire manner. It is the enemy called Clarity.

I always laugh when I discuss this because, really, we think we know a lot. But the fact is that people in our culture are just completely run by their belief systems. This is particularly true of people like you and me. We've had the very precious opportunity of being in a world where we can examine our minds, but unfortunately a lot of pride has emerged in the lives of those of us who have done that. We think we know everything.

Well, the enemy of Clarity is one where belief systems, cultural conditioning, cognitive conditioning, and psychological conditioning obscure our view. To transform the enemy of Clarity into nectar, we must reach a state where there is an absence of any belief system at all. We realize that any belief system that we have will obscure our view and limit our lives.

What happens when the enemy of Clarity is transformed into an ally? The quality that arises is the discipline of Humor. We are suddenly released from the bondage of our belief systems. We as a warrior become an authority that responds moment-to-moment in an ordinary and extraordinary way to life. It's a very exquisite humor that opens up when you see that you are completely in the position of cause, never in the position of effect, with regards to whatever belief system is coating movement, behavior, and the conditions.

Let us now move to the West on our medicine wheel. The West is traditionally associated with the experience of the feminine. It's associated with the experience of death, of magic, and of change. Once we have dealt with our personal history in the South and attended to our belief systems in the North, we realize that we have a physical experience which is outside of any belief system and which is inevitable. And that is the experience of dying and of death. Death is the enemy we encounter in the West. And here we're beginning to really deepen our spiritual understanding.

Gautama Buddha's understanding of suffering is what brought him to engage the world as a way of bringing about the possibility of the cessation of suffering. He came to understand that all life is characterized by suffering. We have birth, old age, sickness, death. We experience suffering when we can't get something we want. We experience suffering when we're separated from something we have loved. We experience suffering when we encounter something unpleasant. In fact, having a human body is simply an experience of suffering in one way or another. And even if we took birth in the "god realm"—one of the six realms of existence described in the Buddha dharma—we would discover after having been there for eons that we are mortal.

So the third possibility for realization in the path of the warrior is an understanding of suffering and the realization of our own mortality. In a way, this is the most exquisite one. Dying into life, realizing that death is an ornament of life, understanding the nature of the dual unity of life and death, is what opens absolute compassion for the warrior.

What happens when the enemy of Death is transformed into an ally? What quality arises? That quality we know as the intent of Honor. What does that mean? It means that we do not exclude death from our experience; we come to understand the relationship between life and death. It means that death is as sacred as life. It means that when we go from the experience of physical, psychological, mental, and spiritual vitality into death, that movement is one of magnificence.

In fact, at the very transition between life and death lies the great possibility for absolute enlightenment. If we can realize this opportunity, then we have a choice: We can stay in the Pure Land, in the completely enlightened state, after death; or we can guide our own process into an auspicious rebirth. So making death an ally is extremely important, not only for individuals who are on the path of the sacred warrior, but also for every individual. It increases, in a very profound way, the possibility of coming back into life in a magnificent manner. So we honor death.

We also realize that everything is composite and subject to dissolution; everything. Even our great sun, which is symbolically associated with eternally awakened consciousness, will die someday. Everything is in a cycle of cause and effect.

The sun has shone upon the earth and has caused the plants to grow; we have eaten the plants, and the plants have supplied us with great nourishment; our brains have become active to understand the far reaches of the universe and have created a machine which will take us beyond this envelope that we know as air, beyond this spinning mudball which know as the earth, and perhaps even beyond this galaxy to a parallel universe. Perhaps there will be space colonies that our offspring, millennia from now, will be living on even as our sun dies. And all this has come about because one day someone ate a carrot that the sun and the earth made in an act of union. So everything is in an absolutely extraordinary cause-and-effect relationship. Everything dies, except for the constant cycling of life. So the intent to honor all also includes the honoring of death.

The next gateway on the medicine wheel is the gateway of the East. In many traditions, this direction has been associated with the experience of illumination, the experience of enlightenment. For example, it is not infrequent in the Native American world that the direction of east is associated with the eagle, the sun bird, the one with great vision. And what have we here as an enemy? We have Power.

When we begin to dance with the enemy called Power, what we begin to understand is that from one point of view we have no power. There is a complete absence of power in our lives. When the eagle becomes involved, we move in the realm of personal power. The personal power that brings mental distortions that create problems is not true power. It's not what Don José Matsua, the Huichol shaman would call *cupuri*, the life-energy force. It is not what we know as divine power or God's power. It is not the power that is intrinsic to Buddha nature.

The true power is not manifested in terms of grasping or manipulation. There's an absence of grasping, an absence of personal will, an absence of manipulation, in this power that we're talking about.

So when one has danced with power and has experienced the distortions that arise in one's nature when contacting so-called personal power, when one transforms this poison into a nectar, what quality arises? Most interesting, it is the responsibility of Harmony.

Realized individuals, completely enlightened individuals, have only one job in the world—to bring about greater balance and greater harmony. Anything we do that contributes to disharmony is coming from a place that is still in darkness. Our mandate, our true job, our great vow is to bring about greater harmony, to help bring about a cessation of suffering.

So these are our four enemies: the enemy of Fear, the enemy of Clarity, the enemy of Death, and the enemy of Power. And the four qualities are very simple. The first quality to arise is the attitude of Humility. The second is the discipline of Humor. The third is the intent of Honor. And the fourth is the responsibility of Harmony.

Joan, would you speak about what's called the book of life in these teachings?

My friend, Swiftdeer, gave me this teaching. It involves the same teachings as are involved in the warrior's wheel, but we move around the wheel in a different manner.

When we refer to the book of life in terms of the medicine wheel teachings, what we're talking about is the totality of who we are. We're talking about our personal history, the history of all our past lives, our entire personal history as something that we are shapeshifting at this very moment. It becomes a rather interesting game to play, because we are making—we have made—our own book of life.

From one point of view, we have read the book of life: This is who we think we are; this is our personal history; this is what we spend a lot of time and money trying to figure out. But as we dance the teachings of the warrior's wheel, we get a very different point of view on who we are in our totality.

There are five movements in the book of life, and they are meant to empty it of its content. When we look at our book of life after having danced on the warrior's wheel and having gone through these five movements, we discover that it's not only empty—it's also a mirror. You'll see the connection between these five steps or five gateways and the warrior's wheel.

The first step we dance to is in the south, and that involves the erasing of our personal history. How do we erase our personal history? Well, it's not by getting a degaussing machine and erasing it like we would if we were erasing audio or video tapes.

In the Native American world, in the Buddhist world, and in most sacred systems, we have methods for erasing our personal history. Whether it's through insight meditation *(vipassana)* or through the ceremonial forms of the Sun Dance path, or through other ceremonial forms from other traditions, it is basically an evocation of the content of our unconscious and our subconscious. It's a calling-forth of the unrecognized content that controls our lives from within. It's finding out about a lot of backseat drivers who are in fact driving us down the road.

For example, in the Native American teachings of the Sun Dance path, there's a medicine wheel called the star maiden's circle. We use the star maiden's circle—which is a kind of philosopher's stone, if you will—as a way of breaking open the delusion code in terms of our basic nature. The star maiden's circle shows us, in the south, how we construct and get entrapped by our own mythology. It shows us the nature of our personal symbols and shows how these symbols are frequently mazes, not mirrors. It shows how these symbols are closed, not open. It shows us how we are entrapped in our daydream and never come into actualizing anything. It shows us how we create rules and laws to constrict our movement in the world. The star maiden's circle is also a teaching device to show us the belief systems which create a sense of limitedness. It also shows us how we design our energy movement in the world. It shows us how we sometimes stay in fantasy, which is our dark mirror, when we could move into freedom and unlimited imagination. And, finally, it reveals our self-concept.

I've just listed the eight points in the star maiden's circle. These eight points reveal eight dimensionalities which determine how we perceive ourself, the world, and our relationship with the world.

In this teaching, we work at freeing ourselves from these factors by inquiring into four aspects of our nature. We make an inquiry of our little child who is vulnerable, of our adult who is socially conditioned, of the other aspect of our adult which is not socially conditioned, and of our little child who is completely outside of all psychological and cultural conditioning—our magical child. And we work the star maiden's circle in relation to these four dimensions of our nature. In the "teaching of the shields," these four are called our child substance shield, our adult substance shield, our adult spirit shield, and our child spirit shield. We make an inquiry of these four aspects of our nature in order to understand our personal history. Only by engaging that history totally—or, as Trungpa Rinpoche says, only by facing yourself completely—can you know it. Having done this, you understand truly what courage is about—courage as derived from *coeur*, the heart. Courage is an engagement of the heart, and true bravery arises when we have engaged our personal history.

The next movement in the book of life is to the west, what we call dancing with death. Until we have made death an ally, death is going to be an enemy; we will be completely controlled, completely at the effect of death.

The third movement in the book of life takes us to the north. The north gateway is what we call stopping the world. What do we mean by stopping the world? Well, the world is how *we think* about the world—that's what the world is. When we have attained beginner's mind, the mind is no longer defining: "This is this, that is that." We literally stop the dialogue which codes our way of being in the world and separates us from the world. When we and the world become one, we have stopped the world. The sense of time—of future, of past, and even of present—ceases to exist.

The fourth gateway we discover in the movements of the book of life is in the east. We call it dancing the dream awake. We can experience the dream from a number of points of view. We can be at the effect of the dream; for example, someone stabs us and we wake up screaming. Or we can look at the dream as if we're watching television; this is what we would call aligning with the observer part of our nature. We're separate from the dream. However, there's a way to be in the dream, where we are not only *aware* of being in the dream but we're also *in* the dream. We are *awake* in the dream.

There are Hindu techniques, Tibetan techniques, and Native American techniques for doing spiritual practice in the dream state. Many teachers will tell you that we waste six to eight hours of every twenty-four, sleeping. So dream yoga is basically about awakening within the dream and doing purification practices within the dream field. We want to do that not only to continue refining our basic nature, but also to realize that we're in a dream right now—even as we fool ourselves that we're awake. We want to awaken within *this* dream, and dance this dream awake. That is, we want to become one with this dream. At the same time, we want to become one with the dream of shape-shifting the dream, creating an absolutely perfect and harmonious dream.

Finally, the fifth movement on the wheel is to assume authority. That is realizing, completely, one's inner authority.

Huston Smith

The Ground of Being

POLLS TAKEN OF the American public show
that there is an increasing interest in things spiritual. And
yet the same pollsters show fewer people attending
church. It appears that the razor's edge is outside the
traditional religious structure, codependent as that is
with other institutional wielders of power. At the same
time that we have increased spiritual longing, there is a
concurrent eroding of core human values, ethics, and
integrity in the society. We may just need to restore our
ground of being in order to meet the challenges of the
present and the future. The great spiritual traditions and
philosophies from cultures all over the planet may
provide us the means.

Huston Smith, author of the classic textbook
The Religions of Man, is well-qualified to provide insights
about what these great traditions and philosophies have
to offer contemporary culture.

MT: *Huston, why have religious structures seemingly lost the Vision, so that people have to seek it elsewhere?*

HS: I think that they, like perhaps all the other institutions in the modern world, were taken in by a development that goes back about three or four hundred years and set the modern world on its course. That development was, of course, the emergence of modern science.

Science in the generic sense had been around as long as art and religion. But what was discovered then—in the sixteenth, seventeenth centuries—was the controlled experiment, which escalated science to a new order of power and exactitude. That power proved to be enough to create both a new world, this world that we now live in, and a new world-view. In the process it brought many, many benefits. But in terms of world-view, it inflicted a great blow on the human psyche by making it appear that life's material side is its most important side. Now this is a logical mistake. Science didn't really *say* this, but because its power derived from attending to the material aspects of nature, and because that power is great and effective and gave us many benefits, the outlook of modernity is unprecedentedly materialistic.

Now, you asked about religious institutions, the mainline churches. Unfortunately, they too succumbed to some extent to that slip. Not intentionally. But transcendence, as that which is not just larger than we are but also better than we are, got pushed into the background and lost our attention. All modern institutions, churches included, have suffered that loss.

Churches are doing many good things—social service causes, taking in the street people, and so on. They're doing very good work. But the reason that they've failed to inspire as they once did is that their grasp on transcendence has slipped. That also accounts for why Asian spirituality has begun to appeal to people in the West. Not having suffered the modern reduction of reality, they have maintained a firmer hold on transcendence.

Asian spirituality puts more emphasis on the experience. I think of my grandmother, for example. She was deeply saddened when the Catholic Church decided to change the ritual and go to an English Mass. The mys-

tery of the Latin—the mystique—was changed, was transformed, in that simple act.

That's right. And the so-called liturgical reform that you're referring to is an ambiguous move. Certain re-emphases were perhaps called for, but there have also been losses. You mentioned one; I'll mention another. I recently was at a gathering with Robert Bellah, the noted sociologist and author of *Habits of the Heart*. He's a wise and right-thinking man. But he claimed that when the priest stopped facing the altar and turned to face the congregation, the Catholic Church gained, for the congregation felt included. Well, I have to confess that my take is just the opposite. Togetherness is nice. But it can't match the symbolism of the priest and the people—*everybody*, the priest included—facing the Cross, as something that is beyond them all. That's what people need, more than they need the sense of together-ness or creating your own theology—the whole anthropological turn. Once more I'll say that the situation is ambiguous. It's not totally black-and-white. Because the gains are tooted more than the losses, it's important to balance the picture. I'm glad you brought up the issue.

The aspect of community also comes up for me as we're talking about the shift. In the previous form—with the priest and the congregation facing the Cross, as you put it—there's a recognition, I think, of each individual on his or her own journey in community.

Right.

Whereas, shifting it around it's like, well, we're all in this "together."

That's right.

But it's not quite that way, it seems. It's different. As you say, ambiguous is a good way to put it.

 Another thing that keeps coming up for me as we're talking about this has to do with the educational system, of which you've been a part for so many years. With the increasing emphasis on business, career, and opportunity— at the sacrifice of what's called the humanities, the bedrock of establishing values and ethics in ourselves—courses on those subjects are going by the by. What about that?

I think it's a serious matter. You may have seen, just in this last week, a poll of students, freshmen, throughout the nation. One of the ques-tions in the poll was, "Why have you come to college?" Seventy-five percent said, straight out, that their top priority was to make money, make more money. Few checked the option, "to develop a meaningful philosophy of life."

That's almost a direct reversal of the way it was twenty years ago, in the 1960s.

Exactly. I see the shift as ominous. The universities and colleges might say, "Well, that's just a problem of our time. We face the yuppies, and that's what they're coming for." But I personally think that we in academia have to take some responsibility for the shift. Again, there's been no wrong intent. We've simply not seen clearly what has happened. And what has happened in academia is, as President Steven Muller of Johns Hopkins said in an interview, "The university is rooted in the scientific method, and the scientific method cannot provide a sense of values. As a result, we're turning out skilled barbarians."

Now, I think that's basically true. But what academics do not see clearly enough is the way that their own disciplines, including their criteria for knowing, gravitate towards scientific ways of knowing which emphasize objective knowledge—public knowledge that can be verified.

All the proper footnotes and bibliographies.

That's part of it. There's also the jargon and the academese, much of which is unreadable. There's the added problem that because such a large proportion of our population is going to college, professors can get their books published just by requiring their students to read them [laughs]. There's an ingrown character to academic writing. Professors speak to their colleagues and their own students. A gap emerges between the university mind and our public consciousness.

Huston, you're mentioning how the scientific paradigm has crept into academic circles, how the scientific model has actually become part of the research into the humanities, and how it can stifle creativity and originality. But in your writings you've also referred to David Bohm's theory of wholeness and the implicate order. David Bohm is certainly one of the foremost theoretical physicists alive today and has pioneered, I think, a theory of physics that almost sounds like a spiritual philosophy.

It does indeed.

One very similar to some of the Oriental philosophies you're so familiar with.

What is your view of the possible coming-together, the linking, with science coming back around to its roots in natural philosophy?

It's an immensely exciting time. The outcome hasn't been determined; we'll find out how things go, but the incursions are fruitful. On one hand, the developments in science have undercut a kind of crass Newtonian view of reality as consisting of ultimate little atoms that are unrelated to other things—our century has undercut that. The interrelation between the parts of being—which David Bohm emphasizes with his concept of implicate wholeness—clearly is a move back towards the unity which traditional philosophies, those of Asia included, emphasized.

At the same time, I think we have to be careful here. Modern science has become a powerful symbol for transcendence—again I use "transcendence" to refer to that which is greater than we are by every criterion of worth we know, including intelligence and compassion. Modern science suggests such a realm, but I do not think that it proves it. Nor do I think that it can, for this reason: The crux of modern science is the controlled experiment; that's what distinguishes modern science from generic science, and what gives it its power by virtue of its power to prove. It can winnow hypotheses and discard those that are inadequate. What we don't see is the corrolary of all this, which is that we can control only what is inferior to us. Things that are greater than we are, including more intelligent, dance circles around *us*, not we they. So there's no way that we are going to get angels, or God, or whatever other beings there may be that are greater than we are, into our controlled experiments. So I think modern science will never prove anything in the area of the human spirit. But it can suggest, and I find it suggesting powerfully. For me, modern science has come to rival, even outstrip at times, sacred art and virgin nature as a symbol of the divine.

Now, if I can continue one more step. I think there's a trap if those who share our kinds of interests—let's just say here "New Dimensions" interests—rush on to say, "Well, that's true of science up to this point. But that only shows that we need a new science that is larger in scope and can prove these transcendent realities." When I hear that, and I hear it very often, my impulse is to say, "In proposing that move, you show me where *your* loyalties lie, namely, in science! [laughs] You're for transcendence, but you won't really believe it exists until science proves that it does. So your move shows that you continue to accept science as the ultimate oracle as to what exists."

That acceptance is the heart of modernity's problem, so the call for a science that proves transcendence only perpetuates the problem.

In probing the physical, material world, science is brilliant; it is a near-perfect way of telling us about that. And to know about nature is a great good, for nature is awesome in its own right.

But science doesn't have to do everything. And if we try to make it do everything, with every step of its expansion we will decrease its power and will end up with a kind of mushy science. Of course, we can define "science" in any way we please. I prefer keeping it hard-nosed, powerful and precise, while insisting that it can only disclose a *part* of reality.

It occurs to me as I hear you present your case here—which I think is very compelling—that it may explain why it's so difficult to get psychic and paranormal experiences to happen in the scientific laboratory.

Exactly. I believe that paranormal powers are real. But to get anything into a laboratory, we have to reduce the variables to a single alternative so we can discover which side of it is true. Where the object in question exceeds us in complexity, we can't do that.

This may also explain why it has been so easy to change the agenda of colleges and universities, through the federal budget and the like. We've made science into some kind of god.

Oh, clearly.

And science has become our religion.

Alex Comfort has a nice line on that. He says, "Science is our sacral mode of knowing." Sacral is a coined word—it comes from "sacred." I think he's right. Science has almost exactly replaced the role that revelation served in the Middle Ages. Then, if you wanted the final verdict on what is true, you would go to the scriptures and the traditions of the Church. Now we go to science. One intellectual historian has pointed out that as far back as a hundred years ago, more people believed, really believed, in the truth of the periodic table of chemical elements than believed anything in the Bible. In the century since then, we've moved further in that direction. Science *has* become the revelation of our time.

And to return to our previous point, it *should* be with regard to the material world. The slip is that we have turned science into scientism—scientism being defined as the assumption that science is the only reliable way of getting at truth, and that only the kinds of things it tells us about really exist.

It may require some sense of humility to admit that we have confused science with scientism.

It will. In a way, we know what we need to know. It's one of these things that we know but never learn.

Or that we know but haven't integrated.

That's right. It has to be assimilated. But everything in our culture—almost everything—works against that assimilation. The visible bombards us from dawn to night. The tangible is so much with us that it's hard to put it in perspective. That's all we need to do, just put it in perspective. But that saving grace is difficult to allow.

Having just a little bit of time to step back, being able to use that observing mind and that observing quality that all of us have to get that perspective, is really important.

Important and, in our time, difficult.

Huston, Joseph Campbell, in his work and through his emphasis on the mythic quest and the symbols of myth, has a lot to do with that missing link, as it were, and why we're not able to get that perspective.

That's very true. Many times he referred to that shape-changing yet wonderfully constant story that all the myths relate. I think it's a beautiful phrase, "shape-changing." In their specifics, their particulars, myths differ; yet the underlying theme is constant. Joseph was a master at going straight for the paydirt—for what the underlying, constant story is—and then making it available to us.

I wonder where we can find that story in the midst of the scientific revolution, because it's obviously present. But how do you bring the symbology out, and how do you make it understandable and obvious to all concerned? Certainly it's there.

Part of it is there. Are you asking how science itself may be exemplifying this underlying story?

Well, in a sense, yes. In a sense, you can see the scientist seeking the ultimate invention or the ultimate product or whatever it is—trying to find the ultimate solution to this disease or whatever—as on the hero's quest, the mythic journey.

We need to distinguish here between science and the scientists.

There's no question but that scientists are on a hero's journey second unto none. Their dedication, their devotion to truth, their ordeals, and then the exultation of homecoming when new truth is discovered—all of that, the whole symbology of the hero's journey is powerfully exemplified by them.

I'd like to illustrate this with an anecdote from MIT, where I taught longer than anywhere else. Ed Land, who later invented the Polaroid camera, came to MIT as a freshman and took a course in optics. Before the semester was over—I tell you the story as it came down to me—the teacher of that course had resigned a tenured position to go with this freshman student and start a company which later become Polaroid. My favorite moment in the story concerns the time when they were right on the cusp of their decisive discovery of how color film could be developed in the small space of a camera. They were working so hard that they were actually living in the lab. When they got exhausted, they would just put their heads on their desks. Finally, the ex-professor said to his ex-freshman, "Ed, I've had it; I just can't go on." "Good," Ed answered. "We'll work in our Christmas shopping today." The professor said, "Ed, Ed. It's January 3!" [laughter]

This story shows the white heat in the quest of science, and the scientists who embody it. Now that has to be distinguished from the expectation that science itself will reveal a world that is full of—saturated, you might say—with a kind of meaning that the myths proclaim. Take Steven Weinberg, the Harvard physicist, for example. In *The First Three Minutes* he says that the irony is that the more understandable—from the scientific standpoint—we find the universe to be, the more meaningless it becomes. Now that's true too if you just hold entirely to what the sciences actually depict and lay out for us. But if we fold it into a larger vision, it fits smoothly.

I was thinking, as you were just giving that white-heat description about Ed Land and that professor, of how the Vipassana teacher might dismiss the student with a wave of his hand, saying, "That's just another one, just another one. Go back and meditate." And I was wondering about how we do get caught up in our life in ways that perhaps remove us from what's real.

We do. But then there are many encouraging signs. You mentioned Vipassana. I was just last December with my wife at the Insight Meditation Society in Barre, Massachusetts. There it came over me again watching those 120 Western yogis sitting and walking for sixteen hours a day in silence, it came over me that this institution goes back uninterrupted for 2500 years, to the "rains retreat" that was instigated by the Buddha himself.

As you probably know, when Buddha formed his *sangha*, his community of monks, he sent them out on the highways and byways for nine months of the year to teach and preach the dharma. But then when the monsoons came along, slamming in and turning the sub-continent of India into a sea of mud, the monks would re-gather for three uninterrupted months of solid meditation in what they called the "rains retreat."

I find it quite thrilling that to this day, 2500 years later, the rains retreat is intact in Barre, Massachusetts. And land has been purchased for a Western off-shoot in California. This kind of extensive retreat and mind-training is being seriously attempted right here in the West.

That's one solution, as it were, to getting off the merry-go-round. But I can hear the critique, "Well, how does someone get three months to go off and do this?" You know, how does one take time out of their busy life? "I've got a family; I've got a career; I've got this, I've got that." There are lots of reasons for not being able to do that in this day and age and in this society. What is your answer to that?

[laughs] My answer is that somebody should tell *me* the answer. My wife has actually gone for three years in a row, and will be going back for a fourth one. She manages her life to do it. I have not succeeded in freeing such time myself. But the real answer is, "Where there's a will, there's a way." To be sure, very few people could just decide tomorrow that they'll go; but, if there is a will, then one can begin with a day, or a weekend. Then, from what one learns and from the encouragement and the incentive one gathers, one can begin to build it into one's life—ten minutes in the morning, ten minutes in the evening. This is not at all to minimize the difficulty of doing that in a busy world. But, again, when we decide that we really want to do it, I think we can free up the necessary space.

Huston, I can't think of anyone more qualified to answer my next query. Am I correct in thinking that Buddhism is the only major religion that hasn't gone to war for its creed? When one looks at Buddhism, one notices its incredible variety and diversity as practiced in different cultures. It seems to adapt to the different cultures. We had the phenomena of Zen becoming very popular in the 1950s, with the beat era. Now we're talking about Vipassana, but Tibetan Buddhism has also become very prevalent as the Tibetans have been spread across the planet after losing their country to the Chinese. As we look at Buddhism, how would you describe the differences? And also, are you aware of Buddhism ever having been in war for the creed?

Yes, but so incidentally that it's the exception that proves the rule. Right now, in Sri Lanka, there's the conflict with the Hindus, and I've been told by field workers that some of those Buddhist monks are becoming fierce politicians. But in the volumes of Buddhist history, this is a small chapter. Basically, I would validate your point. Buddhism seems not to have been violent to the extent that the other religions have.

As I hear the Dalai Lama, it strikes me as very unusual and quite commendable that I've never heard the Tibetans say a bad word about the Chinese.

Nor have I.

One can look at Afghanistan as a relevant, contrasting example. When one looks at Tibet and China, the Tibetans—at least the ones who escaped Tibet—have dealt with that situation much differently than other peoples have dealt with the loss of their country or culture. I'm not suggesting to make a judgment about this, whether it's right or wrong, but just to notice it.

Yes, it does appear to be the case. It is both interesting and impressive.

I want to expand my question relative to Buddhism. As we look at the different varieties of Buddhism, there seems to be a substantive difference between how it's practiced in, say, Sri Lanka or Thailand, and how it's practiced in Tibet and Japan. What about those differences? How do they come together, or do they come together?

It presents indeed a remarkable spread and variety. As for the differences, I happen to have a personal theory on this, respecting the two major branches of Buddhism: Theravada or southern Buddhism which we find in Sri Lanka, Thailand, and Burma, and then Mahayana in China, Japan, Korea, and the like. Usually the two branches are distinguished according to whether the aspirant is out for his own enlightenment or postpones his own enlightenment until others are saved. That kind of thing.

There's something to describing the split in this way, but I think there's an underlying, deeper difference that the historians have missed. Southern Buddhism is the branch of Buddhism that adhered to the Buddha's vision of Buddhism as a total civilization, one that blueprinted an entire way of life—economics and politics included—whereas Mahayana gave up the claim to being a total civilization and contented itself with being, you might say, simply a religion that could be fitted to any civilization and could take up its abode therein.

Original Buddhism presented the vision of a total civilization that was founded on the tripod of monarchy, monks, and the laity. Each of these had obligations to the other, and also was entitled to benefits from the others. Southern Buddhism has adhered to that ideal. This makes the monks more important, for they are one of the three legs on which society rests.

But when Buddhism entered China, China opened its arms to it, seeing that it had psychological and metaphysical resources the Chinese lacked. East Asians aren't strong on metaphysics or psychology. China's social structure, though, was solidly intact. The Chinese Empire was not about to change its groundplan for a foreign import. So Buddhism entered, but compromised: "OK, keep your social structure as it is, and we will deepen its religious component." Therein, I think, lies the fundamental difference between southern and northern Buddhism.

Tibet seems to be an exception to the Mahayana transfer, because there the religion actually became the politics.

You're quite right. In that respect it is more like the southern Buddhist model. This difference between the branches of Buddhism that you brought up is interesting. When Buddhism first significantly entered this country in the 1950s and 1960s, it was primarily in its Mahayana, specifically Zen, form. Since then, Theravada, through the Vipassana meditation, and the Tibetan Buddhism have gained ground. I think that's healthy because Zen—although I have the utmost respect for it—depends on a *roshi* who functions as a kind of guru. Vipassana is something like a democratized Buddhism. It relies on its method more than on a teacher.

It's also interesting to note the seemingly limitless amount of scripture and documentation that the Tibetans have, versus Zen where there's very little traditional scripture at all, if any. Tibetan Buddhism has an incredible pantheon of literature behind it.

It does. And this makes surprising the effectiveness with which the Tibetans have spread their teachings in this country, given the fact that it is so technical and involved. And its meditation is unbelievably intricate. I've made stabs at both Theravada and Mahayana, but though I attempted Tibetan practice, I soon despaired. It seemed impenetrable because of the complexity of the teaching. Yet there are innumerable Americans—you know them as well as do I—who are drawn to that branch.

Yes. There are also Tibetan teachers, who have come to the United States, that are perhaps less strict or less formal or structural—so that there's more allowance for a little informality.

Good point.

So, where do you think we go from here? What do you think the future of philosophy and religion is?

[hearty laugh] I've never been to Disney World, but I hear it has a section called "Tomorrowland." When I first learned of it, I hooted. We don't even know what "Todayland" is, and people are already scripting Tomorrowland.

I don't know. I don't feel like I have much of a feel for the future. We all have our strengths and weaknesses, and personally I feel I'm pretty good with the past. At least it seems solid to me. At least I get some traction there. But the future? Who wrote the song, "I Can't Get No Satisfaction"? I feel like parodying it. I can't get no *traction* on the future. Tomorrow the Bomb might accidentally go off or we may discover that we have burned too wide a hole in our ozone covering. Still, we've managed thus far. I'm not much given to prognosis. What's important is to see the direction in which we should move and let the future take care of itself.

Well, there's certainly something to be said for the value of knowing the past.

Roots. Roots are important.

Who was it that said, "Those who forget history are condemned to repeat it"?

Whoever it was, I agree.

Joseph Chilton Pearce

Adventures of the Mind

THE LATE Gregory Bateson challenged us to "look for the pattern that connects." During the past decade, we have learned more about the brain, the mind, and the formation of reality than we have known throughout all the preceding millennia. In combination with the new image of reality emerging from quantum physics, this new and emerging view of ourselves shatters our previously held beliefs. How we evolve, learn, create, and relate to our universe needs to be re-evaluated.

In times of increasing pessimism over global problems, a corresponding optimism may be arising through the rediscovery of who we really are and what our potential can be. Joseph Pearce is a pioneer in the re-visioning of our capacity for learning and unfolding. He has synthesized a vast amount of research, including such diverse topics as theoretical physics, the holographic brain, aborigine dream time, Piaget's studies of children, and the awakening of personal power through meditative practice. He provides the opportunity and the challenge for us to review the way we perceive and experience the world.

His books *The Crack in the Cosmic Egg* and *Magical Child* have become classics in the field of mind-probing literature.

MT: *Joseph, I want to go back a few years, to a major event that occurred in your life in your early fifties. You had started out doing seminars around the country on the Magical Child, and then suddenly you stopped and went back to build a cabin in the woods in Virginia. What happened then?*

JP: Oh, that was in 1976. You had helped me found those Magical Child seminars, and I was working on my book *The Magical Child* at the same time. I received in the mail a picture of Swami Muktananda, the Indian meditation teacher.

At that time I had a strong cultural and intellectual prejudice against Indian gurus, and this picture—sent by one of my book readers with the suggestion that I immediately rush off to see this person—infuriated me. The result from the picture was what they call *shaktipat*, the descent of power, the descent of grace from a master. And that experience blew me out of orbit. I'd never experienced anything like it before, a whole conscious realm beyond anything I'd ever known happening to me as I sat there. This was a bit much for me to deal with. The experience itself was that God played with me, that I had been tossed from one end of the universe to the other in this ecstatic play. And I wanted it again.

I thought that all I want in this world is to be played with by God one more time, and I had to find out what that was all about. So I resigned from the Magical Child seminars, wrote out a power of attorney, and gave the whole thing over to my seminar director. It was a considerable investment by that time, and we were booked up in advance. I left and left no forwarding address, got into meditation, and found out what that business was all about.

In 1979, I was living and traveling with Muktananda, along with two thousand other people. He said to me, "We don't meditate in caves. We meditate in the middle of Main Street" and sent me back to doing what I had been doing before—which was lecturing and writing. When I went back to that, it was from a different standpoint than before. I had been driven with anger before, rage was the generating force within me. I went back to doing this same thing, except from the heart, generated by love.

After I had given a talk at a medical conference, for example, a doctor came up to me. He said that he had heard me back in 1974, but he hadn't been able to understand a word I had said, because my rage had drowned out everything. And then he asked, "What in the name of God has happened to you? There has been a tremendous change." Well, what had happened to me was that I had come to meditation under a great spiritual master and it had transformed my being, so far as I could tell. That had done it to me. It was not the result of my intellect or anything else. It was simply a grace—a gift freely given.

Your encounter with meditation and the meditative process clearly enriched your understanding of the developmental process and brought you a deeper understanding of where your rage came from. I think that it's a rage common to many male adults, particularly in American society, who are driven to follow a career and have to repress that natural urging. Then, within that repression, the rage comes. Perhaps you could talk about that.

Well, I spend about six months every year overseas, between lecturing in other countries and spending as much time as I can in our central ashram in Ganeshpuri, India. When you come back here after traveling in other countries such as Australia, New Zealand, places like that, there's a certain shock. The rage factor in America is palpable. You can feel it in any city. There is hostility, anger, and a strange fear that permeates our society. And the contrast is greater each time I come back here. Some countries are still peaceful.

I find a deep spirituality in America that just doesn't find its proper avenue of expression. There is also a tremendous vitalism in America, a vital spirit that you don't find anywhere else—including peaceful countries like New Zealand and Australia. And so, while the rage factor is disturbing and distressing, particularly in our young people, there is this tremendous vitalism in America that I find very hopeful. So I'm equally optimistic and pessimistic at the same time.

As our young people grow and mature, particularly within an educational system that isn't too allowing, how does it change, how does it transform?

Well, as far as the educational system goes, certainly we are in some trouble. I gave a lecture at the University of Adelaide in Australia, and a member of the State Board of Education came up afterwards. He said he had just gotten back from a six-week tour of American schools and that it was the shock of his life. He said, "Your education system is bankrupt. It's in chaos, everyone is rushing around trying to sell their answer, and no one is asking the right question." I thought this provocative.

We're training our children simply as dollar-commodity values in our gross national product. We treat them as that from birth on. And they pick this up from us. It's implicit in everything we do with a child that they must get out there and make the Big Dollar. That's the only criterion we give them to measure their own value in the world. And it infuriates them, because it violates their true intelligence. And I think our educational system will not recover from this collapse until we begin to realize the spiritual dimensions of the child.

We must get the word "spiritual" out of sectarian religious connotations. The word "spirit" must be redefined as the true driving force of the child. Waldorf schools, for example, work for the spiritual unfolding of the child and never use the word spiritual. They don't use the semantic-substitute for the function. And another beautiful system in education has been developed by a Sister Grace Pilon, from Xavier University in New Orleans, Louisiana. This woman has worked for more than fifty years with children and developed an educational procedure different from anything else we have had, and it's applicable to a public school situation—if the teachers are willing to undergo the training. Children are flourishing under that system, gaining responsibility and self-esteem. The education takes care of itself, kind of peripherally. The three R's are not the main focus. The main focus is on the children's own unfolding, and they just pick up their learning casually. So these are hopeful signs at the time of apparent collapse of the system.

You had your initial exposure to this "hidden intelligence" within the child—which you wrote about in The Magical Child Matures—*with your five-year-old son, when he came in one morning and sat on the side of the bed.*

Age four to seven, according to Piaget, is a period of development of a type of intuitive intelligence. The child opens up to information about his world, his self, and his relationship with his world, which is non-sensory. It doesn't have to come in through the sensory system, but comes in through the limbic structure of the brain—which is the emotional/cognitive structure, the energy and the quality of relationship. The child begins to resonate with that between about four and seven, and opens up to the possibility of bringing in information through a non-sensory process. Now, we put occult labels on this natural function.

My son, at age five, came in one day and gave me the answer to a passionate quest I had been on for a couple of years concerning the relationship of man and God. He had no recollection of it afterward and I knew that there were capacities in the child's mind that are not developed, because a child cannot develop any intelligence unless he's given the stimulus and the model of someone who has developed that intelligence.

Another example of that—you refer to it in The Magical Child Matures— *is of the young woman who was found in an attic that she had been left in since she was six months old. She had no consciousness of what was happening.*

The young woman was fourteen years of age when she was found. Her name was Jenny. She was tied to a potty seat in an attic and never saw a human after six months of age.

A pan of food was slipped in to her every day and miraculously, no one knows how, she stayed alive. By age six months a tremendous amount of development has happened in a child, but in that sensory isolation even that regressed. When she was found fourteen years later, she was literally mindless, and dwarfed. There had been no development. Nothing could be done for her. She couldn't learn to speak, she couldn't learn anything because all of the developmental stages had long since passed.

It's both a tragic and a fascinating case. You can't say it's tragic for her, because there's not enough consciousness there to base a tragedy on. With a lack of stimulus from her external world, no potentials could unfold. A law of nature is that any built-in intelligence must be given its stimulus from an outer intelligence that has already been developed.

So the child's development is directly related to the stimulus that the child receives?

Howard Gardner at Harvard University points out that the intelligences that make up a human being—mathematical intelligence, musical, spatial, linguistic—all of those are inherent within us, within our genetic system—we don't know quite how—kind of complete, whole potentials at our birth. But none of them can unfold unless it is given its corresponding model out here in the world, one who has developed that potential. So, for a mathematical intelligence to unfold, you must be given the mathematical model or a teacher out here. Language, which begins in the womb, can only unfold if the child is given an actual language spoken around it. The stimulus of the outer physical process brings about a response from the internal potential. The brain neurons fire to handle the flow of energy from a potential state into an actualized state that gives us what we call a structure of knowledge. And we find that the structure of knowledge that results is determined by the quality, the character, and the nature of the model given the child.

Now, if you think about this a little bit, it's both wonderful and chilling. It means that the emotional, intellectual, physical state of the child is determined to an unknown extent by the emotional, intellectual, physical models that the child is given in the world. Give the child a French language from the seventh month in utero on, and what kind of a structure of knowledge builds up? French. Give him German, you've got German. Japanese . . . Japanese. And so on. And it's the same with all other intelligences. The quality and the nature and the character of intelligence are determined by the quality and the nature and the character of the models we're given.

I'm wondering about that technological gift to baby-sitting—television—and the remarkable use to which television is put as a place for children to get their entertainment.

The damage of television doesn't have anything to do with content. There is certainly damage from content, but the main damage of television has to do with substituting critical functions within the limbic structure of the brain, where emotional energy acts on our cognitive process. The damage television does is in substituting processes for internal image-making.

The primary stimulus that the image-making factors operate around are words. Words—through play, story-telling, let's pretend, fantasies, mythologies, ancient legends, and so on—bring about an internal image response, imagery within the child's brain. In every culture throughout history, stories are told to little children. Through that, the child builds up an internal image process which is metaphoric and symbolic and through that metaphoric/symbolic imagery the brain translates its information from a sensory/motor level up to the high brain, the intellectual process. And through that very same transference device of imagery within the limbic structure, the high brain—the intellectual brain—can create its ideas and translate them through the sensory/motor system to the outside world.

Television has broken down the capacity of the brain to create metaphoric transference imagery and symbols. The result is functional illiteracy. By functional illiteracy, we mean that children can go through the sensory/motor motions of literacy—carving out the words, saying what the words mean—but in context they cannot derive any meaning from what they see. The reason is that there are three separate sections of the brain, as Paul MacCleane points out, that handle this. The sensory/motor brain responds to signals and sends them up to the emotional/cognitive brain for transference into metaphoric symbolic imagery which can be received by the high brain, which operates in abstract imagery. We make our response through the same transference of metaphor and symbol to our sensory/motor system. That's what has broken down. It's a physiological breakdown in the child.

More and more school systems are bringing computers in for children to work with and use as creative tools. That would do the same thing as television, wouldn't it?

It simply completes the journey that television started. The average American child sees six thousand hours of television before entering kindergarten at age five. This has taken the place of what would have been the child's ordinary imaginative play. You see, play is the critical way in which the brain develops in the first seven years and on up until age eleven. And it really can't develop except through play. Imaginative play, imitative play, and so on, is verbal in early childhood, and is based on transference of imagery and metaphor. Television has supplanted that in many American children, replaced interaction with parents, and so they fail to learn to play. So we have boredom as one of the major factors in the American child and adolescent.

But far more severe is the breakdown in the brain's capacity to transfer imagery. The brain operates primarily through image transference. It's said that even congenitally blind people think in imagery. So television cripples development of intelligence. People say that it gives so much information, but the child needs visual information of that sort like a hole in the head. It simply plays no part in cognitive development in the first seven years. Information is not what nature's after, she's after ability. The capacity to create imagery is the way by which all learning takes place in the first eleven years.

I think it was in your book Bond of Power *that you mentioned the power of sound without images—radio for an example, audio—to really motivate the developmental process.*

This is simply fact. Look into the work of Dr. Frank Bar and his profound discovery of the existence of the melanin molecule, following on the discovery back in the late 1950s that the eye could not transfer light waves to the brain. The eye cannot transfer light waves to the brain; therefore, the brain must create its own light, by which imagery is constructed. We do not see through the eyes as through a pane of glass—we've known that for a long time. We see with the eyes if it's an external image. But what about the internal images of your dreams at night, all the brilliant color—where does the light come from? From the same source that it does when you open your eyes and see the sun.

Now, this can only really be explained by ancient yogic literature or by quantum mechanics. David Bohm refers to the universe as frozen light. The fact is, the process is created within the brain structure as it translates energy from a potential state into an actualized state. The melanin molecule—not melatonin that has to do with pigmentation of the skin or color of the eyes, but a related one—can transfer energy and change its characteristics. This may be how light is produced within the brain by which we create the images that we see.

We don't know how the images are put together, but our picture of the universe out there is an internal creation. The imagery that we see at night in our dreams and the images that we see outside during the day are produced by the same image factor. Biologists at the Santiago School and Roth and his associates at the University of Hamburg in Germany have reached the same conclusion that the ancient yogis had—that the brain creates its own reality and projects it and we experience it as "out there." The brain does this not through stimuli from out there, but from what's discussed at the level of quantum mechanics.

We're discovering that we're more than we have conceived of before—that the whole universe takes place within our brain. With all due respect to a brilliant man, we're going to have to modify Karl Pribram's model: The brain is not a microcosm of the macrocosm or a little hologram of a great hologram. That which we see as a three-dimensional hologram out there is simply a projection of the hologram which is the brain itself.

Until we understand where *process* comes from, education will be at its present standstill. Nature is after process, not products. We've designed an educational system and our children around products, but nature doesn't care for products. She cares for ability, which means process.

What I found in my ten years of experience in Siddha meditation is that we're led from our attachment to and identification with product—meaning body, brains, physical world—into an identification with and attachment to process. And the process is non-localized, non-time/space oriented. It is not related to any physical orientation but to the creative process which lies underneath or beyond all physical process. And so our relationship starts shifting toward process, and then our anxieties, worries, and fears about products and the interaction of products disappear.

Identifying with the state which *gives rise* to products, we're free of the relationships of products. This means we're free of all the physical ramifications of our life, able to interact physically without having to demand from our physical world all sorts of results. We stop trying to predict and control, because we're moving into process rather than product. That sounds abstract, but the issue is that we move out of time into eternity, so to speak—that's the way Meister Eckhart would have put it back in the fourteenth century—and from that standpoint of eternity, we are free to move into time without any demands being made on it. That's where change really starts: when you're not demanding that your world conform to a lot of intellectual ideas.

It also relates to having to let go of thinking that we control our reality.

Mike, some research is mind-boggling, in that respect, and a bit frightful. We've thought that intellect runs the whole show within this threefold sensory/motor, emotional/relational, and intellectual brain. But thousands of decisions are made instant-by-instant by all sorts of lower brain processes and initiate responses to the world out there before the result even reaches our conscious awareness.

So the unconscious is making decisions that the conscious mind isn't even aware are being made.

Until after the fact. And then we find that our conscious self up here on the surface spends most of its time trying to rationalize something which has already happened. We do and don't know why we do it—like Saint Paul, "That which I would do, I do not do. That which I would not do, I do, and there is no health in me. My members are at war one with another." And that's because those three brains are out of synch with each other. Paul MacCleane at the National Institute of Mental Health Brain Research Center said that until these three brains are integrated, we are at war with ourselves. We are in this internal civil war and it will always reflect outwardly on our society. My teacher, Gurumayi, certainly one of the great saints of history, says, "Until that which you think, feel, and act are a single integrated unit, you have no power in your life. And you fragment every child you come across." That's because children imprint to our state, not to our instructions to them, not to all our brilliant teaching. They imprint to our state—physical, emotional, and intellectual. That is, they become who we are and not who we tell them to be.

That's why our example is so important. The doing is what matters, and not the saying.

What we're crying for are whole models to follow. You see, we *think* we're looking for great ideas to follow. No, we're looking for real living models to follow. Some ninety-five percent of all learning and memory takes place beneath our conscious awareness.

That's amazing.

Ninety-five percent of the whole psychic machinery of the brain is involved in creating our five percent ego awareness, so to speak. And the majority of that imprinting and learning goes on from early in utero. It takes place without our being aware of it, or without the parent and the teacher and the society being aware that they are teaching the child in the ways that they are. So the only way that we can possibly heal the current crisis which our children are facing is to heal the models that they're following. Until those models are healed, this downhill trend has to continue.

I want to go back a few minutes, Joseph, to where you were talking about the power of our projection and how we're projecting outwards. You had a great story in The Magical Child Matures *about the English researcher who had wanted to film the Indian* fakir *doing the rope trick. It's a great example of what you were talking about. Perhaps you would relate it.*

This, again, is best explained within the complementarity theory of quantum mechanics. Relationship takes place on a wave level and is acted out on a particle level. That is, we act out on a physical level— with our bodies and our world out there—relational processes and forces which are not physical, not time/space oriented. Under certain circumstances we share imagery that stems from this wave process, from this other dimension. Sheldrake's morphogenetic theory fits in here.

I think it's important to remember that the particle is physical and the wave is non-physical and they are mutually exclusive.

You can't have one without the other, and you have to have both to explain any event. Within the classical logic of science, a paradox exists. Contradiction means an error in logic, but *paradox* is a threshold over which logic won't go. Beyond the threshold of paradox there's a new logic operative, and to understand that you must operate in that reality. The Santiago biologists have pointed out, for example, that you cannot perceive in a different reality until you behave in it. That is, you must simply plunge into the new reality and act within it in order to understand what the rules of that new perception are. We have to drop classical logic in order to understand what the logic of this new dimension might be. The old logic is valid within its framework, but it won't apply to this other mode of consciousness.

We utilize a hundred percent of the two animal-brain structures—the sensory/motor and the emotional/relational that we share with all the mammals on earth—and perhaps only five percent of the great human brain. We once thought everything translated through the human brain, that it was the whole show. Now we find that it is undeveloped, only used for the development of intellect, and that's an intellect which is locked into the service of the sensory/motor system. This means that the development of our new brain of causation, the ability to create, is on behalf of sensory/motor information. That's all the stimulus that the child ever gets to use that brain on. A fragment of the highest evolutionary structure of brain is used on behalf of the lowest and most primitive brain, the sensory/motor or reptilian brain. But because of the incredible power of the new brain, because pure potential energy and consciousness translate through it, because of the power of it, even the five percent or ten percent of it we do develop is very impressive. It gives us our physics, our mathematics, all of our sciences and technologies, all of our philosophies, art, religions. All these have been developed with five to ten percent of the new brain.

Now the issue is why don't we use the other ninety percent? Because that's for our capacity for process, not product—with wave form, not with particle. And until we bring up a child who is oriented toward process and ability and not toward product, we'll never develop the other ninety percent of the brain. And what is that ninety percent for? Spiritual development. The scientific framework deals with sensory/motor process, the most ancient of all of our brain systems. The other ninety percent or ninety-five percent of nature's latest development is left out, because it deals with this internal world and universe—an unfolding universe of process, creative process.

So you see the possibilities, what we could do if we opened up to that aspect of the human personality. We now call it the spiritual aspect but it's our true biological aspect. What dimensions we would have, if with five percent of it we now do all these things!

What's amazing is that there's some intelligence operating, because we've always had this kind of source-adage that we only use ten percent of our brainpower. But of course, our solution for how to use the other ninety percent goes back to a form of the ten or the five percent.

And that's a self-encapsulated trap. You cannot activate the other ninety-five percent through sensory/motor process because the high brain is so powerful that only five percent of it is needed to handle anything physical—including the seven-year-old child's ability to walk a pit of coals that will melt aluminum on contact. Any physical process can be overcome and gone beyond with only five percent of the high brain. And that, again, is explainable within quantum mechanics or within ancient Sanskrit literature.

I haven't forgotten about that fakir *story, though. Let's get that story. This was about an Englishman who went to India and wanted to film the Indian* fakir's *rope trick.*

After a couple of years of searching, he found it in a little village. He saw the *fakir* throw the rope up, and it hung in the air. The whole crowd of about 150 people saw the rope go up into the air and stay. The *fakir* sent his little boy climbing up the rope, and then he took out a huge knife and . . .

The little boy disappeared.

The little boy disappeared, yes. And then the *fakir* goes up the rope and he also disappears. Then, all of a sudden, the little boy's members come falling down. His arms and his legs and his mutilated head fall, and everybody gasps with horror. Now this Englishman has his automatic camera recording the whole event, and he sees it all. Then the *fakir* comes down the rope, wipes the blood off of his sword, picks up all the pieces of the little boy and throws them in his basket, puts the sword in the basket, and then bows. He pulls the rope down, and puts that in the basket. At that point, the little boy jumps out of the basket, whole and complete, and everybody applauds and throws him some coins.

Now, the English psychologist was blown out of orbit because this is what he had witnessed. He questioned everybody, and they had witnessed exactly what he did. So he couldn't wait to get his film developed.

He develops his film, and this is what it shows: The *fakir* throws the rope up in the air, the rope falls down as it should by gravity, and nobody moves. Heads move up and down as they watch all this activity, while the *fakir* simply stares straight ahead. He is creating an image which is shared by everybody else, you see. A mutual image is shared that arises from some other level and acts on the sensory/motor system. Everybody takes part in this wonderful play of death and resurrection. When the little boy resurrects from the dead and everybody applauds, the show is over.

Now the film can't record that, so we say that the reality is, of course, the film. It exposes the whole play. The truth of the matter is that the only reality is within our brain structure. The film can only record the particle structure. What's going on within the real creative processes of the brain is that we create this mutually shared story that has been handed down for generations in India, like a dream which is manifest and projected on the outer world.

That's why, perhaps, so many psychic phenomena and paranormal experiences cannot be verified with current scientific apparatus.

A physical apparatus that's dealing only with particle process cannot deal with this huge dimension—worlds upon worlds of possibility, of process. We have the access to that process, but we've made this error of identifying ourselves only with the most primitive of our brain structures—the sensory/motor—and denying all of the interior worlds of possibility. We hate being trapped in this body and our identity with it, because they're going to shovel this body six feet under and that makes us angry.

In Siddha Yoga, through grace my teacher would pass her power, send me into other worlds, other processes. Little by little, she expands my frame of reference and capacity as I'm moving more toward process and being freed from product. I can then move into the world with a freedom and capacity that I never had before. I find that my intellect is sharpening. I can pick up and understand books now that I could not have cracked the cover on ten years ago.

Gurumayi says that your intellect must be perfected to its highest point in order to be a proper instrument of the heart. When she talks about the heart, she's talking about that fourth level of intelligence—pure process, pure creativity. You can call it the realm of God or any other term that you want to use. Gurumayi bonds our mind and our heart together—bonds our narrow entrapped, encapsulated little ego to the great ego of God and the creative process of this universe.

I'm giving up most of my ordinary activities and spending more of my time encouraging people to look into meditation, and particularly Siddha Meditation, as a way of opening up these channels that got cut off in our enculturation. Being cut off drove us to rage, anxiety, and despair. But this bond can always be re-established. It is not stage-specific. There's an optimal period for its development—in late adolescence—but if we don't get it then, we can get it at any time. Here in my sixth decade of life, I vouch for the fact that this intelligence of the heart can be awakened at any time. When the intelligence of the heart awakens, it develops the intellect as its tool for access to the world—so you get the best of both worlds then. Your outer world becomes rich and your interior world opens. That's what Siddha Meditation is all about, and that's why I'm such an enthusiast of it.

So as we move more to process as opposed to product and take more responsibility for our own meditative reality, then we can also develop our intellect at the same time.

The intellect is automatically developed to a higher point than it was. Evolution has built all of her higher structures on the foundations of lower structures. There is no exception to this. Every higher structure has to be built on the foundations of lower structures. When nature adds a higher process, such as a higher brain to the two animal brains, the higher brain immediately incorporates the lower brain structures into its service and transforms those lower structures.

We have the same sensory/motor system in us that the higher chimpanzees do, and that's why animal research pays off to a certain extent. But from here to eternity, you'll never get a higher chimpanzee to play 1600 separate articulate notes on a piano to create a Chopin étude or a Beethoven sonata. Do you see what I mean? The very same sensory system incorporated into the high evolutionary structure is radically transformed, leaving a discontinuous gap between.

So when we come to someone like Gurumayi, who spent twenty-five years of intense training to have this state passed on to her—completing her brain structure and integrating it into the heart, integrating her individual ego into the intelligence of God—then we are dealing with a discontinuous leap from our ordinary intellect. Our intellect can never bridge this gap itself. But as Meister Eckhart, that fourteenth-century genius, says, the higher energy flows into the lower energy and transforms it, changes it. So our intellect becomes the avenue for this transformation of the heart, and at the same time the intellect itself is transformed. Ego is the avenue for the transformation of the heart, and yet in that process ego also gets radically transformed; we win the best of both worlds. And we're designed by nature to have the best of both worlds.

What are young people looking for? They're looking for this great internal world. Some try to get it through drugs. Some haven't even imagination; they don't have the capacity to create the internal world of imagery. Boredom is a chief factor that they try to get around through drugs, and that's a major tragedy.

Patricia Sun

New Thinking

AS THE LATE great J. Krishnamurti, the world-famous religious philosopher, said many times: "Thinking is the problem." What he meant was that we have to go beyond the rigid patterns of our mind-brain, and into another realm of knowing which is beyond conventional thought and decision-making. To address the times we live in and to fully engage life may require a new form of thinking, seeing ourselves and the world around us in a completely different way, radically altering our perceptions of what's happening.

Patricia Sun's work directly relates to re-creating thought patterns and re-perceiving experience. For more than fifteen years she has traveled the world, empowering people with ways to hold experience more expansively and to tap the inherent creative capacity within, which results in new ways of thought. Patricia is the founder and director of the Institute of Communication for Understanding.

MT: *Patricia, what does the term "new thinking" really mean?*

PS: It has very profound implications. For more than ten years, I have been traveling around the world and discussing what has come to be called an "evolutionary leap" in people's consciousness. This evolutionary leap is more than just new ideas. It's an actual expansion in our *capacity* to perceive. We are actually expanding how much our brains can hold and what we see.

What I have called a new style of thinking is itself the process, the mechanism, the medium through which our brains can integrate this change in consciousness. It has a lot to do with integrating the left brain and the right brain. It means using your intuition, thinking with imagery—pictures and feelings and spatial wholes—as well as the linear and verbal thinking that we consider normal logical thinking. Both of these modes are valuable, and both are necessary.

In different cultures and societies, one or the other of these modes tends to dominate. Globally, right now, we're predominantly linear and logical. This is true even in the East, which has been noted for its intuitive style of thinking.

The new style of thinking expresses a "win-win" instead of "win-lose" attitude. The common "either-or" type of thinking sets you up to always have a loss; it is always *locked* in some way. A spatial-whole style of thinking gives an overview, lets you get more information at a single glance, lets you be receptive.

In our culture, to say that someone's not logical is tantamount to saying they're stupid, or at least wrong. But alogical thinking, acausal thinking, thinking that just *gets* an answer, is the essence of creativity. You go into a kind of daydreamy place, and something pops in.

Abraham Maslow, a psychologist who studied creative people, showed that the creative process always involves a fallow moment, a still moment, where you're not trying, and you open up; you ask earnestly, and then you let go. And then something pops in that's bigger than anything logic can give you, and sometimes it delivers information that never existed before. It's a process of using the hemisphere of the brain where music comes from.

Where do composers get music that never existed before? They don't create it in a logical way like you build a chair by putting this rung here and the seat there and the back there. The process is quite magical and unique to experience. It is an aspect of human intelligence, an aspect of our ability. But we have censored it because the linear mind, the controlling mind, gives us the illusion of control: "I'll only let this in; I'll only have this many chairs; I close this door, I open this door." To have something just appear, just come to mind, smacks of magic and some kind of peculiarness that we're afraid of.

My job, my work, is to help people see that we have been at a crossroads long enough to be ready to go beyond "crossroads thinking" and leap to a kind of thinking that can see the overview. Getting that overview will give us the capacity to forgive, to understand, to be empathetic, to really create new solutions.

I find it very interesting that human beings use only one-tenth of their brains, because that's a very peculiar phenomenon in nature; nature doesn't waste anything. When I first read that, I thought, "Oh, that means we're not finished yet!" We're a very young species, and we're in development. We're not finished.

The next level in our development involves a new style of thinking, expressing what I call the "win-win" attitude: You get what you need and I get what I need; and *I care* about you getting what you need, and *you care* about my getting what I need. This attitude affects everything—from the most personal things of human relationship among men and women, parents and children, to all the difficulties in our culture and our society. It brings light to all our psychological blind spots, ranging from drug abuse to child abuse to toxic waste disposal to even our romantic connections, our ability to be in love. What does it mean to love, for example, and how do I get hurt? Our ways of involvement with all of these things—from big to little and from technical to very human and emotional—are empowered by a style of thinking that lets you integrate these two hemispheres and have a win-win view that respects logical data and information.

Many people listening to your words have been brought up in the American system of education, which is a system that emphasizes one way of thinking—the logical, rational, linear process. We not only haven't been taught to value the form of thinking that you're talking about, but we're all actually conditioned to think the other way. And it's through that conditioned thinking that we try to hear what you're saying. How does the breakthrough happen with people who have been conditioned to hear what you're saying in the other way? Isn't it sort of a "chicken or the egg" kind of thing?

You know, it's interesting. I have lots of little examples I use to talk about that. One of them appeared in *Life* magazine years ago.

When people from our culture were first adventuring into the Amazon, some of the white men took photographs of the Indians there. At first, the Indians couldn't see anything in the photos but black-and-white blotches. Their minds had not been conditioned to see the photos as anything but black-and-white blotches.

The white men would say, "Look, this is, you know, Sam over there. This is him. These are his eyes—see his eyes and his nose?" They did this kind of thing for a long time. And then suddenly, like in a flash, the Indians saw the face. And they were horrified. It was a *shock*—out of these blotches on a flat paper, suddenly they saw the soul or the spirit, the dimensionalization of this concept.

I use that example because I know that often only a small fraction of what I'm saying really penetrates through the conditioning you mentioned. Evolutionarily speaking, we're just evolving into an ability to see this way. So it isn't only programming. As you said it has a certain "which comes first, the chicken or the egg?" quality about it. I mean, the programming is there because we can't see it and it reinforces itself.

To make a breakthrough, I use things that help people love one another, love themselves, be healthier, be empowered, be more creative, and communicate more authentically, more truthfully. People can feel good about that and gain value from it. I'm very pragmatic at some level. The bottom line is: Is it wholesome? Is it real? Does it work? And is it good? So, with that as my anchor and my real goal, the rest follows.

Any problem that any human being can conceive of can be facilitated if you look at it in the context of this overview and have a Zen-like or Taoist-like attitude of being receptive, having a good intent, and being open to an unexpected kind of solution. It's much more effective than trying to be in a position of controlling an outcome, especially when you don't have enough information to even choose your control properly. But it takes a certain amount of trust, which at first seems too scary to our defense mechanisms.

In my work, I try—kindly, carefully, and thoughtfully—to *show* how this process works. I try to show it by helping people *be* it or actually *do* it, not just understand it intellectually. As you said, intellectual explanation may mean very little, because it has to go through a filter that already doesn't understand.

Imagine, for example, trying to explain the color green to someone who has never seen green. You can't explain it; you can only *show* them green. I believe that the human race is going to make a leap which is much like being able to see color after having been color-blind. We're going to be like those South American Indians: We won't really understand it at first; it won't make sense, and that's as it should be.

People who *can* see, who just happen to already have a piece of this, need to *kindly* show and point it out. Then, as people are ready, they will see. It's not a matter of coercion. It's not a matter of being right. It's a matter of offering, in a innocent way, what you perceive as your reality.

Your conclusions may be wrong, and somebody else may come to another conclusion. That's fine. There's no investment in being "right." It has to do with encouraging authenticity. It has to do with helping to make an environment where each person, without entrenchment, without a polarizing need to destroy anyone who doesn't agree with them, is willing to get the overview.

I made a T-shirt recently that shows a picture of the planet with words wrapping around it. The words go upside-down around the "bottom" as they wrap around the perimeter of the earth. It says, "You can't take sides when you know the earth is round." In a graphic, pictorial way, it shows that when you're in a sphere, which we all are, and you're seeing the whole, one person's upside-down is another person's rightside-up. One person's up is the other person's down, and they're both correct. And the empowerment comes from each of us being receptive to the other's experience.

Patricia, you made reference to Zen and Taoist thinking. In the East there is a nondualistic view of the world, and in the West we have a dualistic way of seeing. What about that?

In the East, the intuitive, acausal mind is not so dominated by the controlling mind. Though much of the Eastern teaching is also religious, it isn't *only* religious. It really is a philosophy. This philosophy influences their medicine and many of their dealings with the world. The *I Ching*, for example, emphasizes duality and balance and feeling life as a dance. To dance well with someone, one person takes a step back as the other takes the step forward.

In Taoism, the duality is described in terms of yin and yang. Yin is the receptive: the void, the room. Yang is the linear: How do you get something, how much is it, where is it, and do I want to buy one?

Lao Tzu, the father of Taoist thought, described the yin as the nothing, the nothingness in the lump of clay that makes it a very valuable vessel. Yin thinking is a kind of thinking that makes our minds go, "What?" The yin emphasis explains why Eastern people sometimes seem strange to us, or impractical, or paying attention to something not relevant from our point of view. The difference in emphasis shows in how people from different hemispheres might give you directions if you asked how to get to some place. A Westerner would say, "You go left right here, and you do this, that, there." And a Chinese might say, "Oh, you move over to this garden, and that's where my sister got married," and he would talk about all kinds of emotional feelings that connect to that garden for him. He would paint a picture that we would call extraneous and unimportant, but for him it would be a rich part of the connection.

So I think that the yin force that appears in Taoism and Zen, the so-called mystery or transcendental kind of concepts, really expresses a phenomenon that is basically human. That capacity of our creativity and our intelligence and our human nature is not really specific to any culture; it is inherent in all human beings. Different cultures develop, allow, deal with, use certain parts of it. And I think part of the evolutionary leap that's happening is that the human race is going to realize itself as one species on one planet. Part of that realization will come from not needing to polarize against anyone, knowing that if I have something poisonous and I dump it to my so-called enemy, it will come around and get me anyway because it's just one little world.

I think that one very strong example of the yin force operating is Jesus Christ. He said, "Love your enemy." He talked about paradox all the time. First would be last, for example. He spoke in parable, and not literally. He talked about love as a power that *was* God, and paradoxically healed evil. He said that you have to bring love into evil; you have to deal with the publicans and the tax-collectors, and you have to *love* them and talk to them and sit with them. From one point of view, that's a very illogical way of thinking. It is a mystical way of thinking, though, a spiritual and powerful one.

I think that all the religions of the world at some level are valid. They come from God or that cosmic unity, that consciousness, and they all have a value. But they've also all been dogmatized by people. The dogmatization is the literalization, the linearization of it, the trying to gain control, to be right: "I'm right, you're wrong. We're right, they're wrong." If we all say *"Sieg heil"* to something, it'll make us right. If we all agree, we're right. But that isn't so! We can all agree on something that's not true.

Because of our way of viewing things, we have many different compartments that we put things into. We have religion, business, politics, education, and so on. And there's not a whole lot of cross-over between the compartments. The values we may apply in the religious compartment, for example, don't necessarily get applied in the business compartment or in the political arena. In business, the bottom line is often to get your competitor, no matter what. What do you think about the way that values change as we go from one area of the society to another?

Well, I think it has to do with part of the crisis and the growth we're going through. Very interestingly, we often use logic to be very illogical. For example, we say that it's important to love our enemy, but we still want to bomb the Russians. I mean, there's an illogic to that.

As you were speaking, I thought of a very dear friend who's a fundamentalist Christian. This woman said to me, "Well, I don't know why people in the world don't love Jesus." And I said, "You know, people in the world *do* love Jesus; it's Christians that they have a problem with." Most religions of the world see Jesus as a Bodhisattva or a prophet, as a divine person, inspired by God, very real and very good. Any person who really looks into what Jesus taught can see that it's very profound.

It is a *challenge* beyond measure to live that way, and we need to forgive ourselves and one another when we can't do it. But we have to have the integrity to keep noticing that we didn't do it, and to do our best to rectify that, so that in business we are honest. That doesn't mean you don't make a profit; it's part of being in business that you make a profit; that's reasonable. But you don't lie, and you don't rip people off. Out of integrity and dignity as a human being, you don't produce products that harm people or that poison the planet.

I'm not trying to say, in a sort of left-handed way, that the people who do these things are not nice people. It is a matter of consciousness and awareness, not a matter of blaming certain companies or the military-industrial complex. Everybody has a reason for doing what they do. My experience, from doing a lot of conflict resolution, is that everybody has a valid point.

We need to look for the other person's valid point, respect it and incorporate it. We must not let our belief and our fears of being powerless keep us from doing that. Being wholesome in this way will create, ultimately, our best security. People usually think about security in the short-term, and they don't realize that the resistance they're getting may be coming from the fact that they're hurting someone else. That's true often enough that it's important to consider.

Thinking this way doesn't mean that you violate yourself. It doesn't mean, as some people have extrapolated some Christian thought to say, that "you sacrifice yourself for the other." One of the hallmarks of win-win thinking is that "I must also be wholesome and good to myself, as well as to you." It's not either-or. It's as much for yourself as for the other. You respect your needs and simultaneously respect the other person's needs. And then, with both those pieces of information, you have to be even more thoughtful about what you really need.

Win-win has to do with being able to hold both parts at the same time. Most of us find that too tedious, too difficult. We also don't believe that others will do it, so we're afraid that if we try it we'll lose. And that becomes a self-fulfilling prophecy.

Whatever you really think and feel is generated, even if you don't speak it. People have a capacity, a sort of biological-intellectual geiger-counter system, to read one another. Some part of us knows when someone else tells a lie.

To begin to get people in workshops to understand the level of authenticity that I'm speaking of and what an empowerment it is, I say, "One thing you can do to help this evolutionary leap happen is to begin to consider, from this moment forward, that everyone can read your mind." When I say that, the audience goes silent, or people sort of twitter, because it's very scary. But there are two good reasons why we should consider it. First, it's going to happen anyway; so we might as well begin now while the fog is in and we have a mutual agreement not to know. Second, developing the capacity to consider it lets the linear, logical mind begin to have a new program. It has to say, "What do I think?"

When we really ask that question, we realize that we have been responding to a lot of things without knowing what we think. We discover that we think complexly, often contradictorily. I can like you and not like you, for example. Nothing is ever one little flat thing; it's always part of a huge, complicated circle-sphere of many sides and parts and points. We begin to see that a flat answer is not enough.

And being able to think in this way opens us to the next dimension.

Patricia, as I listen to you talk, it sounds very promising, very hopeful. But when one sees the news on television or reads about our world-situation in the paper, one is struck by how much seems to be going wrong. Institutions are breaking down, millions of people have been in wars throughout the world in recent years. We can't really say that we have peace on the planet. And so, though everything you say sounds wonderful, one can't help but have a little shred of doubt.

A big shred of doubt.

Can we really do it? Can we really make it, or are we going to blow ourselves up?

If you look at the world situation with your logical mind, it's even worse than you think. Believe me, I do know that. But what we're talking about *is* possible to do, because the capacity for change available to human beings is *astounding*. The only thing keeping us from having heaven on earth right now is that we can't believe it's possible. We can't consider it's possible. We could be *so* wrong if we considered it.

This planet is an extraordinary phenomenon in the universe, and we as intelligent living beings can make it heaven on earth. That, incidentally, is what Jesus said to pray for: Thy kingdom come, Thy will be done on earth as it is in heaven. All of the religions of the world have a premonition of our coming home, remembering, waking up. I don't think that's a delusionary, just hopeful wish. Environmentally, mechanically, physically, it's possible. We actually have to work very hard every day to keep ourselves starving, hurt, unwell. We work hard to hold in place the many systems and beliefs and things we hang on to. And our attachment is to being right.

But it is much more powerful to want to be good. Good is more powerful than right. Right is always in a context. It is always polarized against a wrong. But good covers everything. Good is allowing, in religious terms, the experience of God to live in you. To really love God is to love this planet, to love the universe, to love the animals and the trees, the water, the oceans, to love your children, your fellow man, your husband, your wife, your friends, the people you live with, to care about Russian children, to care about American children. It has to do with really letting love be *in* your body. And this, paradoxically, is also what makes you heal yourself when you are in stress. All the conflict and all the fears about loss are what precede and require us to develop this capacity.

It's, as you say, too big to hold. It seems almost unthinkable. It's so easy to criticize. It's so easy to say, "What a delusion, just look around you." I think, though, of how the media covered the Harmonic Convergence. At first, it was derided. And then, sort of begrudgingly, different reporters all over the country started to say things like, "Well, it's really not such a bad idea, to think of us all maybe loving one another and working well together—not a bad thought at all."

But the criticism and derision are understandable, too. We have to admit that too many people go off to make demonstrations instead of living these things in their daily lives.

Nonetheless, it is an empowering thought to consider that there *can* be peace. It is an empowering thought to consider that human beings *can* love one another. It is empowering for husband and wife to realize they can someday truly be intimate and honest with one another. It is empowering to know that we will become conscious enough to raise our children in a wholesome way.

This is what the evolutionary leap is, and the goal that the new style of thinking serves. There is nothing to lose but your pride and your ego in saying that this is possible. We could love one another. We could be honest.

We can *tell* when people are being dishonest. Instead of hating them, we could say, "Excuse me, could you tell me that again? Something felt funny about that." That could be more constructive than saying, "You liar. I don't trust you. You're no good." Everybody lies sometimes. It's part of our growth to learn that we don't need to lie, that it is more powerful to tell the truth. In the long run, that's what freedom really means.

Freedom and liberty are very real things, and this country was founded in their names. I believe in them fervently, and they are very, very important. They are things you create from the inside out when you have the freedom to live telling the truth. Anything can come in, and anything can come out. You don't need to project onto someone else, because you are taking full responsibility for being all that you are and can become.

Now, this is a tall order, but the job is to get on with it. Do it as best you can, without blaming or hating yourself, little by little each day.

About New Dimensions

INSPIRED BY the need for an overview of the dramatic cultural shifts and changing human values occurring on a planetary scale, New Dimensions Foundation was conceived and founded in March 1973 as a public, nonprofit educational organization. Shortly thereafter, New Dimensions Radio began to produce programming for broadcast in northern California. Since then, more than four thousand broadcast hours of programming intended to empower and enlighten have been produced. In 1980, "New Dimensions" went national via satellite as a weekly one-hour, in-depth interview series. More than three hundred stations have aired the series since its inception, and "New Dimensions" has reached literally millions of listeners with its upbeat, practical, and provocative views of life and the human spirit.

Widely acclaimed as a unique and professional production, New Dimensions Radio programming has featured hundreds of leading thinkers, creative artists, scientists, and cultural and social innovators of our time in far-ranging dialogues covering the major issues of this era. The interviews from which this book was compiled are representative.

As interviewer and host, Michael Toms brings a broad background of knowledge and expertise to the "New Dimensions" microphones. His sensitive and engaging interviewing style as well as his own intellect and breadth of interests have been acclaimed by listeners and guests alike.

New Dimensions Radio provides a new model for exploring ideas in a spirit of open dialogue. Programs are produced to include the listener as an active participant as well as respecting the listener's intelligence and capacity for thoughtful choice. The programs are alive with dynamic spontaneity. "New Dimensions" programming celebrates life and the human spirit while challenging the mind to open to fresh possibilities. We invite your participation with us in the ultimate human adventure—the quest for wisdom and the inexpressible.

For a free *New Dimensions Newsletter*, a list of radio stations currently broadcasting the "New Dimensions" radio series, or an audio tape catalog, please write New Dimensions Radio, Dept. LEB, P.O. Box 410510, San Francisco, CA 94141, or you may telephone (415) 563-8899.

New Dimensions Audio Tapes

These audio tapes are the word-for-word recordings of the original conversations from which *At the Leading Edge* was compiled.

A NEW WORLD VIEW with **WILLIS HARMAN.** Social scientist and futurist Harman leads us through the historical roots of science and into an ever-widening vista of new ways of thinking and perceiving. According to Harman, we are living through one of the most fundamental shifts in history—a change in the actual belief structure of Western industrial society—which points to extraordinary new possiblities for human consciousness. Harman is the president of the Institute of Noetic Sciences and author of two books, *Global Mind Change* and *An Incomplete Guide to the Future.*
Tape #2083   1 hr. $9.95

CREATIVE CHRISTIANITY with **MATTHEW FOX.** A refreshing perspective of the Judeo-Christian tradition is presented by Fox, Dominican scholar and innovative educator, who describes the creation-centered tradition as contrasted with the "fall/redemption" ideology. Since we all share creation in common, and share responsibility for that creation, we are called upon to re-create religion, exploring the mystical streaming kept alive down through the centuries by artists, poets, mystics, and others within and without churches. Fox's message is provocative and challenges us to re-examine our religious roots with new eyes. Fox is the author of *Original Blessing* and *The Coming of the Cosmic Christ* and the director of the Institute in Culture and Creation Spirituality at Holy Names College in Oakland, CA.
Tape #1892   1 hr. $9.95

ECUMENICAL VISIONS: A NEW SPIRITUAL PARADIGM with **MATTHEW FOX.** In the Fall of 1988 the Vatican ordered Dominican priest Matthew Fox to be silenced. This dialogue was recorded just prior to his entering a period of silence as a result. He expresses his dismay with Vatican authorities and at the same time reveals the reasons why his views are being challenged. Creative though controversial to some, Fox speaks of a new cosmology to include a recovery of earth wisdom, reverence for the Goddess tradition, elimination of patriarchal values and more. He also shares his profound vision of an ecumenical Vatican III which is extraordinary.
Tape #2117   1 hr. $9.95

DAILY LIFE AS SPIRITUAL EXERCISE with **MARSHA SINETAR.** This is an inspiring and relevant dialogue about being true to one's deepest motivation. Choosing a lifestyle which blends inner truth with daily life is possible according to Sinetar, who has interviewed many everyday people living unconventional, simple, yet rich and satisfying lives. She emphasizes the importance of solitude, silence, and self-awareness for following the spiritual path. Sinetar is an educator, a psychologist, and the author of *Ordinary People As Monks and Mystics.*
Tape #2007   1 hr. $9.95

FROM PHYSICS TO PEACE: FINDING NEW TRUTHS with **ROBERT FULLER.** This is an inspiring, engrossing tale of one man's odyssey from physics professor and college president to citizen diplomat, searching for "a better game than war." Finding your passion and responding to it are the keys to living fully, according to Fuller, who has spent the past twenty years pursuing his passion for peace. Fresh, candid, and compassionate, he challenges us all in new ways to think about our values, the nature of change and risk. Fuller is past president of Oberlin College and the founder of the Mo Tzu Project.
Tape #2091   1 hr. $9.95

BEYOND POWER with **ANDREW BARD SCHMOOKLER.** "No one is free to choose peace, but anyone can impose upon all the necessity for power." The necessity for power during civilized history has carried humanity to the brink of its own destruction, and most of us still don't know the why and how of it. This dialogue explores the effects and influence of power and how we are its willing and unwilling victims. Schmookler presents an original and penetrating analysis of the evolution of power in society, one which clearly challenges us to perceive power and human aggression in a new light, posing profound questions for human survival. Must listening for anyone interested in the possibility of peace.
Tape #1906   1 hr. $9.95

BEYOND THE THOUGHT OF WAR with **ANDREW BARD SCHMOOK-LER.** Drawing on such widely diverse fields as psychology, anthropology, literature, philosophy, and religion, Schmookler brings new insight into the inner dilemmas that have created the warrior spirit. He suggests that there is a direct link between our personal fears and the drive towards war. So if we can heal the wounds on the inside, there is a greater potential for peace on the outside. He is the author of *The Parable of the Tribes* and *Out of Weakness: Healing the Wounds That Drive Us to War .*
Tape #2159   1 hr. $9.95

THINKING REVERENTIALLY with **HENRYK SKOLIMOWSKI.** Modern thinking, and especially institutional decision-making, increasingly disregard the basic elements and processes of nature, resulting in widespread ecological crises, species extinction, and human misery. Henryk Skolimowski is of the emerging school of "deep ecology," which argues that we need to fundamentally re-orient our thinking about nature and society. Here Dr. Skolimowski points the way toward a "reverential thinking" that can restore the lost balance in our relationship with our environment. A must for anyone concerned about our planet's future.
Tape #1768   1 hr. $9.95

ECO-MIND: REVERENCE FOR LIFE with **HENRYK SKOLIMOWSKI.** A philosopher who breaks through mind-sets and preconceptions, Skolimowski sees the process of evolution working through us. Recognizing the unique role each of us plays within the whole, and meeting the challenge with grace and harmony, can lift us into an ever expanding sensitivity to life and its infinite possibilities. He provides an opportunity to view evolution in personal terms and inspires us to think in new ways about living on planet earth. A professor of philosophy at the University of Michigan, he is the author of *Theatre of the Mind* and *Eco-Philosophy: Designing New Tactics for Living.*
Tape #1976   1 hr. $9.95

WHEN GOD WAS A WOMAN with **MERLIN STONE.** One of the pioneers of the women's movement and the reclaiming of the Goddess tradition, Stone speaks of her own inspiration and vision. Drawing upon a spiritual wisdom extant long before any of the great religions, she reveals the Goddess as the flow of life energy, nurturing and sustaining the planet. At a time when the planet is threatened with destruction, the return of the Goddess embodies a profoundly ecological vision for the future, according to Stone. She provides a multitude of reasons why Goddess wisdom needs to be universally embraced. Merlin Stone is the author of *When God Was a Woman* and *Ancient Mirrors of Womanhood.*
Tape #2116   1 hr. $9.95

CREATIVITY, NATURAL PHILOSOPHY, AND SCIENCE with **DAVID BOHM.** One of the foremost theoretical physicists in the world, Bohm tells why science has become specialized and fragmented at the cost of its soul. He describes his theory of the implicate order and goes on to explore its implications for human consciousness. Thought is based in memory, and true creativity depends on getting beyond a thought process dependent on memory, according to Bohm. In this remarkable dialogue, he delves into the innermost reaches of what it means to be human and alive. David Bohm is Professor Emeritus of Birbeck College (U. of London), the author of *Wholeness and the Implicate Order,* and the co-author of *Science, Order and Creativity.*
Tape #2071   1 hr. $9.95

SACRED ODYSSEY: SEEKING FREEDOM with **RAM DASS.** A 1990 return visit with the spiritual pilgrim whose personal journey during the past three decades has served as a reflective mirror for so many. He speaks about where he is now in his life, how methods are traps, overcoming fear in the midst of change, spiritual potential, the true source of change, facing adversity, the challenge of doing good, the possibility of compassion, and a great deal more. Ram Dass shares himself deeply and profoundly.
Tape #2186   1 hr. $9.95

THE PAST IS PRESENT with **RUPERT SHELDRAKE.** A 1988 update and review of Sheldrake's controversial theory of "morphic resonance," which challenges some fundamental assumptions of established science. Sheldrake offers a revolutionary alternative to the mechanistic world-view and points toward a new understanding of the nature of life, matter, and mind. One of the more profound implications of Sheldrake's account here is his suggestion that the brain may be more like a tuning system than a recording device. He is the author of *A New Science of Life* and *The Presence of the Past.*
Tape #2080   1 hr. $9.95

WAY OF THE WARRIOR with **JOAN HALIFAX.** In our own time, the ancient exercise of martial virtues has been made obsolete by nuclear weapons. This dialogue explores the nature of the "warrior within," the one who defends the future against the aggressor still lurking in one's own psyche. Halifax weaves a magical web of myth and mastery as she speaks of living with courage and compassion. She is the founding director of the Ojai Foundation and the editor of *Shamanic Voices*.
Tape #1857   1 hr. $9.95

THE GROUND OF BEING with **HUSTON SMITH.** A dialogue with one of the world's foremost scholars of religion and philosophy about the role of spirit in modern life, focusing on how to understand the difference between the secular and the sacred in a scientifically biased world. Professor Smith is the wisdom guide as he spins the mystical mandala pointing to the unity of all the great traditions. For those seeking to stretch their spiritual horizons, this conversation delivers a plentiful panorama. Huston Smith is the author of *Forgotten Truth: The Primordial Tradition*.
Tape #2074   1 hr. $9.95

ADVENTURES OF THE MIND with **JOSEPH CHILTON PEARCE.** Understanding the basis of learning and how the brain works lay at the core of Joe Pearce's message, which is both disturbing and inspiring. His natural fervor and steady presentation of facts challenge the mind to recognize its limitations while seeing its possibilities. Borrowing liberally from the visions of physicists as well as mystics, Pearce shows us how, through understanding Nature's astonishingly magnificent process, we can literally change our world. He also delivers a powerful indictment on the inherent dangers of TV watching, especially for young children. Joseph Pearce is the author of *Magical Child* and *Magical Child Matures*.
Tape #2040   1 hr $9.95

NEW THINKING with **PATRICIA SUN.** Moving beyond *either/or* (dualistic) thinking to perceiving with the whole brain underscores this dialogue with Sun, whose message of wholeness and balance has empowered thousands of people throughout the world. During recent years she has traveled extensively in the Soviet Union, and here she applies her transforming vision to helping us see the Russians more clearly as fellow citizens of this planet Earth. New ways of thinking are required in order to create a more peaceful world, says Patricia, the founder of the Institute of Communication for Understanding (ICU).
Tape #2073   1 hr. $9.95

TO ORDER TAPES

Mail check or money order (with Visa or MasterCard give expiration date) and add $1 ($2 Canada, $5 foreign) for first tape ordered for postage and handling. For each additional tape in the same shipment, add 50 cents for U.S. delivery, $1 for Canada and $3 for foreign. California residents add 6.25% sales tax (Bart counties 6.75%). Send to New Dimensions Tapes, P.O. Box 410510, San Francisco, CA 94141. (Telephone: 415-563-8899)

Bibliography

Bellah, Robert N. *Habits of the Heart: Individualism and Commitment in American Life*. Repr. of 1985 edition. Harper & Row.

Bohm, David. *Causality and Chance in Modern Physics*. Repr. of 1957 ed. University of Pennsylvania Press.

_____. *The Special Theory of Relativity*. Addison-Wesley, 1988.

_____. *Wholeness and the Implicate Order*. Routledge Kegan Paul, 1981

_____, and Krishnamurti, J. *The Future of Humanity*. Harper Religious Books, 1986.

_____, and Peat, David. *Science, Order, and Creativity*. Bantam, 1987.

Capra, Fritjof. *The Tao of Physics: An Exploration of the Parallels between Modern Physics and Eastern Mysticism*. 2d rev. ed. Shambhala, 1983.

_____. *The Turning Point*. Bantam, 1987.

Dass, Ram. *Be Here Now*. Crown, 1971.

_____. *Journey of Awakening: A Meditator's Guidebook*. Bantam, 1982.

_____. *Miracle of Love: Stories about Neem Karoli Baba*. Dutton, 1979.

_____. *The Only Dance There Is*. Doubleday, 1975.

_____, and Gorman, Paul. *How Can I Help? Stories and Reflections on Service*. Knopf, 1985.

_____, and Levine, Stephen. *Grist for the Mill*. Celestial Arts, 1987.

Fox, Matthew. *The Coming of the Cosmic Christ*. Harper & Row, 1988.

_____. *Meditations with Meister Eckhart*. Bear & Co., 1983.

_____. *On Becoming a Musical Mystical Bear: Spirituality American Style*. Paulist Press, 1976.

_____. *Original Blessing*. Bear & Co. 1983.

_____. *A Spirituality Named Compassion, and the Healing of the Global Village, Humpty Dumpty, and Us*. Harper & Row, 1979.

_____. *Western Spirituality: Historical Roots, Ecumenical Routes*. Bear & Co., 1983.

_____. *Whee! We, Wee All the Way Home: A Guide to a Sensual, Prophetic Spirituality*. Bear & Co., 1981.

_____, and Swimme, Brian. *Manifesto for a Global Civilization*. Bear & Co., 1982.

_____, ed. *Hildegard of Bingen's Book of Divine Works with Letters and Songs*. Bear & Co., 1987.

Fromm, Erich. *Art of Loving: An Enquiry into the Nature of Love*. Harper & Row, 1956.

Grof, Stanislav, and Halifax, Joan. *The Human Encounter with Death*. Dutton, 1978.

Halifax, Joan. Shaman, *The Wounded Healer*. Thames & Hudson, 1988.

_____, ed. *Shamanic Voices: A Survey of Visionary Narratives*. Dutton, 1979.

Harman, Willis. *Global Mind Change: The Promise of the Last Years of the Twentieth Century*. Knowledge Systems, 1988.

_____. *An Incomplete Guide to the Future*. Norton, 1979.

_____, and Rheingold, Howard. *Higher Creativity*. Jeremy P.Tarcher, 1988.

Hildegard, and Fox, Matthew. *The Illuminations of Hildegard of Bingen*. Bear & Co., 1985.

Krishnamurti, J., and Bohm, David. *The Ending of Time*. Harper Religious Books, 1985.

Pearce, Joseph Chilton. *The Bond of Power*. Dutton, 1981.

_____. *The Crack in the Cosmic Egg: Challenging Constructs of Mind and Reality*. Crown, 1988.

_____. *Exploring the Crack in the Cosmic Egg*. Pocket Books, 1982.

_____. *Magical Child: Rediscovering Nature's Plan for Our Children*. Dutton, 1977.

_____. *Magical Child Matures*. Dutton, 1985.

Schmookler, Andrew Bard. *Out of Weakness: Healing the Wounds That Drive Us to War*. Bantam, 1988.

_____. *The Parable of the Tribes: The Problem of Power in Social Evolution*. University of California Press, 1984.

_____. *Sowings and Reapings: The Cycles of Good and Evil in the Human System*. Knowledge Systems, 1989.

Schumacher, E.F. *Small Is Beautiful: Economics As If People Mattered*. Harper & Row, 1975.

Sheldrake, Rupert. *A New Science of Life: The Hypothesis of Formative Causation*. Rev. ed. Jeremy P. Tarcher, 1983.

_____. *The Presence of the Past: Morphic Resonance and the Memory of Nature*. Times Books, 1988.

_____. *The Rebirth of Nature*. Bantam, 1991.

Sinetar, Marsha. *Do What You Love, the Money Will Follow: Discovering Your Right Livelihood*. Dell, 1989.

_____. *Elegant Choices, Healing Choices*. Paulist Press, 1989.

_____. *Ordinary People as Monks and Mystics: Lifestyles for Self-Discovery*. Paulist Press, 1986.

Skolimowski, Henryk. *Eco-Philosophy: Designing New Tactics for Living*. Marion Boyars, 1981.

_____. *Theatre of the Mind*. Theosophical Publishing House, 1984.

Smith, Huston. *Beyond the Post-Modern Mind*. 2d ed. Theosophical Publishing House, 1989.

_____. *Forgotten Truth: The Primordial Tradition*. Harper & Row,1977.

_____. *Religions of Man*. Repr. of 1958 ed. Harper & Row.

Smoke, Richard, and Harman, Willis. *Paths to Peace: Exploring the Feasibility of Sustainable Peace*. Westview, 1987.

Stone, Merlin. *Ancient Mirrors of Womanhood: A Treasury of Goddess and Heroine Lore from Around the World*. Beacon Press, 1984.

_____. *When God Was a Woman*. Harcourt Brace Jovanovich, 1978.

Trungpa, Chögyam. *Shambhala: The Sacred Path of the Warrior*. Shambhala, 1988.

Turner, Frederick. *Beyond Geography: The Western Spirit against the Wilderness*. Rutgers University Press, 1983.

Zukav, Gary. *Dancing Wu Li Masters: An Overview of the New Physics*. Morrow, 1979.

Contributors

MICHAEL TOMS has been exploring personal, social, and global transformation through his work as an electronic journalist and writer for the past two decades. He has been described as a cultural anthropologist and is best known as the host and executive producer of the nationally syndicated and widely acclaimed "New Dimensions" interview series, which is heard on public radio throughout the United States as well as internationally via shortwave broadcasts.

Michael's broad knowledge in comparative religions, philosophy, history, psychology, and consciousness studies, combined with his in-depth work with some of the major thinkers and visionaries of our time, has brought him recognition as one of the leading spokespersons of new paradigm thinking. His personal friendships and work over the years with such figures as the late inventor/philosopher R. Buckminster Fuller, mythologist Joseph Campbell, physicist David Bohm, and others have continued to inspire his comprehensive approach to global learning.

He is Chairman Emeritus of the California Institute of Integral Studies, an accredited graduate school with a focus on East-West Studies, and currently serves as Senior Acquisitions Editor with HarperSanFrancisco. His 1988 book *An Open Life: Joseph Campbell in Conversation with Michael Toms* has become a national bestseller.

DAVID BOHM, one of the foremost theoretical physicists in the world, worked alongside Oppenheimer and Einstein, and spent more than two decades in frequent dialogue with J. Krishnamurti about the nature of thinking, the mind, and consciousness. He is Professor Emeritus of Birbeck College, University of London. He is the author of *Wholeness and the Implicate Order*, *Causality and Chance in Modern Physics*, and *The Special Theory of Relativity*. He is also co-author, with David Peat, of *Science, Order, and Creativity*, and co-author, with J. Krishnamurti, of *The Future of Humanity*.

RAM DASS, aka Richard Alpert, has become a legend in his own time. Through books, lectures, and tapes, he has become a major contributor to the integration of Eastern spirituality with Western philosophy. He received a master's degree from Wesleyan University and a Ph.D. from Stanford University. His books include the classic *Be Here Now* as well as *Journey of Awakening, Miracle of Love,* and *The Only Dance There Is.* He is co-author with Stephen Levine of *Grist for the Mill,* and the co-author with Paul Gorman of *How Can I Help?* He is the co-founder and a board member of Seva Foundation (8 N. San Pedro Road, San Rafael, CA 94903).

MATTHEW FOX is a Dominican priest who in 1988 was censured by the Roman Catholic Church authorities and sentenced to a year of silence because of his views on Creation Spirituality. He is the founder of the Institute in Culture and Creation Spirituality at Holy Names College, 3500 Mountain Blvd., Oakland, CA 94619. The Institute publishes *Creation,* a bimonthly magazine (P.O. Box 19216, Oakland, CA 94619). He is the author of several books, including *Original Blessing* and *The Coming of the Cosmic Christ.*

ROBERT FULLER, citizen diplomat and former president of Oberlin College, has for the past decade criss-crossed the world seeking to better understand the nature of human conflict and our willingness to make war. He received his Ph.D. in physics from Princeton University and taught physics at Columbia University. He is the founder of the Mo Tzu Project, dedicated to resolving world conflict.

JOAN HALIFAX is an anthropologist who has worked with shamans and healers the world over. She is the editor of *Shamanic Voices* and the author of *Shaman, the Wounded Healer.* She is the president of the Ojai Foundation (P.O. Box 1620, Ojai, CA 93023), an educational community that offers degrees in interdisciplinary studies, as well as offering personal and artistic retreats, colloquia, conferences, pilgrimages, and wilderness trainings.

WILLIS HARMAN is the president of the Institute of Noetic Sciences (475 Gate Five Road, Suite 300, Sausalito, CA 94965), a pioneer organization in the field of consciousness studies. The Institute studies the diverse ways of knowing: the reasoning process of the intellect; the perceptions of our physical senses; and the intuitive, spiritual, or inner ways of knowing. Harman is the author of *Global Mind Change: The Promise of the Last Years of the Twentieth Century* and *An Incomplete Guide to the Future.* He is also co-author of two books, *Higher Creativity* and *Paths to Peace.*

JOSEPH CHILTON PEARCE is an author and lecturer on human development and altered states of consciousness. He is the author of *The Crack in the Cosmic Egg, Magical Child, The Bond of Power,* and *The Magical Child Matures.* He has lectured throughout the United States and Canada. He has a master's degree in theology from Geneva Theological College.

ANDREW BARD SCHMOOKLER graduated *summa cum laude* from Harvard and earned his doctorate at the University of California, Berkeley. He is the author of *The Parable of the Tribes,* which earned him praise from *Esquire* magazine as a "militant genius and renegade academic" and one of the "men and women under forty who are changing the nation." He is also the author of *Out of Weakness: Healing the Wounds That Drive Us to War* and *Sowings and Reapings.*

RUPERT SHELDRAKE received his Ph.D in biochemistry from Cambridge and holds degrees from Harvard University, where he was a Frank Knox Fellow. He also was a fellow of Clare College, Cambridge, and Director of Studies in Cell Biology in Cambridge. He is Consultant Physiologist of the International Crop Research Institute in Hyderabad, India. His work has been featured prominently both in scientific journals and in the popular press. He is the author of *A New Science of Life: The Hypothesis of Formative Causation,* and *The Presence of the Past: Morphic Resonance and the Memory of Nature.*

MARSHA SINETAR heads Sinetar & Associates (P.O. Box 83, The Sea Ranch, CA 95497), a human resource development firm, and she works with major corporations throughout America. She specializes in organizational psychology and corporate "change management." She is a graduate of UCLA, holds a master's degree in public administration from Cal State, Long Beach, and a doctorate in psychology from Cal Western. She is the author of *Ordinary People as Monks and Mystics; Elegant Choices, Healing Choices; Do What You Love, The Money Will Follow;* and *Living Happily Ever After.*

HENRYK SKOLIMOWSKI is professor of philosophy at the University of Michigan and author of *Theatre of the Mind* and *Eco-Philosophy*. He has developed what he calls Eco-philosophy, which signifies an active endorsement of frugality, of reverence for life, and of self-transcendence based on hope.

HUSTON SMITH is Professor of Philosophy and Religion Emeritus at Syracuse University. He is the author of the classic text *The Religions of Man*, as well as of *Forgotten Truth: The Primordial Tradition* and *Beyond the Postmodern Mind*. Raised by missionary parents in China, he served long apprenticeships with Vedanta Swami Prakashananda and with the renowned Zen master and scholar Daisetz Teitaro Suzuki.

MERLIN STONE is the author of the ground-breaking book *When God Was a Woman*, which first showed the important relationship between ancient goddess reverence and the status of contemporary women. She organized and directed the CBC radio series "Return of the Goddess" and has written extensively about the history of the Goddess. She lives in New York City and travels and lectures extensively in the United States and abroad.

PATRICIA SUN is the founder of the Institute of Communication for Understanding (P.O. Box 7065, Berkeley, CA 94707). Without the benefit of advertising, television, or a large organization, she has been traveling the United States and the world for more than fifteen years, talking to thousands of people about a "new style of thinking" that she firmly believes will revolutionize human society.